THE
INSTITUTIONAL
IMPERATIV

C

THE
INSTITUTIONAL
IMPERATIVE

HOW TO UNDERSTAND THE UNITED STATES
GOVERNMENT AND OTHER BULKY OBJECTS

ROBERT N. KHARASCH

CHARTERHOUSE BOOKS
NEW YORK

The Institutional Imperative

Second Printing, February 1974

ISBN: 0–88327–039–0
LIBRARY OF CONGRESS CATALOG CARD NUMBER: 72–95169
MANUFACTURED IN THE UNITED STATES OF AMERICA
DESIGNED BY JACQUES CHAZAUD

To Shari,
for faith and sacrifice
of two vacations.

ACKNOWLEDGMENTS

To Mrs. Elizabeth Crovato, written restatement of my many thanks for being a super secretary, typing and re-typing this book, meanwhile catching missing particles and articles. To my wife Shari, thanks for being an expert researcher of obscurely identified quotations. And to Carol Rinzler, demon editor and "which"-hunter, and Dick Kluger, publisher, thanks for help, faith and encouragement.

Contents

"All my life I have known better than to depend on the experts. How could I have been so stupid. . . ."

John F. Kennedy, the Thursday after the Bay of Pigs, quoted in *Kennedy* by Theodore C. Sorensen

PART I

THE LAWS OF
INSTITUTIONAL BEHAVIOR

FOREWORD:
INTRODUCTION TO THE LAWS
OF INSTITUTIONAL BEHAVIOR

Lawyers in Washington, Washington Lawyers and the Art of the Plumber. The Machinery Doesn't Work. The Devil Didn't Do It. Method of the Book. Modest Hope for Improvement.

Lawyers in Washington, Washington Lawyers and the Art of the Plumber

There are a lot of lawyers in Washington, D.C. Some of the time they do what lawyers do in any city: they draft wordy documents, file pleadings, try cases, and generally engage in those lawyerlike activities so properly condemned by nonlawyers until the nonlawyers need help.

But, much of the time the lawyers in Washington—I am one—are busy as "Washington Lawyers." The task of a Washington Lawyer is to obtain for his client a specific action or decision from a part of the government. Although often paid at a higher rate than a plumber (and often not), a Washington Lawyer has objectives just as prosaic and useful. You ask the plumber to plumb in order that the drain may drain. Similarly the Washington Lawyer works in order that your license to truck or broadcast or export be granted, or your taxes be low-

3

ered, or your combination with your competitor be blessed, or your competitor's behavior be damned.

Just as the arts by which your plumber satisfies your justifiable demand for freely flowing drains are ancient and mystic, so also the arts by which your Washington Lawyer seeks to meet your no doubt justifiable demands for Government action may appear to be mystic rituals. There is something of the priest in your plumber, and something both of priest and plumber in your lawyer's incantations to the Government.

The subject of this book is not how to be a Washington Lawyer, nor even how to use, understand and talk to your Washington Lawyer. There is here a more important end in view, and that is: to reveal the few basic laws by which our Government institutions (and any other institutions) function. This is knowledge as vital as it is concealed.

Some years of observation have convinced me that those who successfully practice the Washington Arts use and agree upon a common view of the way Government agencies function. The button to be pushed at the Pentagon is, in all essentials, the same button to be pushed at the Department of Commerce. The machinery of each department is the same. This sense of the common machinery is the knowledge held by all who are effective in Washington. The plumber who arrives may not have seen the plumbing of your house before, but he has a feel for the principles of pipes. The principles by which Government agencies operate are similarly known, though almost never expressed.

While those who prosper within a government agency or other institution sense the existence of institutional laws, their inner knowledge is never precisely stated nor reduced to writing. As a result, the inevitable results of the laws are often not foreseen—with often dreadful results. Even a President who should know much better will cry, as John Kennedy did after the Bay of Pigs: "All my life I have known better than to

depend on the experts. How could I have been so stupid. . . ."[1]
To keep those folks who brought you the Bay of Pigs from
bringing you similar spectaculars, a few written laws capable of
predicting institutional behavior would be useful. Such laws
will explain not only how things work when they work, but also
why the Government and other institutions so often work very
badly indeed.

The Machinery Doesn't Work

Nothing seems to work right. The chief products of our
society are public bafflement, frustration and rage. The great
agencies of government appear to be purposeless, ineffective
and yet curiously incapable of improvement.

Our government institutions bear titles promising allevia-
tion of all the ills of our society. Yet the recipients of the regular
mercies of welfare agencies insist that they are not faring well.
The multiple foreign policy machineries of the United States
government have for a decade yielded to an uncontrollable urge
to drop bombs on Asian grass huts.

The malaise extends to a profound distrust of the workings
of the world's corporations. Even *Business Week,* a journal not
noted as the voice of the underground, reports that big companies are viewed with "a great deal" of confidence by only 27
percent of the scientifically sampled public.[2]

Profit-making institutions are not alone to blame; Russian
industries have polluted the Caspian Sea as diligently as American industries have destroyed Lake Erie. The convergence of
Communists and Capitalists is a popular theme, and is nowhere
better illustrated than by the parallel malfunctioning of the

---

[1]John F. Kennedy on the Thursday after the Bay of Pigs, quoted in Sorensen, *Kennedy* (New York: Harper & Row, 1965).

[2]*Business Week,* June 17, 1972, p. 98.

instruments of production and government. From the right, the
left, and the center there is uneasy agreement that the machinery requires major repairs, and maybe even a factory recall.[3]

The frustration of organized society appears to be wide-
spread, structural and inevitable. It appears to be so, and it *is*
so.

The Devil Didn't Do It

The theme of this book is that there are a few simple and
inescapable laws of institutional behavior. These laws are unav-
oidable: they apply to the trivial and the grand, to the large and
the small—in short, to all human institutions whatsoever. The
laws can be stated in simple terms and they are to be understood
simply and absolutely. Thus baldly stated, the laws run counter
to a number of accepted doctrines.

The professional students of government and institutions
have little aided the general understanding of what goes on.
There is no academically accepted body of theory both (1)
comprehensible to the baffled citizen and (2) useful in understanding and predicting the behavior of the institutions of society. Of course, the scholarly literature contains insights both
true and valuable. The truths, however, are like the ambergris
in the whale—a precious essence wrapped in layers of blubber.
Something more is needed if the present massive dissatisfaction
with the workings of our society is to be explained and dis-
pelled.

The opacity of academic jargon is matched by the woolly

---

[3]Mr. Clark Clifford, lately Secretary of Defense and a practiced intoner of high
credentials, intones: "The history of the rise and fall of great nations discloses
that their decline was not due to lack of power or influence abroad, but to the
loss of the confidence of their own people at home—confidence in their Government and confidence in their economy." *The New York Times,* July 2, 1972.

phrasemaking of those who have dedicated themselves to criticism of things as they are. Today's revolutionary discourse is conducted in terms either antique or unintelligible. What usually emerges is no more than a highly irritable denunciation of a devil called the "establishment." How the errors of the present establishment are to be corrected in the golden days of the future establishment is a question always and conveniently avoided by the righteously disgusted.

At times, the blame for the malfunctioning of our institutions has been assigned to those individual devils who find themselves temporarily at the helm. Foreign policy will be denounced as the evil product of an Acheson, a Dulles, a Rusk or a Kissinger. Economic policy is attributed to the baleful workings of the Wall Street bankers, the Socialists, or the professorial chairholders of the eastern universities. In their least sophisticated form these theories of government amount to fundamentalist theologies calling for the casting out of devils. Joe McCarthy screamed for the expulsion of Commies and their sympathizers. Other plain Joes regularly interpret the morning news from Washington as the gnawing of termites at the timbers of the Republic.

The trouble with the devil theories of government and institutional action is twofold. *First,* government agencies go through the same motions whether a Democrat, a Republican, or a claimed party-liner occupies the Cabinet seat. The Pinkos and the tools of the Wall Street bankers so often and so noisily exposed in the past have somehow been unable to further their secret causes. Asmodeus is just not the Assistant Secretary for Policy and Plans in any branch of the American government. No way. *Second,* the devil theories are unable to explain why Chinese or Russian foreign policy or economic policy bears such strong family resemblances to American or French policies. If the faults of our institutions were attributable to the evil

motives of the bad men running the establishment, then somewhere, sometime, good men ought to do better—but they
don't.

Method of the Book

What is necessary, then, if the functioning of our institutions is to be understood, is a short statement of the laws which
institutions follow. The method here adopted is to begin, without apology, with a few definitions and a few axioms that, like
all axioms, have to be accepted. From these, theorems are
deduced as logical consequences. These deduced theorems in
turn require to be matched to occurrences in the real world, to
see if they fit and are indeed laws of general application. To be
sure that theory and fact agree, an examination must be made
of both the trivial daily behavior of institutions and the great
matters of state where institutions purport to change the course
of national or world history. If the axioms and the laws deduced
from them are valid, they should be applicable to the high and
the low, to bureaucratic trivia and to statesman-like delibera-
tions.[4] If they so apply, then it is fair to conclude that the laws
enunciated are valid and predictive. Such laws are, in an important sense, true.[5]

---

[4] As we shall see, there is in fact no distinction between "bureaucratic trivia" and "great matters of state." Functionally, they are exactly the same thing.

[5] To say that a law of institutional behavior is true is not the same thing as saying that no other laws or factors are at work. For example, we are not concerned here with the effects of bribery or corruption. A government officer may well be bribed: may have been, and may well be. The vice president of an automobile company might also be bribed. A government officer often gets his job by influence, friendship, political power. So does a corporate officer. But the automobile is not assembled as it is because of nepotism, and neither is a government memorandum. The form of a memorandum and its contents are not dictated by personalities but by principles. The principles here enunciated predict what an institution will do in terms general enough to include action resulting from extraneous noninstitutional pressures of money, friendship, politics and all the rest.

Modest Hope for Improvement

The laws of institutional behavior are cold comfort. They teach that all human institutions are held in the same iron grip. A general in the Pentagon, a Ralph Nader, a yippie, and a commissar are alike caught in the same institutional vise.

That laws of institutional behavior exist does not mean that there is no hope for improving the work of institutions. An airplane cannot be designed by ignoring the laws of aeronautics. A government cannot be well designed by ignoring the laws of institutional behavior.

In a society growing constantly more complex, our institutions have gone forth and multiplied. Since the human birthrate promises soon to drown us all in a sea of unhappy people, it is worth some pains to avoid a second immersion in a wash of inept institutions. Most new institutions are cobbled together without regard for the inevitable institutional laws. The pitiful results are not surprising. If only a few of the laws of institutional behavior can be exposed to view, then hope remains that our institutions public and private can be made useful, productive and humane.

1. FIRST PRINCIPLES

The Classic Form. Definition of Institution. Definition of Internal Machinery (Work). Three Axioms of Institutional Action. The Naïve Commissioner (Mild Anecdote). Case of the Moon Shot. Registration. Case Study of a Monstrous Birth.

The Classic Form

The classical method of setting forth a new science requires a structure as formal as it is reassuring. Euclid's *Elements,* Newton's *Principia,* Galileo's *Two New Sciences*—each is formal, geometrical and elegant. First come the definitions: the subject matter of the science. There follow the axioms which state certain relationships of the terms defined. Axioms are not proved, but are to be accepted as self-evident; a proposition not self-evident but nevertheless to be accepted is a postulate. Last, there comes the elaboration of the body of the work, in the form of propositions first expressed as theorems and then, when logically proved, to be accepted as laws.

If, with all proper humility, we are to follow the classic pattern, then a science of Institutional Behavior must begin with definitions and axioms and move on to proof of laws.

10

Something more will then be required: our laws of institutional behavior will predict what happens in the real world. Therefore, if the laws are true, we are put to it to demonstrate their truth in action. Such tests of truth are not hard to come by, for the world is conveniently full of institutions.

The institutions that are the subject matter of this work are human creations, and the first definition is as follows:[1]

DEFINITION OF INSTITUTION

An institution is a continuing recognizable group of individuals working together where the group's existence is not measured by a human life.

By this definition the United States Government in all its awful majesty and bureaucratic proliferation is an institution. So is every other High Contracting Party to any international treaty. So is General Motors, and so is the General Staff of the Army, which is itself a sub-institution of a bigger institution. The Upper Suburban Garden Club is exclusive in its membership, but a perfectly acceptable institution by the definition. The moral beauty of an institution concerns us not a bit: the Gestapo, the Red Cross, the Weathermen and the Hospital for the Destitute and Infirm are all alike subject to the institutional laws.

---

[1]Stating our first principles is a matter of some delicacy. Parkinsonian pith is surely to be desired, but overcompression has the undesirable consequence of losing any meaning except to the author. That "love is all" is true, no doubt, but hardly an all-purpose guide to daily action. At the same time, properly complex and qualified statements lack conviction. History does not report that Galileo said, "under carefully controlled laboratory conditions and all other things remaining unchanged, the Earth may be regarded as moving." He said (or we are told he said): "and still it moves." That kind of effect is worth some effort.

Within every institution, there is a prescribed pattern of activity for those who are members of the institution. This may be filing a form, writing a memorandum or, in the higher reaches of human achievement, arranging for national rehabilitation by aerial bombardment.

In a very general way we can include the pattern of all these scurryings in the anthills by the following:

DEFINITION OF INTERNAL MACHINERY (WORK)

The internal machinery of an institution is the patterns of work established for the individuals who are a part of the institution.

Note, please, that the definition says the patterns of work are "established," but not by whom or for what purpose. In most institutions the reasons for the patterns of work are lost in the mists of time. In some, the reason for the work pattern is sensible and immediately apparent. In all institutions there is a pattern, and whether the pattern first appeared on tablets of stone or an organizational memorandum concerns us not.

Note also, please, the distinction between "the pattern of work" and the purpose of work. The pattern of the work set the Head Torturer is to torture by the accepted means of rack and thumbscrew. The *purpose* of the torture may be declared to be Protection of the Faith during the Inquisition, Protection of the Reich in Hitler's Germany, or Protection of Perversion in a motorcycle gang. Whatever the ostensible purpose, the pattern of work set for all Head Torturers is the same.

Equipped with two definitions, we can now state our axioms. Appropriately, they appear in triplicate:

THREE AXIOMS OF
INSTITUTIONAL ACTION

First Axiom: Any institutional action is merely the working of the institution's internal machinery.

Second Axiom: Institutional existence depends upon the continual working of the internal machinery.

Third Axiom: Whatever the internal machinery does is perceived within the institution as the real purpose of the institution (i.e., function is seen as purpose).

As any geometry student knows, there is no arguing about axioms. They are given to be accepted. Nevertheless, a little discussion at this point is appropriately directed to those who find the axioms either (a) so obvious as to be meaningless or (b) so meaningful as to be offensive.

The Axioms are meant to be taken quite literally. The First Axiom says: "Any institutional action is merely the working of the institution's internal machinery." Is it not plainly so that an institution cannot act unless its internal machinery (as defined) runs? Pick an institution—any institution. The Outer Exurbs Tennis and Garden Club cannot name Creeping Gadwort the weed of the month without the functioning of the internal machinery for proposing, considering and promulgating such weighty decisions. The institution of the Inner City Police Department cannot arrest a suspect unless the internal machinery functions. If a policeman grabs a suspect but does not go through the machinery of "arresting," the suspect has been conked with a billy club, but he is not "arrested" because the institution did not act.

Put another way, institutional action is recognizable only because the institutional machinery has functioned. If you hire a plane and drop a bomb, you are a nut, properly loathed by all. If you drop a bomb as part of the 923d Wing, duly following Air Force procedures, you may be a hero (to some).

An institution may be insanely complex, as the Department of Defense is, so that the machinery is broken into thousands of subdivisions—those who report and those who plan alternatively, and those who weigh alternatives and those who decide, and those who write decisions and so on, and on. The action of the machinery may be so minor as to be ludicrous: perhaps a directive as to the permissible length of sideburns in the Army.[2] But, there can be no action, no memorandum re: sideburns, unless there are internal procedures—machinery— to consider and act upon sideburneal matters.

The working of this machinery *is* the agency's action. There is just nothing else there but the machinery. To say "The White House tonight sent troops" or "The President sent troops" misses the institutional point. Neither the building nor the man did any such thing. The building couldn't, and the man used (or was used by) the established institutional machinery.

The Second Axiom ("Institutional existence depends upon the continual working of the internal machinery") says no more than that if the machinery stops, so does the institution. A little reflection makes this self-evident. If the machinery for issuing license plates for automobiles stops working—for whatever reason—the existence of the institution called the Automobile License Division of the Bureau of Motor Vehicles also stops.

---

[2]One of Jack Anderson's less breathtaking scoops: "Westmoreland Cuts Line on Hair . . . A stern memo to Army staff heads decrees that sideburns absolutely must stop 'at the lowest part of the exterior ear opening.' " *Washington Post,* October 28, 1971.

While an institution can wait for work (say, the Fire Department, or the Office of Civil Defense), if there is no work ever in sight, in due course there will be no institution.[3] Stop to note that the absence of *useful* work is no threat to institutional health. Lots of institutions do nothing at all worth doing, but they are in the pink of condition—busy filing, writing memos and seeking more staff. A mild anecdote about auto licensing makes this clear.

The Naïve Commissioner

Upon his appointment to high office, the Commissioner of Motor Vehicles of a midwestern state surveyed his domain. The walls of one large room were lined with rank upon rank of gleaming metal file cabinets. Inquiry revealed that each cabinet held records of all the leases of all the motor vehicles in the state. The files were beautifully kept by a staff dedicated to alphabetization.

The new Commissioner was impressed by the competence of this branch, and turned to go. But an idle thought struck him. "What do we do with these records?" he asked. The answer, solemnly supplied as a full explanation, was: "Why, we file them."

---

[3]In Washington, the single and quite unimportant exception to this rule is the Subversive Activities Control Board, which does not control subversive activities, because it is not allowed to—even if it could. We can regard the SACB as an aberration, or perhaps more properly use our Third Axiom and say that the real purpose of the SACB is not at all to control SA but to pay salaries to the Board members (as the late Senator Dirksen plainly intended). This is an intellectually satisfying treatment, and in the grand English tradition of offices such as the Lord Warden of the Cinque Ports. The Warden does not ward any number of ports, and the institution *is* the title.

Anyway, the SACB is losing its grip. In August 1971 an Executive Order tried to give the SACB something to do. But in late June 1972 the Senate cut off all funds, and at last report things looked bad for the Board members who may have to look for honest work.

Further inquiry disclosed that never had a record left the file room after it arrived; the filing of vehicle leases had precisely no purpose whatsoever.

The point of the story is not that bureaucracies do nothing with purpose (which is false), but that the institution requires only work, not purposeful work, to survive. This brings us to the Third Axiom.

The Third Axiom declares that Function is seen as Purpose: "Whatever the internal machinery does is perceived within the institution as the real purpose of the institution." Here is a distinction of high significance, offering the clue to much otherwise mysterious institutional behavior. This all-important distinction is between *what is said to be the purpose* of the institution and *what is perceived within the institution as its real purpose.* What is usually said to be the purpose of our institutions is always something noble. Assertions of noble purpose make excellent oratory, but the significant operative purpose is what the worker within the institution thinks is the purpose. The Third Axiom states that the worker thinks the purpose of the institution is *whatever the internal machinery does.*

The Third Axiom is not a pleasant thought, for it means that no confidence can be placed in the sentiments engraved over the door of an institution's headquarters. Quite so, and it would be well to be wary of what is going on inside, too. We pause for two rather expensive examples.

Case of the Moon Shot

Recent reports of dissension within the United States' space program show the Third Axiom in action. The space program, administered by the National Aeronautics and Space Administration, has in at least some senses been a brilliant success. Man, and man from the United States, has walked on the moon, an enormous technical achievement as well as a profoundly moving symbolic act.

Yet, immediately after the first moon landing, and the announcement that only a few others would follow, reports were heard that within NASA two groups were wrestling. The first group consisted of the technicians who had labored so long and so successfully. This technical faction included the engineers, the hardware designers and the operating pilots, drawn from the armed services. In the second group were the scientists. Although they had a few kilos of gritty moon rocks to study, the scientists were heard to grumble that they had no control, that the program was running on not to gather scientific information but to make more flights and design more hardware. The scientific faction claimed that lunar vehicles had become more important than their passengers or their destinations. The scientists demanded a change of emphasis. They all but picketed, carrying signs reading "make experiments, not flights." In 1969 the chief scientist of the Manned Spacecraft Center in Houston, and three others, resigned with public complaints.[4]

The Third Axiom permits a quick and easy analysis of the fight within NASA, and a prediction of the outcome with substantial certainty.

The NASA program had continued a decade and spent a score of billions of dollars. Every focus in the early years was on hardware—not what to do on the moon, but how to get there. The internal mechanisms of NASA were devoted to the design and procurement of new, outlandish and exciting hardware. Included in the shopping list was the procurement of trained superpilots, the astronauts. By our Third Axiom, making the space vehicles and then the trip itself must be envisaged

---

[4] *The New York Times,* August 15 and 17, 1969.

by those within the institution as the purpose of the institution's activity. The choice between the scientists who wanted to go to the moon and the astronauts was no choice at all. The astronauts had to win, for the purpose of the program was building and flying the equipment, wasn't it?[5]

Registration

Institutional behavior is not, of course, confined to government bureaus. Universities are fine old institutions and offer fine mossy examples.

At many institutions of higher learning the barbaric rites of mass registration open the academic year. The school's largest hall is set aside. Quantities of desks are arranged in rows, aisles are created with standards and ropes, temporary bookkeeping and cashiers' cages are erected, the faculty is called in, and the agony begins. For one, two or three days students shuffle in despairing lines, trying to register for courses, get their selection approved by their advisers and pay their bills.

The mass registration always fails, because many courses are always quickly filled. The faculty then huddles, regroups

---

[5]The prediction is confirmed by a letter from Prof. Brian O'Leary of Cornell, who resigned as a scientist-astronaut and explained:

"The gap between science and engineering in NASA's manned space program seems to be widening, and the scientists are coming out on the short end. . . .

"Perhaps the most dramatic example of this regrettable situation is the August 7 [1969] announcement of the Apollo 13 and 14 crews. Each crew includes two rookie test-pilot astronauts who joined the program more recently than several of the scientist-astronauts (one is a geologist). . . .

"The excuse given for leaving the scientists out of the picture is that Apollo lunar landings will continue to be 'operational' rather than 'scientific' missions."

Letter to *The New York Times,* August 15, 1969.

(Late note: One scientist went on the last Apollo flight.)

and opens new sections. Students return, learn the new hours, have their programs re-reapproved by their advisers and stagger through the aisles again. After the close, several weeks are spent by all concerned changing times, places, and courses of study and repairing their nerves.

While the mass registration does serve the function of introducing the student to institutional behavior, it makes no administrative sense. Clearly the job would be better done by earlier notice, by signing up separately by schools (not many take Early Delphic Poets and Crop Rotation 201) or in a hundred other ways devisable by any instructor in logic.

Our diagnosis is simple. The institutional machinery conveys to the university administrator the sense that registration *is* bringing everybody together for three days of frustration. The purposes of registration (notice, planning, scheduling) have not been forgotten—they are simply not seen as purposes. "The purpose is to get registered—see?" (Third Axiom).

Case Study of a
Monstrous Birth

Thanks to the indignation of Mr. Ernest Fitzgerald, there was told the wondrous story of the birth of an enormous airplane, the C-5A.[6]

The C-5A was conceived within the recesses of the Pentagon as fulfilling an ideal, a very Galatea of a cargo plane, reflecting the purest aspirations of the Pygmalions who conceived her form. In less high-flown language, a planning group began to list their objectives: the plane must supply troops in

---

[6]Thanks to the indignation of Senator William Proxmire, the parent Lockheed Corporation had some difficulty in surviving the delivery.

an instant, and a lot of troops. A requirement for 1,700 square feet or more of usable level floor space was stated, and a capacity to airlift a great weight, over 200 tons, was desired. By now the planners had a great lumbering plane that required a major airport. As practical men, the planners knew that a great lumbering plane that required a major airport was not useful in the average war. Instead of shrinking the monster, they inflated the specifications to include the capability of taking off and landing under difficult conditions. Add a few requirements as to range and speed, and the end was in sight: a truly formidable craft, an agile leviathan, a severe technical challenge.

For its own institutional reasons, the Lockheed Aircraft Corporation was panting to accept the challenge, and development began. Costs for the first 120 planes were estimated at $3,423,000,000, or a bargain price of $28,500,000 a plane. A willing Congress responded with funds. The wisdom of the expenditure could not be doubted, for after all, the most advanced managerial techniques had been prescribed for the procurement, assuring that this was absolutely the most economical way to meet a vital military need.

As work continued, Mr. Fitzgerald, an Air Force auditing officer, began to notice a disturbing fact. Expenses were far outrunning estimates. Such cost excesses are politely called "over-runs," as if all that is wrong is that the contractor ran too hard.

The over-run on the C-5A of about $29 million a plane struck Fitzgerald as a useful sum, and he began to talk about it. The rest of the story is as familiar as the plot of a television comedy. Fitzgerald blew the whistle first in private and then shrilly in public. The Air Force was not amused. Fitzgerald was first exiled to the equivalent of Siberia and then chucked out. The crusading Senator Proxmire took up the fight, the newspapers took notice, Lockheed suffered financial anemia and had to be saved by a transfusion of public money. The Air Force will end up with only eighty-one fat, expensive planes, at a cost of $4.6 billion,[7] and with egg on its face.

The usual reaction to the C-5A fiasco by those who are devoted to viewing such charades unsympathetically is a murmur of "military-industrial complex." This explains little, but is taken as a satisfactory analysis. It has the virtue of showing that the murmurer is wise in the ways of the Pentagon and its suppliers.

Unfortunately, for reasons that must wait for a later chapter for full explication, the "military-industrial complex" is about as real as "the Pentagon." Both exist, but one term describes a business relationship and the other a building. Neither term tells how or why anything works; neither building nor relationship is good or evil in itself.

The plot of the C-5A story all flows from a single original error. The mistake was in assembling a group to specify the design of the plane. Once that step was taken, the end was foreordained. With the inevitability of Greek tragedy, the inexorable institutional laws operated.

A group to specify the design of a plane is a sub-institution. In the military way, such an important sub-institution confers, briefs, coordinates with and relates to scores and hundreds of other sub-institutions within the web. (It is impossible to use and distasteful even to report the proper Washington verb for this activity. The verb is "to liaise." A liaison officer "liaises.")

As our Third Axiom requires, the plane-planning group begins to see plane-planning as its sole purpose, not the conservation of the public purse, nor for that matter the winning of wars. Further, owing to the accommodation of many other sub-institutions in the planning group, and the constant coordi-

---

[7]Figures from the General Accounting Office staff study, reprinted with Mr. Fitzgerald's testimony in the *Hearings* before the Senate Committee on Banking, Housing and Urban Affairs on Emergency Loan Guarantee Legislation (92nd Cong., 2d Sess.).

nation, everybody's ideas must be accommodated in the piece of hardware. For example, the Army's demands for carrying supplies for a large number of troops must be met. The sub-institution, the planning group, has built into it machinery for meeting all participants' demands—and that assures that meeting all demands is seen as a purpose and an end in itself. The busy coordination and consultation leaves no time for reflection on extraneous matters, and the object being planned is taken as a goal in itself. The result is inevitable—a Great Auk of an airplane, monstrous and monstrously expensive.[8]

Most military procurement suffers from the C-5A symptoms (elephantiasis and high-budget pressure). The F-111, McNamara's multiservice aircraft, cost a mint and is still infirm despite months of rest on the ground. Ward Just, in *Military Men* (Knopf, 1970), reports the case of the M-551 Army tank (the Sheridan), another frantically complex and expensive vehicle. According to Just, the Sheridan cost estimates range from $1.2 billion to $1.5 billion. The need for this Cadillac of tanks can be explained only institutionally: "The United States did not have a reconnaisance vehicle as required in Cav [Cavalry] doctrine, and it is immaterial that no other nation did either. What is important is that the requirement was there, and because it was there it was imperative that it be satisfied."

That last sentence quoted is gloriously suggestive, and we follow the suggestion at once.

---

[8]Also inevitable was the fate of Mr. Fitzgerald. The last thing an institution needs is an inside expert telling the world the institution is manned by simpletons. Common sense as well as theory predicts Fitzgerald's ouster, but not the explanation given ("to save expenses"). Someone had a sense of humor.

2. THE INSTITUTIONAL IMPERATIVE

The Imperative and its Corollary. The Story of the Blank Tariff (A Tale of Simple Virtue). The Librarian's Librarian. The General's General. The Case of the SST (Guilt-Inducing Quiz).

Those readers who are logicians, systems analysts, or attentive will have noticed a circular aspect of the Three Axioms of Institutional Action.

If whatever the institution's machinery does is perceived by the workers as the real purpose (Third Axiom) and the working of the machinery *is* the action of the institution (First Axiom), and existence depends on continued operation of the machinery (Second Axiom)—well, then the whole business is circular, self-perpetuating and without higher purpose. If you saw this, you saw clearly. It is this axiomatic circularity that leads us at once to the prime directive controlling all institutional action, the Institutional Imperative.[1] Bold-

---

[1]The name of the Law obviously calls up memories of Robert Ardrey's *The Territorial Imperative* (New York: Atheneum, 1963). Ardrey says: "I submit, of course, that the continuity of human evolution from the world of the animal to

faced type is again indicated, as we are in the presence of
truth.

THE INSTITUTIONAL
IMPERATIVE

**Every action or decision of an institution
must be intended to keep the institutional
machinery working.**

And, as a natural corollary to the Imperative:

COROLLARY TO THE I.I.

**To speak of any goal or purpose of an
institution other than keeping the institutional machinery running is no more
meaningful than to speak of the goal of an
automobile exhaust or the purpose of the
hum of a sewing machine.**

The Institutional Imperative is an absolute law of action,
never broken in practice. It is felt in the bone and gut by every
person working in every institution. Yet language has such
strange powers to overcome both instinct and reason that the
workings of the Imperative are never revealed to outsiders.
Inside the walls, there is a terrible and irresistible compulsion;
the outsider is told the institution acts only from the highest
motives.

Again, we pause to consider a few examples.

the world of man ensures that a human group in possession of a social territory
will behave according to the universal laws of the territorial principle." So here,
our inquiry is whether there are universal laws which bind institutions. The
institution is something beyond a human group. Institutional behavior is as
necessary an object of study as human behavior, and as much in need of illumina-
tion. The lash of institutional necessity is as imperative as any biological drive.
Ardrey teaches much about man in his animal aspects; here we consider, with
a bow, the behavior of groups of men with human aspects suppressed.

The Story of the Blank Tariff
(A Tale of Simple Virtue)

A tariff, be it known, is a schedule of rates and conditions charged by some public utility.

The ostensible purposes of tariff-filing are high ones. They are: to inform the public of a utility's charges, and to assure that the charges are equally applicable to all. These are, let us concede, most useful and admirable goals, to be accepted with satisfaction. We accept with less satisfaction the operations of the institutional machinery established to carry out such high purposes.

Each regulatory agency has a Tariff Office, or Section, or Bureau. The excellent public servants in the Tariff Office devote themselves to assuring that the tariffs filed by the regulated utilities meet the standards laid down for tariffs by the agency's Tariff Circular. The Tariff Circular contains all the rules and regulations about where, when and how to file tariffs, on what paper and in what form. In general the Tariff Circular deals with matters of form, not substance; it tells how to express a rate, but not how high or low the rate should be.

Many tariffs nowadays appear in loose-leaf form, for easy and cheap revision. As revisions are made, an earlier page is canceled and a new page substituted. A system is prescribed, by Tariff Circular, for recording these changes. The upper-right-hand corner of the seventeenth revision of a tariff page will look like this:

United Carriage Company
Tariff No. 6
17th Revised Page No. 10
Cancels 16th Revised Page No. 10
Issued: April 1, 1984
Effective: May 1, 1984

The system is simple and effective, and hardly seems worth the labor of description. But, we learn as much from an ant as from an elephant. We cannot understand matters of state until we know in the smallest detail how the machinery of the state operates.

A generation ago, an agency which could be nameless but will not be—it was the Civil Aeronautics Board (or "CAB" to its many friends)—required all international airlines to file tariffs. These airline tariffs could be altered only on thirty days' notice. A certain airline—call it Air Anterior—had, on March 1, filed a tariff page as the ninth revision of page 21 of its tariff, to be effective April 1. This ninth revised page named rates which, the page stated, would become effective April 1 and *expire* on April 30. Since future rates had not been decided on, a tenth revised page 21 was filed which was perfectly blank, except for the legend stating it was effective May 1. A few days later Air Anterior filed an eleventh revision of page 21, now naming rates effective May 1, and subsequently filed a twelfth revised page 21, duly canceling eleventh revised page 21, and naming rates effective May 10.

Disaster struck! Air Anterior received a curt notice from the CAB stating that twelfth revised page 21 and eleventh revised page 21 had been rejected for noncompliance with the CAB's tariff circular. A call followed to the airline's regular Washington law firm, and the youngest and hence lowest lawyer on the totem pole was dispatched to the CAB to investigate.

Upon inquiry, the head of the CAB's tariff office revealed that twelfth revised page 21 had been rejected because eleventh revised page 21 had been rejected. And why had eleventh revised page 21 been rejected? Why, because it failed to say "eleventh revised page 21 cancels tenth revised page 21," which meant that tenth *and* eleventh revised page 21 were both still

effective, which violated the tariff circular's plain commandment. So also, twelfth revised page 21 had to be rejected because
it canceled only eleventh revised page 21 and not tenth revised
page 21. All quite correct; thine tariff circular is a just tariff
circular, but thine tariff circular is a jealous tariff circular.

But, the eager young lawyer was quick to point out, everything on tenth revised page 21 was perfectly blank. No harm
could come by failing to say the magic words "cancels tenth
revised page 21" because the tenth revised page was a mere
blank—a smile without the Cheshire cat.

This argument was rejected: a violation of the tariff circular was a violation. A blank page is a page, and a page must be
canceled. So, the lawyer tried an appeal to grace. Pray grant
"special permission" to publish on short notice a new eleventh
revised page 21 bearing the proper incantation canceling tenth
revised page 21. The chief of the Tariff Bureau, who has such
discretionary powers, refused. Making a mistake was not a
justifiable reason for asking for special permission.

Next, the lawyer tried an argument on a higher plane. The
purpose of tariffs is to notify the public, and if the tariff pages
were rejected and could not be immediately refiled, either (a)
the airline could not operate for the first two weeks in May,
having no valid tariff on file, which would leave the public with
no air service, or (b) the airline would operate without a tariff,
leaving the public open to all the dangers of tariffless transportation. In fact, the lawyer said to the Tariff Bureau Chief,
"If you report my client I'll tell the world and the judge just
what happened, and they'll laugh you out of court."

The Tariff Bureau Chief's response to this impassioned
logic is the point of the parable. Looking with some astonish-
ment at a lawyer so young and unsophisticated, the Bureau
chief said kindly: "It's not my job to enforce the tariffs, it's my
job to see that they're filed right."

The Librarian's Librarian

Never underestimate the strength of the established work pattern of an institution. Consider the following anecdote handed down from the 1920s, and compare it with the next one:

When the University of Maryland was still a small school, a professor met the school librarian, a Miss Tippett, striding purposefully across the campus, wearing a smile. "Where are you going in such a hurry, Miss Tippett, and why so happy?" "Why," she said, "there's only one book out of the library, and I'm on my way to get it."

The General's General

The Seventh Air Force is an institution somewhat larger and more destructive than a University Library. General John D. Lavelle, lately Commander of the Seventh Air Force in Vietnam, was held as tightly in the grip of the Institutional Imperative as any other institutionalite.

General Lavelle was hastily retired for running his own air war by bombing unauthorized targets in North Vietnam. The concept of a general running his own war is a slippery one— like an elevator man buying his own elevator. General Lavelle's testimony explains it all: it was the Imperative that made him do it.

According to the general's statement: "In certain instances, against high priority military targets, I made interpretations that were probably beyond the literal intention of the rules. *I did this since the crews were operating in an environment of optimum enemy defense.*" (Emphasis added.)[2]

---

[2]A short document titled "Statement of General John D. Lavelle (USAF, Retired) before the Special Subcommittee on Armed Services Investigating of the Committee on Armed Services of the House of Representatives." (Undated; June 1972.)

Translating from the Pentagonese, what General Lavelle is saying is that he bombed places because they were firing at his planes which were bombing the places because . . . and so on. A really beautiful[3] example of the circularity of the Institutional Imperative.

Newsweek (June 26, 1972) charges that "Lavelle's superiors had made a concerted effort to cover up his offense." If so, it would not be surprising. Practically everybody in Washington has his own war in one way or another.

The Case of the SST
(Guilt-Inducing Quiz)

Self-improving books give the reader a quiz from time to time, in order to create a feeling of guilt, remembered from school.

The case of the Supersonic Transport (SST) is almost too simple to mention. Treat it as a quiz, and assume the following:

1. The Department of Transportation has in its budget a multi-hundred million dollar item for development of a supersonic transport.

2. The SST has the following qualities:
   (i)   it is supernaturally noisy;
   (ii) it will sell for a super-expensive price, at a time when the prospective buyers (the airlines) are in a financial bind;
   (iii) it carries fewer passengers, over a shorter range, than existing aircraft;
   (iv) it is claimed to have a substantial chance of polluting the upper atmosphere, even to the extent of

---

[3]"Beautiful" in the sense you hear a doctor talk about a beautiful liver abcess.

causing irreversible changes in the protective layers shielding the world from ultraviolet sunstroke or skin cancer, or both; and

(v) it is going to cost a potful of money to develop, even by Washington aerospace standards, at a time when the government deficit is high.

Quiz Questions:

1. What position did the Department of Transportation take as to funds for the SST?
2. Why?

Quiz Answers:

1. The Department supported money for the SST, declaring that the SST was an economic necessity and an ecological boon.[4]
2. The Institutional Imperative.

Take full credit if you answered as above,[5] and go on to the next chapter.

---

[4]Secretary of Transportation Volpe: "Our purpose is not to push this program come what may. Our purpose is to recognize that this program is a key component of the employment picture in the United States." *The New York Times,* January 14, 1971.

[5]Take no more credit for predicting Congressional refusal to appropriate funds for the SST, for political prediction is a much more complex matter, beyond the scope of this book.

Take no credit, either, for predicting the SST will not rise again. *The New York Times* of May 21, 1971, reports: "William Magruder, director of SST development for the Transportation Department, said . . . 'we continue to believe that a U.S. SST will ultimately be proven to be beneficial to the nation and that the means to develop and produce a second generation SST will be found.' "

3. THE EMBEDDED INDIVIDUAL

Definition of the Relation Between Institution and Individual (Discipline). Field Expedition in Search of the Attributes of Importance (New Federal Obesity Scale). The Five Attributes: Activity, Authority, Security, Urgency, Panoply. The Personnel Postulate (The Institutional Employee). Petty Bureaucrats (Law of Attributed Importance and Theorem of Irrelevancy of Attributes). Personal and Institutional Equivalents.

The ideal logician, said Sherlock Holmes to Dr. Watson, from the sight of a drop of water "could infer the possibility of an Atlantic or a Niagara." So also, if our body of Laws of Institutional Behavior is to be logically satisfying, we must show that by adding up the acts of individuals, a sum is reached that equals the institutional actions required by the Institutional Laws.

We proceed as follows: first, an additional definition is needed; second, a field trip into the Washington bush is required to gather specimens; and finally, we must add to the Three Axioms of Institutional Action a postulate about individuals. When all this is done, the theoretical foundation is complete: all else will be deductive, and we can proceed to derive the Laws of Institutional Behavior.

A Definition of Discipline

Every normal human being is regularly gnawed by self-doubt. No normal institution declares the slightest uncertainty about the total rightness of its every action. While individuals within the institution can doubt the wisdom of what they are doing, they tend to say nothing of their doubts and they rarely do anything about them.

Individual doubts cannot be converted into institutional uncertainty, because of the institution's internal discipline. The rule of discipline of every institution, military or civil, is the same. To keep his job, the individual must accept the rule that the action or decision of the institution is more important than his personal opinion. The Air Force pilot may believe the bombing mission is wrongly conceived and perhaps even evil, but his views are of no effect so long as he continues to push the bombs-away button. At the moment, several of the higher functionaries of the Johnson Administration now let it be known they always had their doubts about the Vietnam war. Some of them probably did. Messrs. Townsend Hoopes, lately of the Pentagon,[1] and George Ball, lately of the State Department,[2] may indeed have believed most sincerely that the Vietnam war was a futile disaster, but they kept discipline, and the institutional actions continued. It must be comforting to the bombee to know the bomber had a moral doubt.

Our theoretical structure requires a definition of this necessary disciplinary relationship between the individual and the institution. This requirement is supplied by the following:

---

[1] *The Limits of Intervention*, (McKay, 1969).

[2] George Ball, former Under Secretary of State for President Johnson, has earned a lot of credit for his "often eloquent and remarkably prescient warning" in 1964 of the perils of the Vietnam war (*Newsweek*, June 19, 1972, p. 47). The 1964 memorandum was publicly printed in July 1972 by *The Atlantic Monthly* at a time when prescience was hindsight.

DEFINITION OF THE RELATION BETWEEN INSTITUTION AND INDIVIDUAL (DISCIPLINE)

An individual is a part of an institution if, and only if, the individual accepts the institutional action as more important than his personal beliefs.

This definition does not inquire *why* the individual accepts the institutional decision. It may be because he doesn't want to be fired. Mr. Fitzgerald was fired for exposing the Air Force bungling over the C-5A.

Townsend Hoopes and George Ball would have been dismissed from the councils of the mighty if they had threatened any useful opposition to institutional war policy. The individual may have to accept the institutional decision because he will be imprisoned or shot if he doesn't—when the commanding officer says "Charge!" it is best to charge first and write your exposé of Army brutality later.

Whatever the reason for accepting discipline, if it is accepted, the individual stays as part of the institution, and if it isn't, he is put outside. Note that all that is required is that the individual *accept* discipline. He need not believe the institution's welfare is more important than his individual well-being, but he is supposed to.[3]

---

[3]Business institutions have their recognized discipline. It is hard to tell whether *Forbes'* article "Proud to be an Organization Man" (May 15, 1972) is talking about Proctor and Gamble (it is) or the Army or the Church: "In staying, however, the career riser must accept the necessarily bureaucratic ways and the shared beliefs of a huge organization. He must be willing to follow prescribed procedures and behavioral norms . . . Moreover, he must find it in himself to believe in the essential goodness of the company . . ."

Field Expedition in Search of
the Attributes of Importance

While we have defined the relationship of individual to
institution, we have not yet explained the motivation of the
individual. There is a powerful force impelling the prison
warden, the under secretary, the sales manager; each to serve
his institution in his particular way, so that the sum of individual actions inexorably equals institutional action.

When data are required in the social sciences, a field collecting trip is indicated, preferably at the expense of some foundation. Our unfunded expedition will be to Washington, where
institutions are most densely packed and highly developed.
Here, if anywhere, the forces motivating the individual within
the institution can be observed and recorded.

We begin by asking a very simple question: how do you tell
if anybody is somebody? The external indicia of importance
vary from society to society and within a society from group to
group and time to time. Within the United States Government,
as in all institutions, there are both formal schedules for indicating rank, and unwritten, shifting indicia that are accepted as
declaring personal importance.

Government jobs are classified on a scale from GS-1 to
GS-18 (and above to Cabinet level). The scale of pay is fixed by
law, and from time to time as the pay scale is shifted upward
by a generous Congress in an election year, the new scale is
published in all papers. Gradations of pay reflect presumed
importance.

In a less dollar-oriented society, importance might be signaled by a more intriguing characteristic—say, weight. If
weight were in as an index, you may be sure that tables would
be published:

New Federal Obesity Scale

GRADE	OBESITY	MAXIMUM WEIGHT*
GS-1	Total emaciation	110 pounds
GS-5	Thin as a rail	120 pounds
GS-7	Scarecrow	130 pounds
GS-9	Fit	160 pounds
GS-11	Mesomorph	180 pounds
GS-13	Fat	200 pounds
GS-13	Very fat	225 pounds
GS-18	Extreme fatty	250 pounds
Sub-Cabinet	Gross Corpulence	275 pounds
Cabinet	Immense Corpulosity	300 pounds
White House Staff	At discretion of President	

*Annual increase in weight: 2 pounds, but total weight not to exceed 1 pound less than starting weight in next higher grade.

The Civil Service Commission would then conduct annual weigh-ins and send stern warnings to all departments that there were too many employees in the fatter grades.

While weight is not an accepted Washington index, other measures only slightly less bizarre are in constant use. To mention only a few of the items doled out by rank: size of office; rug (if any); conference table (if any); chairs by type (from Cabinet full leather to standard wooden) and by number; cars with chauffeurs (high-level stuff); water bottles; secretary (or better, secretaries—a very high level official has a personal secretary *with* a secretary); and so on.

Aside from these carefully dispensed authorized privileges of rank, there are far more significant attributes of personal importance. Again, these shift like the tides of fashion, but they can be classified under five broad headings: (1) Activity, (2) Authority, (3) Security, (4) Urgency and (5) Panoply. Each is dealt with briefly below.

1. Activity.

By this is meant simply a high degree of personal activity by the individual. He is *busy.* Of course, this activity must not appear to be self-generated. On the contrary, the official must appear to be driven by the all-consuming demands of his job.

Activity is a very significant index of personal importance within an institution, because activity is directly work-oriented. The individual's value to the institution is his work, and hence, if the man works very hard he must be very valuable. Thus the message projected by activity is: "I am so busy because my job is so important."

It is as unacceptable for a Washington official to speak of the demands on his time as of his sexual powers. Not acceptable: to say during a meeting, "The White House has been after me all morning." Better: secretary puts head into meeting and says to boss, "The White House is on the phone . . . [pause] . . . again." Best: *after* the meeting, your secretary says as a visitor is leaving, "The White House must be anxious; they called twice during your meeting."

If possible, an official should arrange for statements to the effect that the demands of his job imperil his health. The President is *ex officio* always declared to be in imminent danger of destruction by the pressures of his job: "My God, he's aged twenty years in office." He may be enjoying himself hugely, but by convention he is worn with the strain. The same effect should be striven for by lesser men: "That Bureau of Algae Operations job must be a killer—Jenkins lost 30 pounds [alternative: went gray] at it."[4]

2. Authority.

Naturally, it is always important to command great legions or have dispositive authority over spending of billions. Quite often, unfortunately, authority over such matters is widely diffused. (The Assistant Secretary of Defense can do nothing because "The Generals" are recalcitrant, while each General will declare his hands are tied by the unmentionable civilians.) Accordingly, in Washington the meaning of authority is often redefined in order that the supply may meet the demand.

Where "authority" pure and simple resided in Caesar at the head of his legions, today in Washington "authority" more often means *the power to insist on being consulted.* This is a negative concept—perhaps "consultative authority" is a better term.

Note that having "consultative authority" is not equivalent to having veto power. There is a sharp and recognized distinction. A veto power is a real power to affect the decision or action. Ultimately only the President, Congress and the Supreme Court have such veto power. "Consultative authority" is something weaker: it resides in *the right to be called to the meeting.* Once at the meeting, you may serve no function whatsoever. No matter, you have been called in and your consultative authority thereby respected.

The message sought to be projected by the holder of con-

----
[4]The necessity of appearing constantly busy has a strongly deleterious effect on the ability of high officials to discharge their significant duties. More on this subject in Chapter 15.

sultative authority is: "My job is so important I must be consulted on everything."[5]

It is immediately evident that one with a great deal of consultative authority may use his entire working day, week or official career in consulting, without any further work being produced. This indeed happens, and is predicted by theory (Law of Attributed Importance, below). By the Third Axiom, the perpetual consultee views consultations as the purpose of his work. Great pulpy hunks of many Federal agencies are purely consultative organs. With the recent transfer of all foreign affairs activity to the Presidential Assistants, the entire State Department has become a consultative leftover.

3. Security.

In the present sense, security has no meaning of security in the job. Employment security is, in fact, a negative mark on an importance report. Everybody knows that even people in unimportant jobs have Civil Service protection. The "Security" that evidences importance is Secrecy, and the machinery necessary to maintain Secrecy.

Really important officials have locked safes, are visited by messengers with attaché cases chained to their wrists, and read (or at least receive) documents stamped "TOP SECRET," "EXDIS"[6] or other and rarer designations. They talk on telephones with scramblers or communicate in code because their talk is so important. They have special "clearances" and badges evidencing the same, so that they may see what the uncleared may not. Even their scribblings are glorified by being shredded,

---

[5]Secretaries of those with consultative authority should not announce: "You have a meeting at eleven." Rather, at five after eleven, announce: "The eleven o'clock meeting is waiting for you in order to get started."

[6]*Ex*ecutive *Dis*tribution.

incinerated or dissolved in acid under approved procedures.

The glamour of secrecy is universally recognized. Max Weber noted it long ago; our literature and our motion pictures glorify it daily. You, important you, know about project Alpha, Beta or Zeta. Such knowledge is denied to unimportant mortals. As Weber says: "Every bureaucracy seeks to increase the superiority of the professionally informed by keeping their knowledge and intentions secret . . . The concept of the 'official secret' is the specific invention of bureaucracy and nothing is so fanatically defended by the bureaucracy . . ."[7]

All this is a terrific game, exciting and quite safe for the participants. It is immediately evident that secrecy, secret communications, secret meetings, the whole bit, need have no practical consequences at all.

Secrecy in Washington is usually as devoid of content as nonsecrecy in Hollywood. In movies or television, "secrecy" is replaced as an attribute of importance by "publicity." Everything a movie actor does is made public, as well as a lot of things he does not do but would like to. Neither the imaginary public love life of an actor or the imaginary secret work of a bureaucrat is meaningful except as signaling the importance of the love-maker or the policy-maker.

4. Urgency.

Important things are done by important men with important jobs. Important things are urgent; do not wait until tomorrow to apply the tourniquet, seal the breach in the dike or deal with the international crisis. Urgency is recognized as an attribute of the important job and, hence, the important man.

In a hospital, urgency is recognizable in the dash to the

---

[7]H. H. Gerth and C. Wright Mills *From Max Weber,* (Oxford, 1958).

emergency room, the heart massage, the tracheotomy with a penknife. Sheer physical hurry is not much use in Washington. The Secretary of State is not seen galloping up to the White House out of breath. Indeed the rules of the game require display of a certain phlegm: "Purely a routine meeting to review certain developments" is the announcement following an all-day flap after Liberia and Texas declare war.

In Washington the signals of urgency are threefold: priority, ability of the individual to be communicated with, and breach of routine.

Priority is a self-explanatory concept. In the movies and in Washington, when the terrestrial or extraterrestrial menace threatens, scientists, James Bond or important officers of government are summoned. They all then stop whatever they are doing and report to the White House, to Doctors Strangelove or Kissinger or to secret underground headquarters to isolate the Andromeda Strain. The signal of importance is *priority;* the work takes precedence over what James Bond does on his day off.

To be urgently summoned, one must be reachable at all times. This *ability of the individual to be communicated with* appears in several degrees: (1) leaving word where to be reached (very weak); (2) wearing a radio "beeper" on the belt (better); (3) having a telephone in the car (still better: a secure, secret, telephone); (4) (only at the *very* top) carrying a complete communications system around with you.

Breach of routine is the well-recognized signal of urgency. On a point system a late meeting counts one point, a Sunday meeting two points, and anything after midnight five points. Special consultations out of the country earn extra credit. (Despite the weakness of the pound, "I must fly to London for consultation" still has a good solid heft to it.)

5. Panoply.

The fifth attribute of importance is *panoply,* under which is subsumed the whole formal rag-bag of rituals, marks of self-esteem, and grooming gestures.

There remains in government much of the good old-fashioned *ritual procedure,* the panoply of the Durbar or the Court Crier. Attending a formal meeting with the Secretary of Defense is like taking part in the changing of the Guard. The large conference room, the carefully arranged places with names boldly lettered (the Secretary's place located at dead center in accordance with best practice, of course—not at the head), the assembling of all concerned with quiet introductions by the staff, and finally, the announcement: "Gentlemen, the Secretary of Defense." Golly! And then, of course, the Secretary himself is charming and informal, inferentially dismissing all the ritual as not impressive to such insiders as the participants. A superb performance.[8]

Another harmless aspect of panoply is *titles.* Washington delights in titles. Every few years, whenever someone looks in the telephone directory of a large agency called an "administration," the following title is rediscovered: "Administrative Assistant to the Assistant Administrator for Administration." (Translation: the helper of the man responsible for internal housekeeping in the agency.) A good practical rule of thumb is that the longer the title, the smaller the job. To be *the* President, *the* Secretary, *the* Administrator is the stuff. The title gets longer as it is necessary to describe what the title-holder does. Remember also that a Deputy stands next

---

[8]The author's all-time favorite is the ritual cry in the Supreme Court: "Oyez! Oyez! Oyez! All persons having business before the Honorable, the Supreme Court of the United States, are admonished to draw near and give your attention, for the Court is now sitting. God save the United States and this Honorable Court!" (A sour colleague says that the invitation to all with business to "draw near" means that after spending two years and $10,000 you have a one-in-twenty chance of the Court taking your case for decision.)

to his Chief, and an Assistant below him. Deputy is better.

Perquisites are prized in Washington institutions as in all others. When someone is temporarily taken into a formal institution, he may be given an "assimilated" rank, entitling him to perquisites, such as parking his assimilated self in the executive dining room, and his car in the executive lot.

In most Washington institutions, a very significant form of panoply is *technological panoply*. Most of the technology is devoted to communications: instant telephone contacts, conference calls, rattling teleprinters, giant displays and so on. Even in private Washington life, the possession of means of communication—particularly international communication—is a mark. A Washington law office should have a Telex machine.

Technological panoply is also achieved by the computer. A good big computer print-out on the desk is a caste mark worth having, since it demonstrates both (a) importance and (b) progressive ideas.

Perhaps the oldest but still the solidest form of panoply is *staff*. Sheer number of attendants and outriders is still impressive evidence of importance. One would think it an insult to an official to say he had to have assistance to think, but not so— a "policy" staff is a normal incident of an important office.[9]

The pernicious concept persists that the act of thinking can be administratively transferred from the overburdened top official. In Laputa the officials were followed by flappers, in Washington they have Deputies for Ratiocination.

---

[9]The continued vitality of staff as an attribute of importance is confirmed by the linguistic evidence. The English language, whenever it receives official Washington attention, suffers. The transmutation of a noun to a verb is a frequent and reliable indicator that the word has received much official use. "Staff" has undergone the sea change and the importance of staff is evident in the following usages:

"Staff this around." (Translation: Give it to the staff for comments.)

"Give it to me and I'll staff it out." (Translation: My staff will consider your proposal.)

"Sorry, it didn't staff out." (Translation: The answer is "no.")

The Personnel Postulate

Returning from our field trip to Washington and sorting our notes, we detect a significant pattern. We noted down the activities of an individual part of a Washington institution[10] directed to asserting the individual's importance. The list was a long one, beginning with keeping busy (Activity) and ending with handing over the job of thinking to a staff. In fact, the list was so long *that it included everything an individual does as part of an institution.*

Here is a most valuable insight which must be added to the foundations of our body of Institutional Laws, along with the Axioms. Since we pretend to a mathematical structure of our science, the urge is irresistible, and with apologies to Euclid, Lobachevsky, and Riemann[11] we call this:

THE PERSONNEL POSTULATE

"What I do is important": Each action of the individual who is part of the institution affirms the importance of his work.

The Personnel Postulate is a personal imperative declaring that whatever else my actions as a part of the institution may do, my actions will at least affirm the *importance* of my work. Affirming importance is, according to the Postulate, the prime requirement of all individual activity within the institution.[12]

---

[10]Some better phrase than "individual part of an institution" is needed, but not available. "Bureaucrat" will not do, because its overtones already condemn the worker. "Institutocrat" is foolish, and "human being" is incorrect for someone caught in the institutional web.

[11]Note for the nonmathematician: the parallel postulate of Euclid's plane geometry was altered by Lobachevsky and Riemann to create non-Euclidean geometries valid not on a plane but on a sphere or a pseudosphere. It's an academic sort of a pun.

[12]"So, we would expect man's organizations to be designed to feed the ego and development needs." Townsend, *Up the Organization,* (Knopf, 1970).

Whether the activity is useful or beneficial is only a secondary consideration.

The Institutional Employee

There are absolutely no grounds for believing that those who work for institutions are either dumber or lazier than the run of mankind. On the contrary, the Government employee is demonstrably smarter than the average. The Government employee is educated. He is master of at least two languages: he speaks English and he commits degraded prose in Governmentese. Nor is the average Government exployee any lazier than his non-Government counterpart; indeed, at some of the higher levels the top officials are full-time slaves to their jobs.

Why are these generally superior people in Washington? John F. Kennedy, when asked the same question, is reported to have said: "I want to be where the action is." Others, when asked why the devil they gave up positions of unquestioned authority and fat financial rewards to come to Washington to engage in jurisdictional infighting at much smaller pay, have said: "You can't turn down that call from the White House."

Common to these responses is the feeling that *important* things go on in Washington, that the most *important* people are in Washington, that the call from the White House is *important,* that serving one's country is *important.* Friends from underdeveloped countries frequently bemoan the overattraction of Government for all their educated citizens—but the friends are, of course, in Government work.

Feelings of self-importance are surely not absent in institutions that are not parts of government. Doctors feel a good deal of self-importance in their dealings with life and death, duly reflected in the institutionality of hospitals. A distinct air of pompous self-importance permeates courts and rubs off on lawyers. A big bank is so suffused with importance it looks like a church. The importance of big business is signaled by corporate ziggurats and private jets.[13] A belief in the importance of one's work in the institution is universal.

Not only are Washington workers generally intelligent, diligent and filled with a sense of self-importance, they are also convinced that they are doing right. You or I may judge an action or decision to be wrong, to be useless, to be a lie or at worst to be brutally immoral. Only those with no experience of dealing with Government fall into the error of conceiving that the Government man *thinks* he is doing wrong, doing a useless thing, lying or committing a brutal and immoral act. Such a conception is the error of the inexperienced and uninformed. If, when you call a policeman a "pig," you mean that the policeman thinks he is doing brutal, piggish things, you are simply wrong. If you say more precisely that a policeman almost always *thinks* he is doing important work, vital to society, and that this belief of the policeman may lead him to some incidental brutality, you are right, and you know something about the operation of an institution.

Petty Bureaucrats

The Personnel Postulate teaches at once why all petty bureaucrats, inside and outside the Government, have the same offensive habits. The forms, the rubber stamps, the air of fussy self-importance, the treatment of the applicant as an undesirable nuisance, are the same at the admitting desk to a hospital, or the draft board, or the commission for licensing go-go danc-

---

[13]". . . The underlying cause of the [executive's] stress is not so much the personality of the offender as the feeling of the troubled executive that his security or prestige is threatened, or that he is being denied earned recognition." Albert Z. Carr, *Business As A Game* (New American Library, 1969).

ers. The maltreatment is of a special kind: the applicant must wait, must go through the formal motions, must go to window C in room 101 for a pink ticket. Maltreatment of the waiting public comes not from spite or bad upbringing. Not so, for if infliction of pain were the only purpose, the person behind the official counter might just as well step on your foot.

The common characteristic of all petty bureaucratic chivvying of the public is the affirmance of the importance of the bureaucrat's work. It was so in Imperial Russia, as reported by Gogol; it is as true today in Peoria as in Petrograd. There is no cure for the condition, for it is one of the fundamental Institutional Laws. All that can be done is to understand the phenomenon and apply the teachings of the Laws.

For example, there is the

LAW OF ATTRIBUTED IMPORTANCE

Each institutional job will be given the maximum quantity of attributes of importance (activity, authority, security, urgency, panoply) which it can sustain.

This follows directly from the Personnel Postulate: each action of the individual affirms the importance of the work, therefore the individual acts to add as many attributes to the work as the work will sustain. The less the job really entails, the more urgent the need to assert its importance—which means, the longer you will wait on line. When a man is really important, he often evidences it by dispensing with formality.

As a practical matter, in order to deal with any institution's bureaucracy, it is frequently necessary to use a working knowledge of the Institutional Laws. Two practical rules much used are the following:

1. Admit importance.

Go along with the game; never attack the importance of an official's job. To tell a man his job is unimportant all but requires him to demonstrate its importance by denying you what you seek. If you want your auto license plates, you had better not tell the clerk he is overdoing the fancy work with the rubber stamps. He will overdo it a little more by letting you walk for a month. Similarly, do not tell the staff of the Federal Communications Commission they are engaged in useless Talmudic disputations, even if they are. You will end up with a license restricted to broadcasting *Readings from the Lesser Rabbis* on alternate Sabbaths. Shalom!

2. Recognize puffery.

Subtract from the job every shred of Activity, Authority, Urgency, Security and Panoply; what remains will be instantly recognizable as important or not. For example, if the question is whether the job of a judge is important, strip from the judge his bailiffs, his bench and even his robes. With His Honor thus left standing in his underwear, ask, is what he is doing important? The affirmative answer follows at once. The rule of recognizing puffery is in constant, almost reflex, use by everyone who deals with any institution. You must apply it to know who is doing what.

If the secret labels, the air of urgency, the titles and the rest are stripped from some jobs, the jobs are obviously trivial; others are honestly important. A real crisis is usually recognizable as such by men of good sense. Fire, flood, riot, are solid emergencies without benefit of secret memoranda, staff thinking, or high-level midnight meetings. Absent his rubber stamps, the issuer of licenses is seen to be doing a job equivalent to that of a postage meter. Absent the car, the conferences, and the cables, the Deputy Assistant Secretary for Bedouin Sheiks and Laotian Princelings may not be much more than a mailbox.[14]

Personal and Institutional Equivalents

The Personnel Postulate is the last assumption in our theoretical structure. All further laws must be deduced from the Three Axioms, the single Postulate and the Definitions. Before turning to the task of deduction, it would be well to ask whether all that we have so far set down is self-consistent. If not, then any deductions will be gibberish, for it would be possible to deduce one Law from an Axiom and another, contradictory, Law from the Personnel Postulate.

A simple test for consistency is to compare each formal statement we make about institutional behavior with the equivalent statement about individual behavior within the institution. For internal consistency, a one-to-one correspondence is required, and so the following table reveals:

---

[14]A Final Note on Importance: please note again that nothing said above implies in the least that the government official does not honestly *believe* his job is important. You miss the whole point of the Personnel Postulate unless you see that (a) the official does want to believe he is doing important work and (b) does so believe. It is just that belief which makes the institutional machinery inexorable. The length of the list of Attributes of Importance simply illustrates the soundness of the Personnel Postulate: every action evidences the Importance of the Work.

Table of Equivalents

STATEMENT ABOUT INSTITUTIONAL BEHAVIOR	EQUIVALENT STATEMENT OF THE INDIVIDUAL
First Axiom: Any institutional action is merely the working of the institution's internal machinery.	My important work is the institution in action.
Second Axiom: Institutional existence depends upon the continual working of the internal machinery.	The institution's existence depends upon my important work.
Third Axiom: Whatever the internal machinery does is perceived within the institution as the real purpose of the institution (i.e., function is seen as purpose).	I perceive my important work to be the real purpose of the institution.
The Institutional Imperative: Every action or decision of an institution must be intended to keep the institutional machinery working.	Above all, my important work must continue.
Corollary to the I.I.: To speak of any goal or purpose of an institution other than keeping the machinery running is no more meaningful than to speak of the goal of an automobile exhaust or the purpose of the hum of a sewing machine.	If you understood my institution, you too would see that my work is the real purpose of the institution.
Every institutional job will be given the maximum possible quantity of the Attributes of Importance (i.e., the Law of Attributed Importance).	My work shows that what I do is important (i.e., the Personnel Postulate).

This table of parallels can be extended to each and every Law of Institutional Behavior which we shall deduce from the

Axioms and the Postulate.[15] The parallelism never fails. In every instance, the institution's action is a reflection of the insistence of the individual on the importance of his work. This unbreakable link, converting a person to a cog in a machine, is what makes the institutional laws so inexorable and the typical institutional action so inhuman.

---

[15]For further proof, consult the Appendix, where all the later Laws are listed with the equivalent statement of the individual within the institution.

PART II

THE LAWS OF RELEVANCE: WHAT COUNTS AND WHAT, UNFORTUNATELY, DOES NOT

4. INSTITUTIONAL SELF-OCCUPATION: THE PARTICULAR AND GENERAL LAWS

Secret, Stale Trivia. Case of Project Zeta: The Securest Secret. Special Law of the Security Office. General Law of Institutional Self-Occupation. Crisis Declared and Crisis Effectuated. A Rule of Safe Institutional Design. The National Emergency (Quiz).

Secret, Stale Trivia

A secret, as we have seen, is a most delightful invention. It is cheap, it provides hours of innocent fun, and its possession makes the bearer an important fellow. Best of all, secrets can be made easily at home by any institution with a rubber stamp and a locked file—and therein lies a danger.

Many things are institutionally as well as personally pleasing; cars with chauffeurs, for example. An institution cannot make its own Lincoln Continentals, or, for that matter, print its own money. A secret, though, is both (1) the subject matter of fascinating institutional machinery (security officers, dossiers, phone taps, locks, files, codes) and (2) easily capable of self-generation by the institution itself. With secrecy offering such irresistible temptations, we must predict that all institutions will succumb. Succumb they do, and the United States Government is awash in secrets, most of which have no justifi-

53

cation other than their own existence. The average classified document is stale trivia—and yet its secret triviality is defended to the death.[1]

The Institutional Imperative declares that *every* action of the institution will try to keep the machinery operating. Secrecy machinery is machinery, and therefore must be kept going. This prediction was crisply confirmed not long ago when a Republican Administration was suddenly faced with the public printing of masses of old secrets proving the ineptitude of the previous Democratic Administration (the Pentagon Papers). One would think this a politically happy result, to be encouraged by the Republicans in power. Not so, for the Institutionally Imperative need to protect secrets transcended politics. So, the Republicans tried to enjoin newspaper publication of the Pentagon Papers. This failed, and the master war planning of the Johnson Administration was publicly exposed as comic book stuff—a politically happy but institutionally repellent result. Therefore the Justice Department is, at this writing, still busily turning the screws on the alleged purloiners of the Papers.[2]

Our concern now is with the institution's self-absorption in its own secrets—what we might call the ability to play with

---

[1] *The Congressional Record* of June 28, 1971 (E 6650) reports testimony to the House Government Operations Subcommittee that: (1) the Department of Defense alone has over 20 million classified documents; (2) the same Department has 31,000 employees allowed to exercise "original classification" authority (803 "Top Secret," 8,000 "Secret," the rest—poor fellows—only "Confidential").

Improving the supply of secrets is the "derivative classification" gimmick. All of any document quoting any part of a "secret" document is "secret" and so on.

Secrets are, of course, leakable in the institution's best interest. "But our entire foreign policy and defense posture remains secret except for what the federal establishment thinks is in its own interest to make public."—Jack Anderson's *Washington Merry-Go-Round, The Washington Post,* June 27, 1972.

[2] More about the Pentagon Papers in Chapter 6. One last corroborating note here: A pretrial motion filed by the Special Assistant U.S. Attorney prosecuting Ellsberg and Russo complains that the government had been characterized as "secretive, abridging freedom of the press, concealing information from the public, opposing Congress' right to know; corrupt and inept in bringing the case . . . [etc]." *The New York Times,* June 11, 1972. Note how "the government" merges the past and present administrations of different parties.

itself. The Third Axiom declares that what the institutional machinery does is perceived within as the institution's real purpose. In an extreme case, then, we can predict that the institution will become autistic—self-security becomes its only purpose. The following true story proves the point.

Case of Project Zeta: The Securest Secret

Following World War II, the best research scientists at leading schools were reluctant to work on military projects. Among the reasons for their refusal were included the collective sense of guilt of the scientific community for the creation of the atomic bomb, as well as the less high-minded reason that military research was not publishable. Personally modest or not,[3] few scientists yearn for obscurity for their work.

In the early 1950s a General commanding an Army service sought the help of a valued friend, a professor at a noted midwestern university. By appeals to patriotism, promises of fat research funds, and other arm-twisting, the General persuaded the Professor to head a new project—call it Project Zeta. The Professor was to enlist the help of a dozen or so of the ablest young men in the field working at other universities. Project Zeta would conduct secret military research of the most terrible kind, never to be revealed publicly, and designed to cause none of the researchers to sleep as soundly should they succeed as they would if they failed.

After many months of travel, argument and persuasions of all sorts, the Professor was able to induce a dozen selected scientists to join him in Project Zeta. The dozen names were submitted to Army Security for Top Secret clearance, and time began to pass.

---

[3]Usually not.

The early 1950s were the Dirty Joe McCarthy era,[4] and clearance took some time. Almost a year passed, and then a letter arrived for the Professor from Fifth Army Headquarters, Security Branch. The letter contained, not the clearances for the twelve co-researchers, but a formal "Notice of Suspension of Security Clearance" for the Professor.

According to Fifth Army Security,[5] the Professor was forthwith denied further clearance because "You have regularly been seen in the company of a person named as a Communist Sympathizer by the House Un-American Activities Committee." In the style of the time (and today), the "Communist Sympathizer" was not named, but the Professor was given ten days to submit information to the contrary. It later turned out that the "Communist Sympathizer" was a Nobel laureate with whom the Professor played cowboy pool on Saturdays.

The Professor had the pleasure of sitting down and writing the kind of letter most similarly accused poor fish are never in a position to write. The letter, addressed to the Commanding General of the service, praised Army Security's accomplishment of the ideal of total security: "Thanks to the splendid work of Army Security, in the twelve months since the inception of Project Zeta, not one single secret has fallen into the hands of the enemy. No secret has been discovered, because Army Security has prevented any research from being done, and has now suspended the Project Chief. Security is total, and so is ignorance."

---

[4]The practice of speaking well of the dead has been unfortunately extended to the late Senator from Wisconsin. It shouldn't be. Joe McCarthy was a liar, and an unprincipled phony. His destructive work product lingers on, in the form of terrified bureaus afraid to tell unpalatable truths. They remember what happened to truth-tellers a generation ago.

[5]Fifth Army Security was later identified as a not-bright lieutenant. Note how well the institutional trappings conceal the reality. A letterhead reading "U.S. Fifth Army Security Branch" inspires fear. A letterhead reading "Dumb Lieutenant in Charge of Security" would inspire snickers. But security—all security—is a dumb lieutenant.

It is satisfying to add that the letter, all fifteen pages of it, was read aloud by the Commanding General to the security officers responsible, from the dumb Lieutenant on up.

The average accused security risk, then and now, has no great credentials and no powerful sponsors. He is accused on grounds vaguely stated and by accusers vaguely identified. He is accused, not of a treasonous act, but of an insecure twist of mind. He might prove he has not committed treason, but never that he would not *think* of it. Therefore, when accused, he writes no indignant letters and he departs quietly from his job. A more perfect device for dissuading the most able men from the service of their country could not be devised.

Special Law of the Security Office

The vulgarities of the Government's security systems teach a valuable theoretical lesson. We need an answer to the question: why did the Fifth Army Lieutenant, stupid or not, choose to suspend the Professor, the Chief Researcher? The answer lies only a little way below the surface.

It will be recalled that Project Zeta was to include only a dozen top researchers, and that during the first year of the Project their dozen clearances were making their way through the security system. Thus, when the Lieutenant had run through the twelve, he was out of subjects—no more important security work. The idea of making the Chief Researcher himself the subject of a security suspension must have appeared a great stroke, and was duly put into effect. It was by no means the first or last time the security system has barred scientists from access to their own work.[6]

---

[6]The most famous case is J. Robert Oppenheimer's. After a famous security trial, the father of the atomic bomb was denied visiting rights to his child.

As we have seen, by our Third Axiom the Security Officer regards the machinery of maintaining "security" as a purpose in itself; he is quite unable to see that the failure of Project Zeta to develop any secrets whatever is slightly undesirable. Of course, it is not a new insight into the outlook of Security Officers to understand that the action of making secure—the operation of the machinery—is, to them, all-important. Dostoevski knew it, and Orwell said it with considerable clarity.

A further truth lies one layer deeper. An office of personnel security shares with an office classifying documents the power of creation of the subject matter upon which it operates. This is by no means a universal institutional attribute. The Coiffeurs and Chauffeurs license bureau will issue no licenses unless some applicant appears to coif or chauf; a Court will try no cases unless some plaintiff sues; letters patent cannot be issued without an inventor; and, at least in the good old days, the Army would not be in combat unless Congress declared war. Quite generally, an institution is not able to create the grist for its own mill.

From the Institutional Imperative, the decision of any institution must be intended to keep the institution's machinery working. Security offices can decide to find security risks, which will keep the machinery working. Therefore:

SPECIAL LAW
OF THE SECURITY OFFICE

Threats to security will be found.

If you are sensitive to the presence of evil, the sentence just printed should chill your blood. We are all potentially either heroes or traitors, and a security office can, on its own initiative, designate anyone as a "potential security risk." Through the centuries the Special Law has been true, and has caused human suffering. Establish an office within the Church to find and deal with heretics, and heretics will be found (else the office machinery would come to a halt). If it be the habit of the times, heretics will be burnt, but at least they will be found. Let there be an institution to judge witches, and so long as that same institution can designate those suspected of witchcraft, witches will be found. Establish an office to search for and find commie sympathizers, or to detect crypto-capitalist revisionist enemies of the people's revolution, and the tree will bear the fruit: Commies or enemies of the revolution will be duly discovered.

The Special Law of the Security Office suggests a minor corollary, and a more general and horrifying extension. The minor corollary is only the thought that if threats to security will always be found, their finding does not prove there are any. We might state the corollary thus:

> **The finding of threats to security by a security office is totally predictable, and hence the finding is totally worthless.**

Heretics, witches, security risks, Commies, crypto-capitalist revisionists and enemies of Chairman Mao may or may not exist, but the announcement of their discovery is meaningless, in the United States, in Russia, in China, in the past, present or future.

General Extension of the Special Law

There is yet more, and more important, matter here. While not all institutions and sub-institutions share the ability of a security office to generate the material they process, many do. There are a number of institutions, some of the very highest

importance, that can claim this generative power. Wherever the
power exists in an institution to produce the subject matter
which keeps the institution's machinery busy, the Institutional
Imperative requires that the power to produce be exercised.
Accordingly, we have the following:

GENERAL LAW OF
INSTITUTIONAL
SELF-OCCUPATION

**If an institution can generate the subject
matter of its operations, it will.**

Perhaps the General Law appears to be too pat to be true.
An early reader of this book[7] translated the General Law as: "If
an egg poacher could lay eggs, it would." Precisely.

The General Law is broadly applicable and invariably
true. It is also rarely funny in its consequences, which reach far
beyond mere Security Offices.

Simple examples of the General Law come easily to mind.
Traffic policemen have a formal or informal quota of traffic
tickets to give out each day. The policeman possesses the power
(by writing a ticket) to generate the subject matter of what has
been defined for him as the function of the institutional machinery (ticket-writing). Accordingly, he writes tickets, fulfilling the
General Law.

If the example of the policeman is too simple-minded,
consider the behavior of your daily newspaper. A newspaper is
an institution, and usually a self-confessed one. The internal
machinery of the institution is set up to print a paperful of news
each day. Clearly, on some days there will be much news of
high interest. Rapes and other sex crimes will abound. On such

---

[7]The author's wife.

days the newsworthy stories will be selected for print—properly
illustrated—and other stories will be excluded. On other days
not much will be happening, but the newspaper must print the
same physical quantity of news stories. So, on the dull days
stories will be printed that would not have appeared in type on
the interesting days. The death of half a million peasants
becomes "news" only because the institution selected it to be
so—in effect generated "news" to fit the institutional need.

While the newspaper staff can claim they are not genera-
ting news, because all that news pours in from the outside, in
reality, the world's occurrences are just that—occurrences—
until the paper creates "news" by the process of selection and
designation.

Carry the thought along. Some institutions find it difficult
to create their own business. The branch of a public health
service devoted to meeting epidemic emergencies does not, one
hopes, go around giving people the plague. Nor is it really
possible (or professional) for an epidemic to be announced
when no one is sick. But suppose the disease were as invisible
as "security risk" is. On that supposition, is it inconceivable
that on a dull day the *danger* of an epidemic of the plague might
be announced? On a dull day prior to the time the branch's
annual budget was being considered? On a dull day at budget
time when the branch chief sincerely believes cutting the budget
would endanger his branch's ability to fight a plague epidemic,
if one occurred? Perhaps you are unwilling to believe that a
doctor's professional integrity would allow him to go so far, and
perhaps you are right.[8]

---

[8]Perhaps you are right, but probably you are wrong. The evidence is that even
the practitioners of the healing art can find their institutional occupations more
compelling than their duty to cure. For example, the U.S. Public Health Service
was running a forty-year study of the effects of syphilis. Such studies require
maintenance of an untreated control group. Therefore: "U.S. Public Health
Service officials revealed Tuesday that under a PHS study, treatment of syphilis
has been withheld from hundreds of afflicted Negroes for the 40-year period [of

Crisis Declared and Crisis Effectuated

One final step is required to bring the newspaper example home to the operations of the very highest reaches of the government. A story is not "news" unless the paper selects it to be. On remarkably frequent occasions a selected story is a story of crisis, national or international. Crises are of course to be dealt with by our Government institutions. Inevitably, the uncomfortable question suggests itself: where does the designation of "crisis" originate? The answer, plainly, is with those Government institutions that deal with these same crises. The conditions of the General Law are met—crises can be generated by those institutions that deal with them.

If there were not some natural check on the declaration of crises, the country would be constantly in the grip of a hundred proclaimed near disasters, and 1984 would arrive sooner than the calendar permits. Luckily, however, there is a natural check on proliferation of crises, which usually prevents their having any effect. This check resides in the diffusion of power in Washington.

Two types of crises must be distinguished: (1) *crisis declared,* which has no effect other than to signify the importance of the declarer and his institution, and (2) *crisis effectuated,* which means something is going to be done. Declared crisis is marked by words of warning of "grave consequences" or similar formulary vapidities predicting what may happen but hasn't happened yet. Effectuated crisis is known by deeds: invasions, devaluations, mass inoculations or the like.

The distinction between crisis declared and crisis effectuated is that crisis can only be effectuated by an institution with the power to act in the crisis it declares. This is an insight well worth having. For the General Law of Self-Occupation

the study]." "Human Guinea Pig Bares 40 Years of 'Doctoring on Me.' " *The Washington Post,* July 27, 1972.

states that crises, being subject matter for institutions, will be constantly found. This inevitable tendency of an institution to keep itself occupied will be of no great consequence unless the institution can act in the crisis it declares. The State Department views everything with alarm, grave alarm, and always fears the gravest consequences. The State Department, luckily, cannot often do much about its constant night sweats. To prevent a runaway of the institutional machinery, except in those cases where the existence of crisis is objectively determinable (fire, flood, riot), it is most vital that the power of acting in a crisis not be lodged in the institution which can declare the crisis. For emphasis, this is repeated as:

A RULE OF SAFE INSTITUTIONAL DESIGN

Do not allow those who act in an emergency to declare the emergency.

This doesn't sound like much, but to the attentive student of Government institutions the rule just expressed has enormous, shattering implications for our foreign policy, particularly our military foreign policy. The violations of the rule of safety, and the uniformly disastrous results, are of course already obvious to the reader, and we will get to the subject in later chapters. Before dealing with such ultimately weighty matters, it would be well to complete our supporting theoretical structure. To test your qualifications to proceed, try the following quiz.

The National Emergency (Quiz)

There are, as you no doubt know, a number of statutes giving the President and the executive departments certain extraordinary powers only in time of national emergency. The existence of a National Emergency is made known by Presidential proclamation. Speaking as of 1972, answer the following questions:

1. Which President declared the last state of National Emergency and when?

2. When was that state of National Emergency terminated?

The answers are:

1. President Harry S. Truman, by Executive Proclamation on December 16, 1950, at the time of the Korean War.[9]

2. The state of National Emergency was not terminated; it has been continued for more than twenty years through five administrations.

---

[9]Proclamation No. 2914 (15 F.R. 9029).

5. INSTITUTIONAL SELF-JUSTIFICATION: THE INVARIABLE EXPERTS

Law of Institutional Self-Justification. The Expert Oracles. Law of Institutional Expertise. Let's Hear It for Nuclear Fall-Out. Case of the Plowshare Program. Case of the Cute Cannikin. Case of Too Many Regulators (Quiz).

Ordinary people, when jostled, pushed, or impoverished by their fellow citizens, expect a certain minimum of justification or excuse. Even the pickpocket offers a word of pardon after bumping you as an adjunct to lifting your wallet. Similarly, when an institution relieves the citizen of his loose cash by taxation, an explanation or apology is expected. All institutional justifications, however, are offered in a consistently weighty tone. The use of such a tone is predictable.

From the Personnel Postulate we know that every action of the individual within the institution affirms the importance of his work. Since his work *is* the institution's action, the next law follows logically.

LAW OF INSTITUTIONAL
SELF-JUSTIFICATION

**Reasons said to be important will be given
to justify every institutional action.**

That the reasons for institutional actions are important reasons, you may be sure. There ought to be important reasons for some of the things that go on.

Such important reasons are supplied to the public regularly, on demand, by every Government man from the President on down. The President gives important reasons for his Vietnam policy on prime time; the Secretary of Defense explains the need for the military budget to Congress; the Air Force General explains the need for a new plane to the Secretary, the aircraft planning group briefs the General on the need for the plane, and so on. All are good, solid reasons, and delivered with conviction. Only the wisdom of experience, and now the statements of our Laws, teach that such good solid reasons are always on hand to justify all institutional actions. The best reasons, of course, come from experts.

The Expert Oracles

The complexity of modern life leaves us uneasily dependent on the opinions of experts. Experts tell us what to eat to stay slim and, when the laboratory mice get convulsions, other experts tell us to stop eating it. In happier times we only prayed for enlightenment from above; today we cannot drive to work without receiving from the sky the expert traffic guidance of a sepulchral voice from a helicopter. Experts are the High Priests.

Nowhere are experts received with more reverence than in

our institutions. Indeed, some of our institutions are nothing more than collections of experts, and, of course, every institution presents itself as the source of expert opinion in its designated field. The assumption of expertness is now enshrined in the law—all government agencies are legally presumed to possess the quality called "administrative expertise."

Daily the branches of government supply the citizen with expert opinion on all subjects. The citizen's life is deeply affected, even in the air he breathes. Expert agencies attend first to the pollution of the air (by expertly building more roads and encouraging more industry) and second to the cleansing of the air thus expertly dirtied. And, of course, the citizen is expertly told to what increasing extent he should pay for more such activities of certifiable merit.

It would be more than helpful to know the standard by which the expert pronouncements of institutions can be judged. We turn again to our statement of the Institutional Imperative. An expert opinion put out by an agency is, surely, an "action or decision" of the agency, and the expert opinion must meet the prime objective of keeping the institutional machinery working.[1] Therefore, we can at once derive the following:

LAW OF INSTITUTIONAL
EXPERTISE

The expert judgment of an institution, when the matter involves continuation of the institution's operations, is totally predictable (and hence totally worthless).

---

[1]Note again that the Institutional Imperative does not declare that every action or decision is *solely* intended to keep the machinery working, nor does the Imperative say that the action or decision is good or bad, right or wrong, true or false. All the Imperative says is that whatever else is true of any institutional action or decision, it must first be intended to keep the machinery working.

The tone of the institutional pronouncement is oracular and impressive, but an oracle, even an expert oracle, with only one opinion is simply worthless.

Of course not every institutional expert judgment involves the continuation of operations. A bureau in the Department of Agriculture will competently tell you when and how to plant; a doctor in the National Institutes of Health will competently diagnose your disease; the National Bureau of Standards will reliably standardize your weights and measures. But when it comes to advising as to the budgets, the scope of operations or the need for existence of such presumptively estimable institutions, their own opinions will be without value.

A pointed example will drive home the truth of this law.

Let's Hear It for Nuclear Fallout

The Atomic Energy Commission has expertise if any institution has. It is the repository of dark secrets, of instruments that threaten the very survival of our civilization. Its secrets are all the more impressive to the average citizen because if revealed to him they would be meaningless.

The peace following World War II had the normal stimulative effect on weapons design. The AEC began a brisk program of testing nuclear weapons. The nuclear tests were conducted conveniently in the open air, thereby simulating wartime conditions of people-crisping. Tests in the open air, as might be predicted, distributed radioactive material into the sky.

What went up began to come down, around the world. Scientists not employed by the AEC began to note an unpleasant rise in the quantity of radioactive strontium-90 in the milk of cows and caribou alike. Geneticists discussed permanent radiation damage to the germ plasm of the race. Slowly, dimly, the idea began to form in the public mind that it was desirable neither to glow in the dark nor to have two-headed children. People began to shuffle in picket lines bearing signs opposing the continued radioactive dusting of the world.

The reaction of the AEC, as chief world-duster, is of value in the present inquiry. The AEC produced a great mass of expert opinion in defense of continued testing. The AEC experts (memory gives them all the generic name of Dr. Teller) opined that the danger to health was minimal. There was radioactivity around us; there always would be. The average radiation increase was footling, comparable to a dental X ray. A little change in the germ plasm was a good thing—it leads to progress —who wants only five toes? According to the AEC experts, fallout was a lesser threat than dandruff, and far more attractive.

The tone of the debate went like this (from *The New York Times* of April 29, 1958):

> Dr. Linus Pauling, leading biochemist, introduced today a new threat in atomic fall-out—a long-lived radioactive atom known as Carbon 14.

> The paper was designed to refute a recent statement by Dr. Teller that fall-out, as far as shortening life span, was as dangerous to human health as being an ounce overweight.

AEC experts thereupon issued solemn warnings that national security would be threatened by failure to test a few hundred more bombs. While it was never made clear exactly why the tests were so inefficient that scores and hundreds were necessary, the public was assured all the tests were most urgently required, even at the risk of a little genetic mutilation.[2]

---

[2]"He [Teller] admitted there might be 'many thousands' of mutations as a result of radioactivity's effect on genetics. But, he argued, mutations were not necessarily all bad . . ." *The New York Times*, April 17, 1958.

Several facets of the atmospheric testing imbroglio are worth attention. First, the institution set up to test bombs followed the Institutional Imperative: it fought fiercely to keep its machinery running. Second, the Law of Institutional Expertise was confirmed. The institution's expert opinion involved continuation of operations, and therefore was of no use. This is not to say that the expert opinion supplied by the AEC was necessarily false; it might or might not be. One has to form an individual judgment, or wait for the judgment of history. But the AEC opinion was not useful as a basis for decision, because it was predictable.

A third interesting facet of the testing fight is its resolution. The open-air testing picnic was closed down when the common sense of the world's people asserted itself. Most atmospheric testing was stopped in 1963, by international agreement (France and China not consenting). Underground testing of nuclear devices continues today, thus keeping the testing sub-institutions of the AEC and its Russian equivalent occupied, although still grumpy. The public, naturally, still does not know whether or not the tests are useful.[3]

Fourth, the testing fight leads to some intriguing speculations about the role of common sense and good taste in institutional activities. As a matter of common sense, it would seem that the AEC could have anticipated public objections to nuclear fallout. People were desperately worried by the creation of the atomic bomb, they feared radiation as an invisible killer, and anyway, who wants a lot of poison in the air? Common sense tells us that our neighbors will not applaud fumes from a backyard distillery, so why should they welcome the nasty by-products of a bomb?

Further, there is a question of what can only be called good

---

[3]Perhaps the usefulness of much institutional activity is unknowable—a subject discussed later. See Chapter 8, Paradox and Law of Invariable Accomplishment.

taste in setting off an indiscriminate number of nuclear bombs. It just did not seem the thing to do.

Case of the Plowshare Program

The suspicion that good taste was lacking in the AEC's view of its business is confirmed by the conception of the "Plowshare" program. This was a 1957 swords-into-plowshares proposal of the AEC to use nuclear explosions for peaceful purposes. Canals, for example, would be dug by nuclear explosions. The AEC estimated a charge of "$350,000 for a nuclear explosive with a 10-kiloton yield, and $600,000 for a nuclear explosive of 2-megaton yield . . . These charges cover nuclear materials, fabrication and assembly, and arming and firing services."[4]

Still in the memory of many were the effects of the wartime atomic bombs that had killed, seared and maimed the populations of two Japanese cities. Thus, whatever its intrinsic merits, the Plowshare program was about as tasteful an idea as using the contents of a cemetery for fertilizer. Somehow, the Plowshare program, as they say, never took off.

Case of the Cute Cannikin

Institutions do not give up easily, and by 1971 the AEC was back drumming up trade with the "Cannikin" test, a five-megaton underground nuclear explosion on Amchitka Island off Alaska. Amchitka islanders are not a large voting block, and there was only one insignificant objection to such a beneficial explosion. Dr. Russell E. Train, chairman of the President's

---

[4]Whitewall tires not included. Quotation from *Plowshare*, U.S. Atomic Energy Commission, Division of Technical Information (1966).

Council on Environmental Quality, had suggested—quietly[5]—
that the test might set off a large earthquake, and perhaps a tidal
wave. The test came off, and the earthquake didn't, which
proves: (1) that one of two sets of opposing experts is right and
(2) "Cannikin" was a much better name than "Plowshare."
Obviously, a Cannikin is a cute, harmless little five-megaton
bomb.

Every year at budget time in Washington—and most of the
time it is budget time—agency experts declare that for the
Republic to stand, more battleships, or crop supports, or poverty programs, or Congressional gymnasiums must be supplied,
and supplied at once. For the unbeliever, charts, tables and
professional expert studies are available on demand in any
quantity.

The Law of Institutional Expertise declares that all this
self-justifying expertness may or may not be right, but it offers
no basis for decision. From the time of Hammurabi no man can
be a judge in his own case, and similarly no institution can be
believed as expert witness in its institutional self-interest.

Case of Too Many Regulators (Quiz)

A clash of experts is always fun to watch. As a quiz, you
are asked to predict what happens when several Government
agencies all want to be the resident experts.

When Congressional wisdom has dictated the regulation
of transportation, regulatory powers have fallen to separate

---

[5]Dr. Train opined very quietly and secretly because what Councils on Environ-
mental Quality do is object quietly to possible "grave consequences" (Crisis
Proclaimed). Quote: "When asked if he advised against conducting the test,
Train said, 'I don't think I'd better comment on that.' " *The Washington Post,*
November 4, 1971.

agencies: railroads and trucks to the Interstate Commerce Commission, ships in foreign trade to the Federal Maritime Commission, and air transport to the Civil Aeronautics Board.

The rapid development of intermodal cargo container service has placed a severe strain on the regulatory structure. These containers, when mounted on a detachable chassis, become trailer bodies for trucks. Without their chassis, containers can be carried on rail flat cars, loaded into special racks on huge new container ships, or even carried by air.

The benefits of modern container transport have recommended it to all except three classes: (1) longshoremen, (2) thieves, and (3) regulatory agencies. Longshoremen don't like containers for the obvious reason that they are efficient, so jobs are threatened. Thieves don't like containers because pilferage is more difficult (a problem usually solved by stealing the whole container). The regulatory agencies find container transport unsettling because no one agency has jurisdiction to regulate the entire journey.

Now for the quiz questions:

1. In the expert judgment of the Interstate Commerce Commission, who, in the highest public interest, should regulate intermodal container transport?

2. In the expert judgment of the Federal Maritime Commission, who, in the highest public interest, should regulate intermodal container transport?

3. What about the CAB?

4. What happened?

Answers:

1. The Interstate Commerce Commission.

2. The Federal Maritime Commission.

3. The Civil Aeronautics Board.

4. Nothing at all, of course; everybody keeps regulating everything, and all the institutional machinery keeps on grinding (The Institutional Imperative).

6. THE INSTITUTIONAL IRRELEVANCE OF TRUTH

Regeneration of the Organs of Belief. Case of the Pentagon Papers. Law of the Institutional Irrelevance of Truth. The Bureau of Counter-Inflationary Affairs. Creation of Facts. Special Exception of the Deliberate Lie (Spy Business, War Business, Fire in the Theater, Boys-in-Blue Lies, National Emergency Lies, Personal Disaster Lies). Practical Rules for Detecting the Truth: Rules of Budget Statements, Communiqués, Grave and Gravest Consequences, Defending the Mess (Law of Institutional Admissions), Rules of Aid and Abet, Debasement of the Language.

Regeneration of the Organs of Belief

Certain lizards possess the facility of growing another tail if the original is lost. Zoological science, however, still knows nothing of a lizard's power to regenerate its lost beliefs. In contrast to the lizard, human powers of bodily regeneration are limited, but human powers of restoring lost beliefs are unbounded.

The American people have a strange but persistent belief that statements by government officers should not be lies. Daily, this belief is proved wrong, and daily, cries of shock and outrage resound. After every demonstration of institutional lying, there occurs an overnight regeneration of the sense of belief, and the next day both press and public are ready to be outraged anew.

75

The persistence of faith in the possibility of institutional truth-telling is a matter more for the arts of psychology or theology than for our present inquiries. The Laws of Institutional Behavior do teach us much, though, of the relevance of truth to institutional talk and action. We proceed to examine the subject of truth both from example and from our theoretical point of view; an example comes first.

Case of the Pentagon Papers

All organs of the bureaucratic body are constantly bathed by a warm fluid of memoranda. When the conscience of Daniel Ellsberg and the invention of the Xerox bled off a quantity of this vital fluid in the form of the Pentagon Papers, parts of the institutions affected went into spasm.[1]

By any standards it was quite a story. The major lesson the Papers taught was that the American public had been systematically lied to about the messy involvement in Vietnam. All those who could be expected to comment on such things commented. Those who looked bad warned that forty-seven volumes of documents were not enough and something called "the

---

[1]For those future generations who read these words and do not remember the Pentagon Papers, they were a forty-seven volume study of the sources of the United States involvement in Vietnam, prepared by a team of researchers at the request of Secretary of Defense McNamara. Upon completion, they were classified Top Secret and apparently never read within the Government. One Daniel Ellsberg, a former Department of Defense functionary repelled by our actions in Vietnam, turned a copy of the Papers over to *The New York Times,* which found them fit to print. The *Times* published the first installment of its story on Sunday, June 13, 1972. After two installments had appeared, a minor Constitutional crisis developed. The Nixon Administration had nothing to do with the Papers, but it had inherited the war. The Justice Department tried to enforce the Top Secret classification by obtaining a court injunction against further publication. Other newspapers then began to print portions of the Papers. Two Federal District Judges decided the Papers were embarrassing, but not a threat to national security. The Supreme Court decided (6 to 3) that publication would not be enjoined. Freedom of the press was saved, Justices Burger, Harlan, and Blackmun dissenting.

full story" was not out. Former President Johnson, who looked very bad, was reported by *Time* magazine to think release of the papers was tantamount to treason. Hubert Humphrey, Senator and former Vice President, commented in triplicate: (a) "I don't think you've been lied to," (b) "the lack of candor is regrettable," and (c) that he had doubts about publishing the Papers because they "will do a great deal to damage confidence in government" and will "only aid and abet the doubt and cynicism and suspicion about government."[2]

For good and sufficient institutional reasons, members of the following (Nixon) Administration busied themselves with condemnations of the breach of security[3] and attempts to enjoin publication and lock up the leaker. Most other institutions reacted predictably.[4] The best comment on the subject was that of a reporter who said only: "What a baloney I was given."

So all in all, in public, there was a great to-do about the revelation of Government deception. The Old Washington Hands, who may be forgiven by Senator Humphrey, did not need their "doubt and cynicism and suspicion about the government" abetted. A typical reaction of such Old Hands, whether

---

[2]Quoted in *The Washington Post,* June 17, 1971.

[3]Herbert Klein, the President's Press Secretary, said "I do not know of any editor who is qualified to decide what is not a matter of military security if it involves Top Secret material." *The Washington Post,* June 17, 1971.

[4]The Veterans of Foreign Wars apparently reasoned that without foreign wars there couldn't be any veterans. H. R. Rainwater, Commander of the VFW, intoned that publication "was very close to the thin edge of treason, if not treason itself." *The Washington Post,* as the local paper supposedly in the know about such matters, managed a creditable combination of surprise and foreknowledge:

> "Taking nothing away from the *Times,* the story that unfolds is not new in its essence—the calculated misleading of the public. The purposeful manipulation of public opinion, the stunning discrepancies between public pronouncements and private plans—we had bits and pieces of all that before. But not in such incredibly damning form, not with such irrefutable documentation. That is what brings you up breathless . . ." *The Washington Post* lead editorial June 17, 1971.

To give the *Post* full marks for prescience, exactly one month earlier (May 17, 1971) it had published a good long piece by Ben H. Bagdikian titled "The Government Is a Crude Liar."

or not they had ever worked in the Pentagon was: what else is new? They *knew* what had to be in forty-seven volumes of institutional memoranda. Any forty-seven volumes. It is not news in Washington that a Government institution has told a lie.[5]

Although some say it, no one really thinks the Government lies all the time or about all subjects. That is a crude overstatement. The kind of lie expected by the professionally disillusioned is the lie necessary to the continued working of the institutional machinery. The question is, then, whether this is predicted by our institutional laws, and the answer is: certainly. Our Laws of Institutional Behavior must include the following:

LAW OF THE INSTITUTIONAL IRRELEVANCE OF TRUTH

When the making of a statement is seen as necessary to the continued working of the institutional machinery, the statement is totally predictable and its truth is irrelevant.

This Law follows directly from the Institutional Imperative. An institution's statement ("we are winning the Vietnam war"; "prosperity is just around the corner"; "there is no possibility of genetic damage from atomic fallout") is an institutional action or decision. By the Institutional Imperative any action or decision *must* be intended to keep the institutional machinery running. Because the statement must be made, the percentage of truth it contains is irrelevant to its being made.

Or, if you prefer, the present Law can be derived from the

[5] " '. . . the Viet Nam papers came as no special revelation to those with experience in Government.' " Leslie Gelb (one of the directors of the project), quoted in *Time*, July 5, 1971.

Law of Institutional Expertise. Most agency statements are made as expert judgments—no one wants the opinion of the Bureau of Mines on our foreign affairs. (Whether anyone should want the opinion of the experts on foreign policy is another question to be considered later on.) Expert judgments, when they involve continuation of agency operations, are without value—which is no more than to say their truth or falsity is unknown.

Please note the specific phrasing of the Law of Irrelevance of Truth. It does *not* say that any institution's statements on any subject are always false. It does *not* say, either, that any institution's statements designed to keep the institution's machinery running are false. These would be clumsy overgeneralizations.[6] What the Law says is that truth is *irrelevant* to the making of any statement that is seen as an institutional necessity. Institutionally necessary statements are not untruthful, they are a-truthful.

Note further that our Law does not declare that those within an institution who tell lies either necessarily, or usually, or even often, believe they are lying. The psychology is more complicated, and worth attention in our next example.

The Bureau of Counter-Inflationary Affairs

Suppose, for example, that you are an important part of an administration's inflation-fighting machinery. You are, in fact,

---

[6]The overgeneralization that all Government statements are lies comes from the permanent anti-establishment institution. The required mouthings of phrases by the anti-establishment are no less unimaginatively mechanical, and no more related to truth, than the press releases whose truth they deny. Example: in some quarters it is received truth that the foreign policy of the United States is always designed to further the interests of big corporations. For instant refutation of this doctrine, try to get the State Department to help a big business abroad.

the Director of the Bureau of Counter-Inflationary Affairs (BCIA). Congratulations. There arrives on your Directorial desk the statistical branch's report that the cost of living is up another one percent last month (March). Rats. What do you do?

If it is unnecessary to issue any statement at all, you might issue none. At least, you will not be out there trying for a banner headline announcing another month's defeat in the BCIA's good fight.

If, however, you know that the news will have to come out, you will cast about for ways to announce it. Being a Director, you call a meeting and direct your staff to think of a way to break the bad news. With practiced ease, they will produce, and you will make a strong, positive announcement. For example:

1. You may examine the components of the price index. Are artichokes up sharply? Aha, then you may say:

"The BCIA announced today that owing in part to a temporary sharp rise in the cost of artichokes, the cost of living rose one percent in March. Prices of kumquats and buttonhooks remained stable."

2. You may notice that prices rose one percent in March, but two percent in February. Perfect, for now you may say:

"The BCIA announced today that the rate of increase in prices had been cut in half between February and March. Reporting this victory over inflation to the President, the BCIA Director said modestly, 'It was nothing, Chief, we'll do better next month.' "

3. You may remember that while prices are certainly rising fast, you did a good job in March by killing that proposed 37 percent hike in paper clips. You sincerely think you did a good inflation-fighting job on paper clips. You really believe the BCIA is doing good, solid, necessary work. So your statement reads:

"The BCIA announced today that during March its fight on inflation had held down prices on paper clips by 37 percent. Prices on other commodities rose a relatively modest one percent. The BCIA Director pointed to the need for a continued vigorous battle against inflation on all fronts . . ."

The series of hypothetical press releases need not be continued, since it bears an uncanny similarity to the monthly economic word from all national capitals. Let us make one thing perfectly clear, and that is, you are not going to issue a press release saying, "The BCIA said today it had totally failed in its job during March, owing to incompetent personnel."

As Director of the BCIA, you are an honorable man and also one who doesn't like to be caught, and therefore you are ready to defend every release against the charge of being a provable lie. (Of course, if you can classify some of the facts Top Secret, it isn't so hard to defend your press releases.)

As for the question whether you believed any of the BCIA releases to be lies—why, banish such evil thoughts. The human capacity for self-deception is unlimited, and you simply never had any intention of lying. You put a good face on things, that's all.

This is an important point, known to all Washington operatives, so mark it well: the man (or institution) saying the opposite of what you believe to be the truth does not think he is lying (except in one special case, to be discussed shortly).[7]

---

[7] If you think cigarette smoking causes cancer, and you find a tobacco-state representative saying it doesn't, do not be quick to assume the tobacco man is lying. He doesn't think he is, and he will have facts and figures from an Expert Institute to back him up. One of the foundations of senatorial courtesy and of successful operation on the Washington scene is the assumption that no one thinks he is lying (with that one same exception). Thus, say, "The Senator's facts are mistaken." Do not say, "The Senator knows he is lying."

Creation of Facts

Institutional statements are not deliberate lies; rather, they are created backward from the necessity of making the statement. The order of events is from effect to cause: *first,* determine the necessary content of the institutional statement; *second,* assemble "facts" to be included in the statement. The BCIA staff meeting first determines what the press release must say—good news this month—and second selects "facts" to be good news. The press release is an institutional statement related to the BCIA's machinery, and therefore the press release is neither truthful nor untruthful—it is unrelated to truth because it is foreordained.

The "facts" are selected or suppressed as required. In a real sense, the "facts" are created as needed, by the BCIA or by any institution. Among the institutions busily fact-creating have been the real-life equivalents of the BCIA. The monthly news from the inflation front has been of defeat followed by disaster. As the bankers of the world fled from the dollar into bubble-gum cards, the Washington script was all sunshine:

The Washington Post, October 23, 1969:

The cost of living scored another big increase in September. . . .

Actually there has been some slowdown on balance in the rate of increase, Assistant Commissioner of Labor Statistics Arnold Chase noted.

The New York Times, June 19, 1970:

Consumer prices continued to rise in May at the rate of other recent months. . . .

Joel Popkin, Assistant Commissioner of Labor Statistics, called the recent pattern a "significant" improvement from that at the turn of the year.

The AFL-CIO News, April 24, 1971:

A sharp increase in food prices—especially supermarket prices—pushed the Consumer Price Index up another three-tenths of 1 percent in March. . . .

"This has to be interpreted as good news, extremely good news", said Paul McCracken, Chairman of the President's Council of Economic Advisers.

The Washington Post, July 24, 1971:

"Viewed solely as a single month, June was not one of our better months on the price front," Secretary of Labor James D. Hodgson said. "But June can also be viewed as the final month of the best half-year performance the nation has seen in some time."

And after such famous victories, there followed the Price Freeze, Price Controls, the Price Commission, the Cost of Living Council and all the rest of the new price-fixing institutions. They are all, you may be sure, proclaiming their monthly triumphs—and will continue to do so when the dollar and the doughnut reach parity.

Special Exception of the Deliberate Lie

The press releases of the BCIA, and most other institutional statements, are innocent acts of faith, not to be denounced as lies just because they prove to be totally false. Institutional lies are deliberate in a few circumstances listed below.

1. Spy Business.

Any good spy is supposed to lie about his spying; the dissemination of false information is an honored division of counter-intelligence work. When the Russians found U-2 spy planes in their skies, President Eisenhower was scolded for omitting the usual lies (off course; weather research; pilot high on hash, etc.).

2. War Business.

In battle, lies are expected. An army is not expected to say where or when it will strike, or whether it is retreating in disarray. This approved form of lie is often stretched unmercifully to make every communiqué optimistic. Since 1964 all announcements have promised that within six months the South Vietnamese army would be at the fighting efficiency of the Golden Horde.

3. Fire in the Theater.

Lies are expected when public danger would immediately result from telling the truth. California may be in real danger of sliding into the Pacific, but the fact cannot be proclaimed until some weekend when everyone is in Las Vegas.

Newspapers treat racial incidents with caution during times of riot and tension. Announcements are *not* made that "six white (black) youths with bicycle chains beat up a sweet little black (white) lady in the park." Though true, they are not made, because they would be followed by announcements that the city just burned down.

4. Boys-in-Blue Lies.

The police lie in order to catch criminals. Since this is acceptable, it is often hard for the policeman to understand why there is anything wrong with a little working-over to force a confession, or a little eavesdropping.[8]

5. National Emergency Lies.

Institutional lies are accepted policy in times of emergency, when the true statement would itself lead directly to a national disaster. Such an acceptable lie is, for example, the statement of a British Chancellor of the Exchequer that the pound will not be devalued. The accepted conjugation of the verb is: "We shall not devalue, we shall not devalue; we have devalued." American Secretaries of the Treasury have now learned this special grammar. Note that the disaster always comes off anyway, despite the lie.

6. Personal Disaster Lies.

Institutional white lies are told where telling the truth would destroy a career. "Assistant Secretary of the Atmosphere, Otto Zone, resigned today for personal reasons" (he was fired). "The President accepted Secretary O. Zone's resignation with regret" (he was delighted).

Similarly acceptable to some are the self-imposed restrictions of the news media requiring suppression of the juiciest peccadillos of politicos. "The Committee met with the Vice-Chairman presiding" (the Chairman was, and the newspaper knows he was, dead drunk for the last ten days). The Chairman's alcoholism is doubtless a fact of interest to constituents, but no matter. Only Drew Pearson used to accuse the late chairman of a vital House committee of drunkeness. Read:

---

[8]The motto for this is: "Don't tie the hands of the police, they're dealing with criminals."

"The Mayor was unavoidably detained at the Miami Beach
conference," but understand that the real story is: "The Mayor
was arrested for running stark naked around a motel pool
chasing a blonde." The newspaper won't tell if it's the Mayor,
but if it's you—better behave yourself.

All the news that's fit to print doesn't include news that
might upset the news institution's relationship with its subjects.

These known but acceptable lies are not merely false reports to paint prettier pictures. Instead, the known lie is acceptable because the statement itself is not a report but a part of a
present emergency. To tell the truth about the possibility of
devaluation will *cause* devaluation; to tell the truth about troop
dispositions will *cause* defeat; to tell the truth about police
plans will *cause* the murderer to escape.

Unfortunately, the institution that declares the emergency
also decides when a lie is acceptable. Therein resides the danger
to the public good. Since the beginning of the Cold War, the
American public appears to have accepted the idea that it is all
right to lie knowingly in order to confound the Communists.
World Communism is an emergency threat to the United
States, and therefore a knowing lie with anti-Communist purpose is acceptable.[9] News from Moscow shows that the same
doctrine is in force there.

Indeed, in Washington a certain glamour attaches to a job
where lying is regularly necessary. The underlying logic appears to be that since lies are needed in important emergencies,
an official who lies is important. From such logic it is only a

---

[9]As an example, take Radio Free Europe, supposedly financed by private gifts.
It turned out that it wasn't, and the Senate Committee on Foreign Relations said:
"The Committee deplores the fact that this financing—covering some 20 years
—has been kept secret from the American people and their elected representatives. It is indeed regrettable that the Executive Branch of Government under
five administrations deceived the taxpayers . . ." 92 *Congressional Record* S
12756.

To the trained ear, anything that is both "deplorable" and "regrettable" is
understood as damn well going to be continued.

little step to the assertion that "I may lie because I know what I am doing is important."

As an institutional botanist you now know that the deadly combination will be: (a) an institution dealing with emergencies; (b) a power in the institution to declare its own emergencies; and (c) an individual within the institution who can be important by telling important and necessary lies. An institution showing these deadly markings will give you lies as surely as poison ivy gives you blisters.

The appropriate questions are, then, which institutions are asserters of emergencies, and what evidence is there that they lie? The Federal executive departments evidently clothing themselves with the power to declare emergencies are the departments dealing with military matters, whose dealing with foreign affairs, those who spy and of course the Office of the President. The story of the Pentagon Papers is the story of these very departments systematically massaging the truth. The massage was impelled, not by evil motives, but because only these departments appreciated the grave national emergency, which had to be dealt with by their lies.

Practical Rules for
Detecting the Truth

The twin, cold teachings of the institutional laws are (1) that truth is irrelevant to most institutional statements, and (2) that some institutions tell a lot of deliberate lies—from the highest motives, of course. The uneasy citizen needs a test for truth, but an infallible test would depend on exact knowledge of each institution's inner machinery. In practice, there are certain rules of thumb in common use by those whose affairs depend on a quick assay of institutional pronouncements. These are:

1. Rule of Budget Statements.

Institutional statements regarding the urgent need for increased appropriations for institutional operations are to be disregarded as twaddle. This rule is confirmed directly by the Institutional Imperative, for budgets nourish the Institutional machinery.[10]

2. Rule of Communiqués.

A communiqué is an institutional announcement required for an institutional reason at a certain time—e.g., after a diplomatic conference. The content of all communiqués is foreordained and therefore unworthy of belief. The rule is: don't bother reading communiqués. You will learn only either that there was a "useful exchange of views" (nothing was agreed), of that something was agreed but kept secret.

3. Rule of Grave and Gravest Consequences.

Institutional statements warning of "Grave Consequences" if something isn't done *by the institution making the statement* are probably false. If the words "Grav*est* Consequences" are used, the statement is invariably false. The reason for the near certainty is that if the institution could do something about the mess, it would have. "The Deputy Secretary of State for Alarums and Excursions stated tonight that the 'Gravest Consequences' would ensue if . . ." Translation: the Deputy means his institution will do nothing whatsoever.

---

[10]There is also the Rule of Foreign Travel, which declares that institutional statements urging visits by institutional officers to Paris, Rome, London or the Virgin Islands have a minimal probability of being valid.

4. Rule of Defending the Mess.

The Institutional Imperative leads directly to the

LAW OF INSTITUTIONAL
ADMISSIONS

No institution can admit an error.

An admission of error threatens to change the internal machinery, not to keep it operating. Hence, by the Institutional Imperative, error is not admitted.

From this, the practical Washington rule of thumb is: don't waste time reading statements explaining away goofs. Obvious current examples are the statements explaining the many-faceted wonders of the Vietnam fiasco, or the fights to control inflation or smog.

5. Rule of Aid and Abet.

This is one of the most useful rules, especially in its positive form: Senator Humphrey's fear that publication of the Pentagon Papers would "only aid and abet the doubt and cynicism and suspicion about government" is a perfect "aid and abet" statement. What Senator Humphrey means is that doubt, cynicism, and suspicion will be aided and abetted *because* doubt, cynicism, and suspicion will be shown to be justified. A phony criticism never aided and abetted anybody.

In general, any institution's statement objecting to criticism as "aiding and abetting" means that the criticism was valid. Further examples: criticism of police brutality will aid and abet criminals; criticisms of doltish foreign policy aid and abet enemies abroad; uncovering waste of money, arrogance, sleeping in patrol cars or other institutional failures will aid and abet those evil forces the institution purports to fight.[11]

Exception: the "aid and abet" test cannot be applied to the FBI; all criticism of the FBI is "aiding and abetting."

6. Rule of Debasement of the Language.

Every Government document is full of neologisms, "specialty" words and awful jargon. The density of debasement of the English language affords a significant index of truth: the more debased, the less truth. A professor reading the Pentagon Papers cries: *"Has* there ever been a time when men in high office in this country wrote such godforsaken prose as these men put to paper?"[12]

The rule of debasement works for a simple reason: those who wish to convey truth use simple, understandable language. Those who conceal truth do not, in aid of concealment.[13] So, "killing" becomes "attrition," failure becomes "shortfall," and a depression becomes "slowdown in rate of growth." A convenient excuse for immorality lies in these false words. When did the Lord say to Moses: Thou shalt not attrite?

---

[11]Do not omit to apply the anti-positive form of the "aid and abet" rule. It is astonishingly useful to test an institutional statement by asking: If the statement said the opposite, would the institution denounce it as "aiding and abetting"? If so, don't believe the original. For example, suppose the Secretary of the Treasury says: "The dollar is as sound as a dollar." Apply the anti-positive test by supposing that a Senator from the opposition party had said: "The dollar is weak and will have to be devalued." Would not the Secretary denounce such a statement as "aiding and abetting those who would profit from devaluation"? You know he would. Therefore, the original statement ("the dollar is sound") is not to be believed. As an exercise, apply the anti-positive form of the "aid and abet" test to the press releases you approved during your tenure as Chief of the BCIA a few pages ago. You will find the truth shining through.

[12]George Anastaplo, "Preliminary Reflections on the Pentagon Papers," *University of Chicago Magazine,* Jan./Feb. 1972.

[13]"Even the language of the bureaucracy—the diminutive 'nukes' for instruments that kill and mutilate millions of human beings, the 'surgical strike' for chasing and mowing down peasants from the air by spraying them with 8000 bullets a minute—takes the mystery, agony and awe out of violence." Richard Barnet, "The Game of Nations," *Harper's Magazine,* November 1971. More from Mr. Barnet in *The Roots of War* (Atheneum, 1972), Chapter 5.

This list of rules could be expanded to include the rule of impenetrable neologisms ("new terms are invented to conceal the truth"), the rule of incomprehensibility ("statements meant to be incomprehensible are false"), and the 1984 rule ("when you know it's black, don't believe them when they say it's white"). A good supply of such rules is indispensable when dealing with institutions. To list them all would delay our examination of more important matters, including some of the darkest aspects of institutional behavior.

7. THE INSTITUTIONAL IRRELEVANCE OF MORALITY

The Crushed Individual. Law of the Institutional Irrelevance of Morality and Humanity. Minor Illustrative Cases: Hospitals, License Bureaus, Prisons, Concentration Camps. Case of Lieutenant Calley. Case of the Higher-Ups. The Personnel Nature of Guilt.

The Crushed Individual

No more somber theme runs through modern literature than the crushing of the individual by the institution. In Kafka, in Huxley, and of course in Orwell, the machinery of the state is seen as grinding remorselessly and mechanically to destroy all resistance to—what? Resistance, simply, to the further operation of the remorseless machinery of the state.[1]

The impersonality of a bureaucracy, the cold refusal to distinguish one individual from another, or to consider any

---

[1]Motion pictures mirror the same vision of the helpless human caught in the great institutional machineries. The famous image is Charlie Chaplin, in *Modern Times,* trapped between two huge gearwheels of a monstrous machine designed to manufacture we know not what. The innocent bystander caught by mistake in the workings of a spy apparatus has fascinated Hitchcock and given employment to a generation of his imitators. While the audience rejoices when a Hitchcock hero defeats the network, we know in our hearts that in real life the organization would have picked him off in reel one.

human consequence of the institutional action, all this is well recognized. Max Weber noted it,[2] as have all investigators after him. A *New Yorker* editorial in 1971 quotes Simone Weil in 1933:

> . . . whether it calls itself Fascism, democracy, or the dictatorship of the proletariat, the supreme enemy remains the administrative apparatus, be it civil or military . . . the worst betrayal is to consent to subordinate oneself to this administrative apparatus, and, in its service, to destroy, in oneself and in others, all true human values.

Reflecting on Weil in 1933, the 1971 editorialist concurs: the Indo-China war "may prove to have been the assembly area for a vast machine" with "a natural tendency not to be passive and inert but to move and gather momentum. The difficulty is not in setting it in motion . . . but in getting it to stop . . . It is the machine's nature to make war."

To remind us all of the blind immorality of properly designed institutional machinery, we need only remember those who manned the machinery of the Nazi concentration camps, methodically slaughtered millions of innocents and thriftily saved the by-products. Those who administered the camps were men like us; we share a common humanity with the sacrifices and the butchers as well. That the statement below is true we know without reference to the Institutional Laws:

---

[2]See H. H. Gerth and C. Wright Mills, *From Max Weber* (Oxford, 1958) ("The peculiarly 'impersonal' character" of the apparatus.)

LAW OF THE INSTITUTIONAL
IRRELEVANCE OF MORALITY
AND HUMANITY

**If the operation of the institutional ma-
chinery requires an action, morality and
humanity are irrelevant.**

In our theoretical structure, this derives directly from the
Second Axiom and the Institutional Imperative. The Second
Axiom states that the institution's existence depends on continued working of its machinery; the Institutional Imperative
that all institutional actions *must* keep the machinery running.
Thus if an action is immoral or inhumane but necessary to the
operation of the institutional machinery, it will be taken. That
is only to say, morality is irrelevant.

As usual, it is worth noting the precise phrasing of the
Law. It does *not* say that all institutional actions are immoral.
Plainly they are not. Institutions care for the sick, house the
poor, and feed the hungry. But the care, the housing and the
feeding are not—in the usual, governmental, case—performed
as moral acts but as operations of the institutional machinery.
The Division of Improverished Nutrition in the Department of
Hunger feeds because its function is to feed, not from animating
moral impulse. A few examples make this clear.

Minor Illustrative Cases: Hospitals,
License Bureaus, Prisons, Concentration Camps

The aims of the founders of our hospitals are moral and
humane: to care for and heal the sick. Yet it is a universally
observed fact that many hospitals carry on their humane work
in a highly impersonal, brutal way. Some report the experience

of standing bloody while the hospital Admissions Office requires answers to a barrage of questions. Other and more imaginative minor indignities abound. When did you last see a hospital room with a bookcase?

In our terms, both the minor indignities and the major inhumanities of the humane institution are a simple case of perception of the operation of institutional machinery as the institution's purpose. The machinery of the Admissions Office functions to admit you; the fact that you are standing there bleeding does not prevent the Office from discharging its purpose.

Similarly, the impersonal maltreatment of the citizen by minor licensing offices has been noted for centuries. To obtain the boon of issuance of license plates, a citizen is forced to stand waiting in four lines for three hours to receive two squares of painted tin.

The Personnel Postulate provides the required insight into the reasons why all such forms of minor harassment are adopted (in parts of the bureaucracy, importance can be shown only by being rude to the public). Here we note also that the machinery's functioning is independent of its inhumane effect. The perceived purpose of the Office of Nose Rings is to process nose-ring applications, *not* to be humane to applicants (and quite possibly not to issue nose rings).

The minor maltreatments of City Hall become systematic inhumanity in some prison systems, organized torture in politico-military prisons, and butchery in the extreme case of concentration camps in dictatorships. Any suggestion that brutality flows from the personal characteristics of the staff ("it's the guards—they're inhuman") or the national characteristics of the country ("it was the Nazis; we wouldn't do such things") must be rejected.

Ordinary prison brutality is spread throughout the world, from Devil's Island to Attica. The evidence is even clearer that

torture has retained its international popularity: the North Ko-
reans beat the captured crew of the Pueblo; the French in
Algeria favored electric prods as do the ruling Greek colonels;
czars and commissars favor Siberian exile; and Americans are
now reported to prefer advanced methods of interrogation such
as dangling from helicopters.

Thus, the explanation for brutality is neither tainted national characteristics nor the outcropping of a rare genetic trait.
Brutality is a regular part of institutional operations and as such
is susceptible to institutional analysis: brutality appears as a
confusion of the operation of the machinery with the purpose
of the institution (Third Axiom).

For example, our civil prisons neither rehabilitate nor treat
nor train. Nevertheless, the prison machinery operates to punish, such operation is perceived by the prison staff as the purpose, and adding a little more punishment makes sense. When
political prisoners are involved, torture to get information is a
normal and natural functioning of the institution for high and
noble state purposes.

Those most terrible examples of institutional design, the
Nazi extermination camps, are but the farthest extension of the
same principles. An institution was created with machinery
directed to the killing of millions. The perceived purpose of
killing was indeed the intended goal of the institution. The
institution thus created functioned in complete inner harmony,
and the machinery hummed for years. Guilt, if any was felt, was
irrelevant. Similarly well-designed institutions could run in any
country at any time. Generally, they do.

Case of Lieutenant Calley

Every war brings vicious acts. Ugly stories from Vietnam
had circulated for several years before the story of the affair at

Mylai surfaced. At this writing a certain Lieutenant Calley has been tried by an Army court-martial and convicted of the murder of a score of Vietnamese men, women and children in the course of a military operation in the hamlet of Mylai. Calley's conviction is on appeal; the incontrovertible fact is that a ditch in Mylai contained over a hundred bodies.

Two aspects of the Calley case require attention: we wish to know first, the reasons for the massacre, and second, the reasons for the strange public reaction to Calley's trial and conviction.

The reasons for the massacre are not hard to understand, and the Mylai massacre itself was apparently just one of several. The machinery of the Army in the field in Vietnam was designed to kill Vietnamese, to achieve certain results that did not include the well-being, let alone the existence, of an inconvenient civilian population (which could not in any event be identified as friend or enemy). That purpose of the Army's operations, as perceived by Calley and his platoon—and doubtless by many others—was to be served without reference to morality, as the Law of the Institutional Irrelevance of Morality confirms.[3]

While the acts at Mylai were not unusual, the public response to Calley's conviction was astonishing. A multiple murder called up great waves of popular sympathy. Letters to the White House ran 100 to 1 in favor of Calley.[4] "Free Calley"

---

[3]This is not to say that the Army is an immoral institution, or that the Army's prosecution of Calley was not the result of strong moral beliefs that Army men should not kill civilians, or that individual Army officers were not deeply disturbed by the murders at Mylai. Dismiss with contempt those who bewailed the prosecution as "aiding and abetting" the enemy, but give respect to those who prosecuted their fellow officer.

[4]Letters to the Editor, *Time* magazine, April 26, 1971:

"Sir: How can the Army, an organization that trains people to kill, condemn Lieut. Calley for murder?
                                        Marc Iuanic
                                        Eveleth, Minn."

buttons were distributed; ballads of a sort were written; Southern governors came to call. The President ordered Calley freed until he personally had reviewed the verdict. It was not a reaction of the intellectuals, who viewed the Mylai incident as one more example of the Vietnam mistake, but thought the trial perfectly correct. Instead, the sympathy for Calley was a popular emotional spasm, and Calley himself was unable to articulate its cause. Such waves of popular feeling conceal truths.

The essence of the supportive reaction was that Calley was doing *the job the institution really, operatively, assigned to him,* and "there but for the grace of God would go I, if I had Calley's platoon." As we have seen, the popular reaction was based on truth. Morality is not relevant to operation of the sub-institution of an Army platoon in Vietnam and Calley correctly sensed what the machinery he was part of was designed to do. Calley did what many before him had done, and what his public supporters rightly felt they would have done. Whether the buttons should have read "Free Calley" or "Convict Me" is a quibble for philosophers.

"Sir: So Lieut. Calley has been found guilty. Of what? Of having the courage to fight for his country?
                                        Janet Dunlop Schom
                                        College Station, Texas"

"Sir: . . . to punish Lieut. Calley for carrying out his basic mission—to seek out and destroy the enemy—is wrong. . . .
                                        Osborne S. P. Koerner
                                        Captain, U.S.N.R.
                                        Arlington, Virginia"

Or, in a professorial tone: "An otherwise undistinguished lieutenant has been received as a hero, a scapegoat, and a mass-murderer . . . " Professor B. Meltzer, "Some Uneasy Reflections on the Calley Case," *The University of Chicago Law School Record,* Spring 1971.

Case of the Higher-Ups

When Italy attacked Ethiopia, there was first described the aesthetic experience of bombing tribesmen. The reflective pilot flew far above, all the while appreciating the white blossoms of smoke rising below.[5] Aesthetics aside, at the time these views were considered slightly immoral.

Decisions of the American higher-ups in the Vietnam war, while still difficult to believe when they are set down in cold print, provide solid evidence of the irrelevance of morals to institutional actions.[6] Not in the heat of battle with Calley's platoon, but in the air-conditioned planning rooms of Washington, decisions were made:

1. To bomb and destroy Vietnamese towns fom the air, when the destruction necessarily would mean the killing of many civilians, without any possibility of knowing whether the civilians had taken any hostile action.

2. To strip the leaves from the trees and poison the crops in the ground.

3. To waste and level whole towns harboring, or thought to harbor, any sympathy for the Viet Cong.

---

[5]Mussolini's son Vittorio, who flew with Ciano, is quoted in Angelo del Boca, *The Ethiopian War, 1935–1941* (U. of Chicago, 1965):

> "It was always disappointing when I failed to hit my target, but when I was dead on I was equally upset because the effects were so disappointing. I suppose I was thinking of those American movies and was expecting those terrific explosions when everything goes sky-high. Bombing those thatched mud huts of the Ethiopians doesn't give one the slightest satisfaction."

[6]Draft memorandum of Assistant Secretary of Defense McNaughton to Secretary McNamara, March 24, 1965:

"1. U.S. aims.

> 70% —to avoid a humiliating U.S. defeat (to our reputation as a guarantor).
> 20% —to keep SNV (and the adjacent) territory from Chinese hands.
> 10% —to permit the people of SVN to enjoy a better, freer way of life.
> ALSO —to emerge from crisis without unacceptable taint from methods used.
> NOT —to 'help a friend,' although it would be hard to stay in if asked out."

The Pentagon Papers (Bantam, 1971), Document #96.

4. To adopt the "body count" (of supposed enemies killed) as a measure of success. This piece of institutional design inevitably led the troops in the field to kill as many as possible and classify them posthumously as enemy bodies to be counted. (Another example is the method adopted to distinguish from the air those who, as enemies, could properly be machine-gunned: "they run.")

5. To continue the destruction of the country that the American effort was ostensibly designed to save long after the destruction was known and the effort was a failure.

6. Throughout, to maintain a systematic policy of deceiving the public. The public was told not what was going on, but only and always that the military program was succeeding.

These are not the actions of berserk savages, nor the plannings of the Joint Chiefs of Staff of Attila the Hun, but the cold deliberate policies of a group of distinguished Americans from the highest levels of government: the Westmorelands, Taylors, Bundys, Rostows, Rusks, McNamaras and of course in the end the Presidents themselves. Yet no matter how sympathetically these decisions are viewed in any system of ethics they must be adjudged immoral. It is not moral to bomb and strafe innocent civilians from the air, and it is no more moral to kill them on the ground. And it cannot be more moral to make the decision than to execute it.[7]

We require, then, an explanation of the immoral actions taken by a group of men each of whom in private life would be

---

[7]Here is Colonel Anthony Herbert, relieved of command for insistently reporting war crimes:

"None of the people who are really responsible for war crimes in Vietnam has ever admitted doing anything wrong . . . Generals like Westmoreland won't take any responsibility for the awful things that could have been avoided in Vietnam. Instead, they try to sell people this bill of goods about the heavy responsibility of sending men to their deaths, implying that this is so much harder than going out there themselves. What unadulterated horseshit." *Playboy*, July 1972.

expected to display every civilized feeling. Our body of laws provides it, and at once. In Vietnam, the institutional machinery was established and it began to operate. The machinery included—indeed consisted of—the planning sessions of the Departments of Defense and State and the White House staff. Once started, the machinery continued and *the purpose of American action in Vietnam was perceived solely in terms of the operation of the machinery* (Third Axiom). The only operative purpose of the war was to do what the sub-institution, the planning machinery, planned. The Institutional Imperative required all actions, moral or not, that kept the machinery going. The Vietnam war kept the machinery going.[8] The Imperative overrode all human considerations, and the Law of Irrelevancy of Morality was proved again, in action and in spades. Deliberate murder was planned and ordered as achieving the institutional purpose—a purpose no more glorious than keeping the machinery going.

A Law of institutional behavior with predictive power sufficient to forecast the bloody group activity of individually civilized Washington functionaries, is a law as close to being proved true as the nature of proof permits. Such proof, not polemics, was the reason to review even briefly the events in Vietnam. We leave the subject to history, and the souls of those who participated to God in His mercy.

---

[8]"It is impossible to think of a case more intellectually inert than that for the Vietnam War. Yet the war continues. This is because the bureaucracy, the military and intelligence bureaucracy in particular, operates not in response to national need but in response to its own need." John Kenneth Galbraith, "Plain Lessons of a Bad Decade," *Foreign Policy,* Winter 1971, reprinted in *Economics Peace and Laughter* (1972).

The Personnel Nature of Guilt

A final note is appropriate as to the state of mind of those normal and moral people who do abnormal and immoral things as institutional functionaries. Mr. Ellsberg, of the Pentagon Papers, thinks that the power of making decisions "gives their lives an electric excitement to which they are clearly addicted . . ."[9] Excitement there is, and addiction too, but we need to know also why the decisions are as bad as they are. Why not an electrically exciting moral, humane policy? Why not a crusade instead of a defoliation?

The answer lies in the Personnel Postulate. Of course the top jobs seem important, exciting, addictive. All institutional jobs are important, as the Personnel Postulate teaches. These men, with their repellent little vocabularies of "hard knocks" and "raps" and "tilts" are self-important, but not decision makers. There is the illusion, for the decisions have long since been compelled.

Immoral decisions flow from an institution when the machinery is so designed as to function only by being immoral. It is as if the Torturer in Chief is given his important job, and then asked to decide if torture is necessary. His squeezes and turns of the screw will seem immoral to you, but only the natural performance of his important job to him. The trouble with most of our institutional machinery, including most especially the great foreign policy-military machinery, is that it has no moral way *to* function. A hospital can be well or ill-run, helpful or not. The Joint Chiefs of Staff are not now set up to produce anything but moral disaster, because they have no institutional machinery patterned to consider morality. They can count bodies but not good will.

---

[9]Studs Terkel, "Servants of the State," *Harper's Magazine,* February 1972.

Of course, the fact that the institutional machinery calls for immoral behavior does not absolve a Calley, a guard in the concentration camp, or the hard little souls of our Washington planners. Personal guilt remains, even though personal virtue is hard to practice inside an institution. Unattractive as it is, we shall have to return to the subject of virtue at a later point.

8. THE INSTITUTIONAL IRRELEVANCE OF PURPOSE

Paradox of Invariable Accomplishment; Law of the Same. Three Principles of Institutional Design. Case of Union Negotiations. Case of *Illinois v. Allen*. Case of the Brave Protectors of Everything (Fighting the Menaces). Necessary Internal Alterations; Law of Reflexive Purpose; Mount Vernon Rises Curd on Curd. Case of the Commissioned Castrati. The Ever-Helpful Foundation. Peace. Pollution. Hard Answers for Hard Questions.

Paradox of Invariable Accomplishment

The attentive reader—and can you admit to less?—will have long noted, buried in the Third Axiom, a most intriguing paradox. By the Third Axiom, whatever the internal machinery does is perceived within the institution as the institution's real purpose: "I file, therefore our great purpose is filing." But since the machinery is always operating, the Third Axiom thus leads directly to the paradox that: an institution is perceived as always accomplishing its purpose.

Another route to the Paradox is via the Law of Institutional Admissions: no institution admits any error, much less the grossest error of all—that its purpose (the operation of its machinery) is futile. Never in the history of civilization has the announcement been heard that: "The Bureau of Diminishing Returns announced today that all its operations had been determined to be without rational purpose, and the Bureau

104

was closing its doors at the end of its (futile) business day."

There is no logical avenue of escape, and it must be concluded that logic requires the following:

LAW OF INVARIABLE ACCOMPLISHMENT

An institution will always accomplish its internally perceived purpose.

We make a very careful distinction between *ostensible* purpose (the noble publicly declared purpose of the institution) and its *real,* internally perceived purpose (whatever the internal machinery is set up to do). Ostensible purpose is as irrelevant to an institution as truth or morality.

Much irritation is wasted on institutions which function quite well by their own internal standards, but poorly in terms of public service. The Department of Parks does not provide agreeable green space for the relaxation of the citizenry? Are you sure the Department was designed so that its ostensible purpose (to provide parks) was its real, internal, purpose? What is the Department's internal working definition of a "park"— is it a concrete parking lot? Remember that the rule as stated by computer programmers is: GIGO (Garbage In, Garbage Out). If you do not design your institution right, internal purpose will not equal ostensible purpose. And your park will be covered with concrete, not grass.

Three self-evident principles govern all institutional design:

THREE PRINCIPLES OF INSTITUTIONAL DESIGN

FIRST PRINCIPLE: *If the institutional machinery is designed not to accomplish anything, it won't.*

SECOND PRINCIPLE: *If the desired result is not accomplished, the institutional machinery is not designed to accomplish it.*

THIRD PRINCIPLE: *If the desired result of the institution cannot be stated in terms meaningful to design of the institutional machinery, it will not be accomplished.*

Simple as these rules are, they are violated as regularly as the girls in an old-fashioned stag film. The frustrated citizenry fumes and frets, when all that is wrong is that ostensible and internal purpose are confused. A few examples of confusion follow.

Case of Union Negotiations

The behavior of labor unions in wage negotiations often baffles and even enrages the public. Your friendly bridge-tender or steel-smelter suddenly disappears for ten weeks, returning tanned, fit and unsympathetic with your untended bridge and your unsmelted steel. You and the newspapers point out with an edge of hysteria that the difference between the wage settlement and the opening management offer was so small that it would take fifty-six years to recoup the wages lost during the ten-week strike. Your tender or smelter looks at you pityingly, as if you didn't understand. And if you made the fifty-six-year calculation, you don't, as a matter of fact. You are thinking of a strike as a decision of a kind of town meeting of the workers. Wrong.

Wage negotiations and strikes these days are handled by institutions. Unions have strong internal discipline, high-paid officers, staffs, marble office buildings and all the rest of the trappings. The ostensible purpose of unions is to win "fair" wages and working conditions.

Such goals as "fair" wages cannot be stated in meaningful terms (what's "fair"?) and so, the goal has no relation to the activity of the institution.[1] The real purpose of the organization, as always, is the operation of the machinery. Union decisions and actions have as their purpose the continued functioning of the union machinery. The real object of the game is to assure that the officers continue their important work. In blunter terms, the officers want to show that they "delivered" for the men, as much as Congressmen want to deliver for constituents.

This view of labor negotiations makes more sense of the rituals and the waiting periods. On the union side, the strike lasts not until a "fair" settlement has been reached, but until the officers believe the men will accept the settlement as proving "delivery of the goods" by the officers. If the officers are very strong, as Jimmy Hoffa of the Teamsters was, there will be a quick, solid, agreement. If the officers are weak, the men may even reject a settlement—even a "fair" settlement—leaving the officers embarrassed and in danger of losing their offices.

The common sense of the settlement is irrelevant. Union demands quite often put the employers out of business and the men out of jobs. By insisting on practices which make it cheaper to print by lithography rather than setting type, the printer's union has done wonders for the business of lithographers. Remember, the settlement has to make not economic sense, but

---

[1]This was the third of the Three Principles of Institutional Design.

institutional sense to the union leadership. To predict the outcome of a strike, consider the institutional needs of the union
leader.

Case of *Illinois v. Allen*

The founding fathers in their wisdom established the federal judiciary as one of the three separate branches of government. As an institution, courts have considerable scope to
define their own business, and the Law of Institutional Self-
Occupation predicts that they will venture into many fields.

A complete analysis of the reverberations of our institutional theory in the courthouse dome would be difficult and
tedious, and call for a number of those citations lawyers find so
dear. A simple example of the institutional Laws in action can,
however, be supplied. The citation is *Illinois v. Allen,* 397 U.S.
337 (1970).[2]

For centuries, defendants in criminal cases knew their
place in the judicial system. They sat in the hushed courtroom,
whispered to their lawyers, and tried to look incapable of crime.
Since a defendant need not even take the stand, in many a trial
the defendant played no role at all except to shuffle nervously
at the time of sentencing. He just didn't talk much.

In the 1960s the belief was held in certain circles (a) that
courts were part of "the system" (certainly true) and (b) that
courts were responsible in some degree for the evils of "the
system" (almost wholly false). Accordingly, when defendants
holding this faith were brought to trial, their behavior was
creatively outrageous. They yelled, they interrupted cross-
examination, they gave speeches, they accused the judge of acts

---

[2]The numbers are volume and page of the United States Supreme Court Reports,
and year; the names are those of the contestants, with him who came to the
Supreme Court named first.

with his female relatives unsuited to his age and dignity.

The old-fashioned concept of a trial as cousin to a funeral was under attack, and presiding judges did not know what to do. What would you do if you delivered a stern warning with all the majesty of the bench, and the defendant shouted back "____ you!" The natural reply of "____ you, too!" would not advance the judicial ball.

Warnings, threats, citations for contempt being in vain, judges began to turn to gags, chains and other restraints in the courtroom, and to think longingly of trials *in absentia* with the prisoner resting conveniently far from the court.

In the case of *Illinois v. Allen,* the Supreme Court dealt with the problem of disorderly defendants. There were several possible solutions, including declaring a forfeited game. A trial can be considered a contest that a defendant can enter only if he wants to. If the defendant does not want a trial (as he shows by interrupting it), why not just find him guilty as charged, and move on to the next case: "And ____ you, Mr. Defendant!"

The Supreme Court's decision is interesting in terms of our theory. An analysis of the institutional machinery of the court system does not show that it is designed to achieve the ostensible purpose of "justice." "Justice" cannot possibly be defined in terms specific enough to design machinery. Instead, the court machinery is designed to try cases. "Trials" are the product of the institutional machinery, and "trials" should, by the Third Axiom, be perceived internally as the purpose of the system.

So, our theory predicts, by the Institutional Imperative, the Supreme Court should necessarily select a method of dealing with unmanageable defendants that leads to the institution's real purpose: "trials." And so it came to pass, for the Court approved any reasonable and appropriate restraints on obstreperous defendants in order to permit the trial to continue. A result as predicted, in all respects.

Case of the Brave Protectors of Everything

Studded around Washington, amid the bloated federal buildings and the union's marble cubes, are the headquarters of the National Associations. By now, there are National Associations for everything and everybody. There are the professional associations of doctors, chemists and geology teachers. There are industry associations: The American Pharmaceutical Association, The National Coal Association (they have a black marble building), The National Forest Products Association (they have a building with wooden windows), not to forget The National Peanut Council and The National Association of Metal Name Plate Manufacturers.

These organizations are not in Washington because the climate is salubrious. They have direct purposes, not hard to understand, of assuring that official Washington pays adequate attention to their needs, all of which by definition are urgent. The urgent need for a higher depletion allowance on tortilla mining must be understood, the tortilla subsidy must be voted, and the tariff on foreign tortillas (based, of course, on the U.S. selling price) must be maintained. Senator Herbert W. ("Tortilla Tom") Frijole must be supported; January 27 must be proclaimed National Tortilla Day, and a stamp must be issued honoring the inventor of the tortilla, the beloved Jugo de Naranjas.

Often enough, the activities of the National Associations are perfectly consistent with their natural goals—usually the excessive prosperity of the membership. At other times, the Associations appear to be somewhat off the track, for familiar institutional reasons.

The National Rifle Association, for example, obviously has considerable lobbying clout. After the assassination of Senator Robert Kennedy, there was much agitation for gun control laws. The NRA fought the laws, in a campaign criticized both for misstating the proposed law and for raising false fears of unconstitutional disarmament of the populace. "Register Commies, not guns" was the general tone of the campaign. Since the National Rifle Association's members are not rifles, but people, it was hard to see how the membership could benefit from being misinformed by its own Association.

The explanation for the NRA's behavior, in terms of our theory, must be that a good part of the institutional machinery of the NRA is designed and devoted to fighting gun controls, all gun controls, defined as The Menace. The institutional machinery exists, and it operates. Do not ask whether The Menace is really there (Law of Institutional Self-Occupation).

The American Medical Association, similarly, is thought throughout Washington to have done a first-class job in recent years if its job was to project the image of doctors as greedy money-grubbing monopolists, firmly opposed to any aid for the sick and poor. Surely such a public image is not good for doctors, and the AMA is not serving any recognized ostensible goal of the institution. It is not defeating much legislation. The question, though, is not why doctors take such positions— because many doctors didn't. The AMA did, and the AMA is an institution. Somewhere in the past, part of the AMA was set up to fight "socialized" medicine, The Menace. The Menace-fighting sub-institution is operating brilliantly by its own purposes, which are to keep fighting The Menace. At the moment the score is: Menace—2, AMA—0.

The catalog of Association behavior could be continued, but in each case the diagnosis is the same. When the Hollow Noodle Association is not serving the members' ostensible interests, it is serving what are the institution's real interests. A good Menace a day keeps the Association healthy.[3]

---

[3]Final note for the student of rococo institutional forms: there is an American Society of Association Executives.

Necessary Internal Alterations

It sometimes happens that an institution is correctly designed to reach its ostensible goal, but the goal itself proves unattainable. Perhaps the task is impossible, or politically unacceptable, or just foolish. Standard institutional behavior in such instances is not to shut up shop, but to alter the *internal* purpose. This is an institutional law, as follows:

LAW OF REFLEXIVE PURPOSE

If the institutional machinery cannot function, the perceived purpose will be altered.

This follows from the Institutional Imperative, as an example shows.

Mount Vernon Rises Curd on Curd

Suppose that the Society to Build a Replica of Mount Vernon Out of Pot Cheese has been well designed: its ostensible purpose and its internally perceived purpose are one and the same. Yet, sadly, its goal is unattainable. In all such instances the internal purpose is slightly altered to "studying the conditions for" or "doing research in" or "planning for" or "coordinating activities of " the SBRMVOPC. The nasty problem of doing the impossible is avoided, and the organization continues happily to turn over its forever useless machinery.

Many government departments have become Societies for the Exhaustive and Endless Study of some impressive objective. They reach their internal goals daily; their ostensible goals will be achieved the day when that replica of Mount Vernon rises, curd upon curd.

Case of the Commissioned Castrati

We have stated it as a principle that if an institution is designed not to accomplish anything, it won't. To this, the objection may be heard that no institutional machinery is ever designed to accomplish nothing. This objection is observably false.

In less humane times and places, boys were castrated in order to preserve the beauty of their tenor voices. Their place in twentieth-century Washington has been taken by institutions bearing titles reading "President's Commission on [Insert Name of Problem]." Such Commissions are institutions gelded from birth, with machinery designed to produce a report, and nothing else. Many Commission reports have been well done, as lovely as the songs of the *castrati,* but as nonfunctional.

There is, for example, the Report of the National Advisory Commission on Civil Disorders (The "Kerner Commission" of 1967). Well and compassionately written, it warned that the cities of America were tinderboxes, ready to be touched off by smoldering resentments. If the Commission had declared that Gary, Indiana was entering a golden age, it would have had the same effect: nil.

The 1970 Commission on Obscenity and Pornography took its job most seriously. Scientific studies of effects of reading dirty books were ordered (one wonders what a requisition form for thirty-two dirty books looks like). The Commission's comprehensive report said that there was no evidence that pornography, hard-core or not, ever did any harm, except that in quantity it produced boredom, just as Commission reports do. This startling news was greeted by a great political hubbub. Agile Vice-Presidents and Congressmen knocked down aging Senators to be the first to say they rejected the report because "everybody knows reading dirty books is bad."

At times, when even the making of a report by a Commission would be dangerous, extra care is taken to see that the report is ineffectual. A current commission on drug problems has been warned not to recommend legalizing marijuana. The next Commission on Pornography will probably be given full powers to report on anything but sex.

The Ever-Helpful Foundation

The creation of ineffectual institutions is not confined to government. The great private charitable foundations finance piles of high-minded studies of national problems. A story tells of the plight of the small literary magazine: distinguished, deserving, it was broke and would have to suspend unless it got $2000 to pay the printer. In despair, the publisher asked the nearest Foundation to slip him the two grand, and quick. He was promised a telephone call after the next morning's Board meeting, which duly came: "Congratulations! The Board just voted $25,000 for a study of the financial troubles of small literary magazines."

Peace

Our institutional laws teach bitter truths: the faults of our society lie not in our stars not necessarily in the intractability of our problems, and surely not in the machinations of the evil Doctor Fu Manchu. Rather, our institutions are not designed to do what we at least say we want them to do. Whether any high-sounding ostensible purpose has been translated to be a real purpose of an institution is a question always worth asking.

Consider, for example, the activities (if they can be called such) of those sitting in Paris to negotiate peace in Vietnam. For years, the net result of negotiations by the four teams of diplomats was to settle the date of the next meeting. Nothing at all appeared to be happening. Nothing at all was happening. In short, each of the negotiating teams existed to "negotiate," not to get anything done. The institution's effective purpose was indeed met; to sit there. It is plainly wrong to say that the purpose of either side was "peace." Although they said so, it was not so, for each side knew very well how to get peace *if that were the real purpose.* Peace could be reached by the North Vietnamese withdrawing, or the Americans withdrawing, or the South Vietnamese or Viet Cong giving up. Peace, if peace were the only goal, was instantly available. The negotiators of all nationalities were not "peace" negotiators, but negotiators for unobtainable advantage, which, by the Law of Reflexive Purpose, led the real purpose to be perceived as sitting, and sit they did.

Pollution

Efforts to solve the problems of pollution have not resulted in much cleanliness. Despite speeches, legislation and the creation of agencies, city air looks like muddy water and the waters are solid with residues. Here again, what is causing the problem is quite plain. Advanced studies of pollution dynamics and oxygenation rates are not necessary to uncover the cause of water pollution. The river is polluted because someone is throwing sewage in it.

No Commission is needed to debate the real solution to river pollution. Tell everyone throwing sewage in the river to stop doing it by January 2, next year, on pain of fine, imprisonment, or being forced to swim in and drink of the water. That is a simple and efficacious remedy. It is also a remedy presenting no problems of institutional design. An Office of River Purity can be staffed at once and given a directive of model clarity and simplicity: "No crap in the river!"

This marvelously effective solution has not been adopted. A number of hypocritical excuses are given: it would be too expensive, industries could not conform, the municipalities would not want to do it, the problems of "coordination" in this "complex" matter would hold things up. Nonsense. If the *real* objective is to have clean water, adopt the slogan above and set to work. If the objective is to have clean water but cost no one anything and permit all present sewage disposal practices to continue, and make no political enemies, such an objective is phony, and cannot be achieved. Obeying the Law of Reflexive Purpose, our Offices of River Purity will turn themselves into commissions, coordinating bodies, liaison bureaus, and study groups. The river will still stink ten years hence.

But, you may object, a directive as strong as is suggested might cause good old River City to have its municipal sewer outfall cemented up next New Year's Day. The good citizens of the good city would have no sanitary facilities. Mercy! To this the reply is, if the good citizens and their city fathers knew that on New Year's Day 1974 they would flush their last flush, you can bet they would spend 1973 building a sewage treatment plant as fast as they could. If the threat is meaningless, the plant never will be built.

Hard Answers to Hard Questions

More than a few—perhaps most—of our problem-solving institutions appear to be deliberately designed to be ineffective. When a Fire Department is required, one is set up. Those who evade the fire regulations are looked upon with disfavor, and, given a reasonable level of honesty, fires are kept under control. In other fields, the rule is hypocrisy: the real intent is not to solve the stated problem, because the known solution is too expensive, or unpleasant, or politically unacceptable. The institution with the ostensible purpose of solving the problem is designed (or is forced to design itself, reflexively) to accept some other purpose. The national attacks on poverty, on overpopulation, on housing, on crime, all share in this hypocrisy. As a result the agencies ostensibly set up to lead the big "fight" are in fact only crypto-commissions, or worse.

This book is not the place for the demonstration, but an excellent showing can be made that for each major domestic problem there is a known and efficacious solution, or set of solutions. Each solution, in turn, has been rejected, often silently, because it costs too much in terms of money, of time, or in terms of just tough decisions. Institutions supposedly assigned to cope with the problems obviously cannot cope, and show the symptoms of institutional disease predicted by our Laws: they begin to do things without useful results. The institutions appear to fail at their ostensible tasks. Such failures, it must be said, are not institutional; the fault lies with our representatives who designed such institutions, and with those who, in turn, elected them.

PART III

THE INSTITUTIONAL
DISASTERS

9. REGULATORY AGENCIES FOR FUN AND PROFIT

Regulating Rates. Case of the Toll Bridge. The BURP. Tom Swift and the Electronic Earlobe. Institutional Inertia, Theorem of Same. The Regulator and the Regulatee.

Regulating Rates

For an industry to be tagged as a "public utility" is a social disaster. Immediately, the industry is considered a menace, to be left at large only under the supervision of a keeper called a regulatory agency.

Telephone calls are regulated by the Federal Communications Commission (FCC); electricity and gas by the Federal Power Commission (FPC); railroads and trucks by the Interstate Commerce Commission (ICC); steamships and airlines by the Federal Maritime Commission (FMC) and the Civil Aeronautics Board (CAB), respectively. Even the price of a stamp is, since 1971, subject to the decisions of a Postal Rate Commission. Such an alphabetical constellation of regulators surely evidences the accepted belief that rate regulation is desirable and effective. Testing that belief is instructive.

All federal regulatory agencies are subject to the Adminis-

trative Procedure Act, which requires the following procedure
to pass on a rate: (1) notice of hearing; (2) a public hearing
before an independent Examiner,[1] where a stenographic record
will be taken (all parties may call witnesses and offer written
evidence and everybody has a lawyer, including the agency
itself, which has lawyers called Public Counsel, Bureau Counsel, or the like); (3) Written briefs or proposed findings of fact
submitted to the Examiner; (4) Examiner's recommended decision; (5) written exceptions to the Examiner's decision filed
with the agency itself; (6) oral argument before the agency
(discretionary); (7) agency decision in writing; (8) if any party
seeks it (and someone usually does), court review and, of
course; (9) possible review by the Supreme Court. As in playing
Monopoly, the court decision can send everyone back to Go to
start over.

Rate hearings last for months or years. Millions of dollars
appear to be at stake; economists are called in to predict (de-
pending on their side) either bankruptcy for the utility or economic strangulation of the utility's customers.

A single body of doctrine is reasonably common to all
rate-regulating agencies. Rate inquiries are divided into two
main classes: (1) are the rates "reasonable" (too high or too
low), and (2) are the rates "unjustly discriminatory" (i.e., is one
user getting a better or worse deal than another)?

With such brave words as "reasonableness" to guide
them, with the aid of expert and devoted staffs, with the
mandatory observance of the procedural guarantees of the
administrative equivalent of the Bill of Rights, and with an
accepted body of regulatory doctrine carefully supervised by
the courts—with all this surely the regulatory agencies are
eminently equipped to dispense the most informed administrative justice, satisfactory and beneficial to all? It is not

---

[1]The Examiner is an administrative judge, and now has that title.

clear who asks such long questions, but the answer is: no.

As a matter of fact, the procedures for regulating utility rates afford us an almost perfect example of the operation of our Third Axiom and the Institutional Imperative. The regulatory hearings proceed in good faith, with honest attention and hard work by all concerned. What results is a most elaborate ritual, whose purpose is perceived by the participants as "regulation" —easily translated by the Third Axiom to be merely the operation of the regulatory machinery. That there is little public purpose served by the performance of the ritual is demonstrable, and we proceed to demonstrate.

Case of the Toll Bridge

The doctrines of rate regulation come from simpler days. In the primitive faith, the utility is seen as the owner of a toll bridge, and the user as the traveler who must pay toll.[2] Regulating the reasonableness of rates can be conceived in simplest terms as asking what is a "reasonable" toll.

In the standard doctrine, the question of reasonableness of the toll must be subdivided into two issues: (1) what is the toll bridge owner's investment in his bridge—called the issue of the "rate base," and (2) what percentage of investment should the bridge owner receive each year—called the issue of the "rate of return." These two issues can become delightfully complex. Just as a sample, the "rate base" issue can include such niceties as:

1. Is the investment in the bridge to be valued at "original cost" (which may be a few colonial dollars), or "present value"

---

[2]The regulation of rates is conceived as a necessity because the utility enjoys "monopoly." In most instances, though, the monopolies are conferred by licenses granted by the same regulatory agencies, a nice application of the Law of Institutional Self-Occupation.

124]   THE INSTITUTIONAL IMPERATIVE

(which may be high, but depends on what can be earned), or "reproduction cost" of building a new bridge?

2. What about depreciation on the bridge—how much should be allowed each year, and on what basis (straight-line, accelerated, double-declining balance)?[3]

3. How much should be allowed for working capital necessary to make repairs, pay the bridge-tender, and wait out the bridge-tender's strikes, which come once every two years in the fishing season?

4. What about that expensive sheep-walkway on the bridge—is its cost in the rate base? There are no longer any sheep crossing, and should automobiles have to keep paying toll forever to amortize that ovine promenade?

5. How about the bridge owner's souvenir shop down by the exit ramp, and its stock? Is selling shoddy souvenirs part of the business of running a toll bridge, or isn't it?

The "rate base" list could be continued for pages, but shift for a moment to a few of the simplest "rate of return" issues in the toll-bridge case, such as:

1. The bridge has a mortgage on it—will the rate of return be figured on the owner's equity (cost less the borrowed money) or on full cost?[4]

2. Do you figure rate of return before or after taxes? What if the owner is a company with another losing toll-bridge twenty miles away and pays no taxes?

3. What is a "fair" rate of return anyway—5 percent, 10 percent, 15 percent of the "rate base" each year?

4. How many tolls will be paid next year? Will national or local economic conditions affect bridge use? And if you don't

---

[3]Or SOYD, not a health food, but Sum-of-the-Years-Digits. This and other niceties will be the subject of the forthcoming "Everything You Wanted to Ask About Rate Bases* (*But Were Too Afraid to Know)."

[4]I.e., if the bridge cost $2 million, half of which was borrowed, does the owner get a "fair return" on $1 million or $2 million?

know the answer, how do you know how much profit will be made next year? More difficult yet, what is the elasticity of demand—if tolls are raised, will the number of bridge users fall?

5. How about that souvenir shop—aren't you going to figure in the profits as part of the return on the bridge? And how about the profit made by the bridge owner from the bridge-painting company he owns; are you going to let him siphon off the profits that way? And what if the bridge-painting company lost money?

And what if this, and what if that, and what if dozens of other sensible questions? And, since the subject of discussion is only a toll bridge, what if the same questions are asked in much more detail about an electric utility, or a railroad, or *all* the railroads?

The BURP

You will observe that the questions posed in the example of regulation of the toll bridge are difficult and subtle ones. Multiply them by a thousand in the case of a modern multi-state utility, and you may wish to dispose of such matters by leaving them to the judgment of an expert body. By assuming that there must be an expert way to answer a difficult question, you have just created a new regulatory agency—the Bridge Undertaking Regulatory Power (or BURP). Most assuredly, your new agency will look thoroughly into these complex matters, and will through the years engage in the same stylized rituals with respect to the toll bridge as its sister agencies practice in their regulation of communications, transport and power.

Having established a new regulatory agency, you are in the comfortable position of being able to answer the question— what is the agency's purpose? You answer: "To be sure rates

are reasonable." The next question is—how do you know rates
are reasonable? You reply: "The agency regulates them." The
last question is not so comfortably answered—how do you
know the agency's procedures result in reasonable rates? You
are forced to reply, since you are honest: "I don't, but I assume
reasonable rates are the result of the expert regulatory agency
asking and answering all those subtle and complex questions."

In short, your honesty under stiff cross-examination has
revealed that the result of the rate-regulatory activity (that is,
"reasonable rates") *is defined solely in terms of the regulatory
activity itself.* Put in terms of our theory, the Third Axiom
applies in spades. Not only is the operation of the machinery
of regulation perceived within the regulatory institution as its
purpose—it is even so perceived outside the institution.

There is no *a priori* reason to believe that the mere running
of any institutional machinery will necessarily achieve a desirable purpose. Indeed, the corollary to the Institutional Imperative warns that to attribute any purpose to the mere *running* of
institutional machinery is meaningless. As scientific investigators, then, we must consider the question open and inquire
whether any beneficial public purpose is served by the regulation of utility rates under the standard doctrines. To reach an
answer, it is convenient first to propose what should be generally acceptable as the public's goal, and then to see if the standard doctrines fit the public purpose.

Tom Swift and the Electronic Earlobe

The consuming public wants from utilities the best service
at the cheapest rates. If the utility management is properly
avaricious, their desire is: to make the most money.[5] While it

---

[5]We shall shortly demonstrate that rapacity alone is not an acceptable explanation of most business behavior (Chapter 11).

might be supposed that the standard doctrines of rate regulation balance these twin aims, with the point of balance being
"reasonableness," the fact is otherwise. Both aims are demonstrably frustrated by current regulatory doctrine.

To begin the demonstration, let us consider a utility—say
a telephone company—with the following vital statistics:

Hypothetical T&T—1970

"Rate base" (phones, wires, etc.)	$100,000,000
Annual gross business (one billion calls at 10 cents	$100,000,000
Rate of return	10%
Profit (after tax)	$10,000,000
Common stock of HT&T	5,000,000 shares
Profit per share	$2.00

Rates look nice and "reasonable"—a 10 percent profit on
the rate base surely is not extortion. But consider what happens
if Hypothetical T&T were to be approached by the inventor of
the Electronic Earlobe. This device, at a fifth the cost of telephones and wires, allows instant communication by microwave.
If the phone campany were to convert to the microwave system,
its financial picture might be (making some simplifying assumptions about labor costs, depreciation and so on):

Hypothetical T&T—Electronic Earlobe Service
(Before Regulation)

Rate base (microwave devices)	$20,000,000
Annual gross business (one billion calls at 10 cents)	$100,000,000
Annual profit (after taxes)	$20,000,000
Rate of Return	100%
Profit per share (5 million shares)	$4.00

Note that the microwave service is *better* service than the old-fashioned phone-and-wire service, and the public is paying no more for it. The telephone company is gaining a substantial reward for its progressive adoption of the new device, and everyone should be happy. Will this satisfy standard regulatory doctrines? It will not. Standard doctrine does not permit an annual profit of 100 percent of rate base. Instead, after regulation the telephone company's business would look about as follows:

Hypothetical T&T—Electronic Earlobe Service
(After Rate Regulation)

Rate base (microwave devices)	$20,000,000
Annual gross business (100 million calls at 5.4 cents)	$54,000,000
Profit (after tax)	$2,000,000
Rate of return	10%
Profit per share (5 million shares)	40 cents

By accepted regulatory standards, the rate of return must be held to ten percent of rate base, and the price of calls must be cut until this profit limit is met. Therefore the reward of providing better service at no more cost would be to cut the company's profit per share by four fifths. You may say, that after all, regulation is a good thing because the price of a telephone call would be reduced from 10 cents to 5.4 cents. To this the reply is a question: what incentive is provided by regulators to cause a profit-making concern to cut its stockholders profits by four fifths? In other words, who says the microwave system would be installed?

Try another supposition. Suppose this time that the inventive wizard dreams up a way to add color pictures to the telephone call. This marvel of modern technology is available at only twice the investment of the old phone-and-wire system. Now, the telephone company's investment will have to be doubled. The company will want to raise its rates and —lo and behold!—the regulatory agency will agree that rates have to be increased to reach a reasonable rate of return, thus:

Hypothetical T&T—Color TV Service (After Regulation)

Rate base (color TV)	$200,000,000
Annual gross business (one billion calls at 15 cents)	$150,000,000
Annual profit (after taxes)	$20,000,000
Rate of return	10%
Profit per share (5 million shares)	$4.00

This is more like it, from the point of view of the company's stockholders and the executives who must keep them happy. Profits per share have doubled and the regulators have smiled approvingly. True, costs per telephone call are up moderately (to 15 cents), but the public is getting that glorious full-color picture with every call.

The figures set forth are simplified almost to vanishing (and those initiated into the regulatory arts are urged not to write in with amplifications and corrections). Still, the lesson these simple figures teach is clear. Under the rate base/rate of return system of regulation, it is vital to *increase* investment in order to *increase* permissible profits. The utility's profit does not depend, under the current doctrine of reasonableness, on giving the public what it most wants (best service and cheap rates). Instead, profit depends on investment, which need be only accidentally related to public benefits.

Consider the utility executive's decision when he looks at his old desk and tries to decide whether (a) to buy a new desk or (b) to rent a new desk or (c) to make do with the old desk. If the executive chooses alternative (c)—keep the old desk—he has increased neither the rates the public pays nor the permissible profits of his company. Alternative (b) will increase rates (because desk rental is an allowable expense) but will do nothing for company profits. But alternative (a) has the real charm: rates will go up slightly to cover the new desk depreciation, but at the same time the company's rate base increases, and so do its "reasonable" profits.[6]

Institutional Inertia

Public utility regulation consists of layers of elaborated doctrines and procedures enfolding a very dubious premise:

---

[6]Memorandum to the regulatory initiates: please do not try to make the point here that regulation takes account of the capital gain on disposition of old assets. While the standard doctrine can be patched up here and there to avoid its silliest results, it still has no tendency at all to reward actions which lead directly to public benefits.

that the purpose of regulation is to punish the regulated industry, because it is an evil monopoly.

It is true, of course, that alternate and more sensible methods of rate regulation can be devised. The regulatory machinery
can be retooled so that its purposes are related to public benefits. A private-enterprise society should not be afraid to pay
a profit if it gets what it pays for. If the regulatory machinery
were designed to measure the degree to which the public received the best possible service and the cheapest possible rates,
then a utility might be allowed to make a good fat profit if, and
only if, the service was good and the rates cheap. The net cost
to the public might well be lower and the regulated industries
more innovative and efficient, as well as wealthier.

While such thoughts are interesting, our purpose here is
not to speculate on a better scheme of rate regulation. Rather,
we see in the present regulatory system solid confirmation of
our Laws of Institutional Behavior, in two respects:

First, the activity of regulation, the sheer running of the
machinery processing minute inquiries and complex questions,
is itself the only "purpose" of regulation.[7] This is so because the
machinery defines the purpose: you cannot say whether a rate
is reasonable without establishing a rate base, and the question
of what goes in the rate base is a question so surpassingly
difficult as to be decided only by the machinery of regulation.
So, only the operation of the machinery defines the purpose of
its operation. The Third Axiom is perfectly illustrated.

Second, the *effects* of operation of the rate regulatory machinery are quite unrelated to any public benefit, but the procedure is repeated at great length. In terms of our Laws, the
reason is obvious. From the Institutional Imperative we know

---

[7]The objection that without regulation a monopoly might overcharge the customers brutally is answered neatly by the observation that in almost all cases the
regulation *confers* the monopoly. You cannot set up a new, competing utility
without a license from—guess who?—the regulatory agency.

that every institutional action must be intended to keep the institutional machinery working. Continuation of rate base regulation keeps the machinery working. Consideration of other factors (such as the public benefit) might not keep the same machinery going. (It should be clear that there is no absolute legal barrier to the agencies altering their regulatory doctrines.) Further, the Third Axiom declares that "public benefit" or some other good which might appear to an outsider as a legitimate "purpose" of an institution is not seen as meaningful within the institution. What is meaningful is regulation. Thus we may propose the following:

THEOREM OF INSTITUTIONAL INERTIA

The same institutional procedure will be repeated without reference to the results (if any) achieved.

The Regulator and the Regulatee

Whenever a utility gets a rate increase, dark rumors circulate to the effect that the agency has been bought off. The utility got what it wanted (higher rates), the users did not get what they wanted (lower rates), and the fix must be in. Usually the fix is not in.

All the regulatory agencies see themselves as one half, and only one half, of a two-part relationship. For there to be a regulator, as the old joke goes, there must be a regulatee. The utility initiates, files rates, and does things. The machinery of the agency reviews, regulates, corrects and generally nags. Since it thus operates its institutional machinery, it sees this as its purpose.

It is this two-part relationship, almost marital in its exclusion of third parties, which is inaccurately called "captive agencies." Most agencies are not captives of their industries and do not regard themselves as such. They are properly termed not captive, but symbiotic. The regulated industry is as necessary to the operation of the agency's machinery as the peanut butter in a peanut-butter-and-jelly sandwich. Agency action will therefore, by the Institutional Imperative, be intended to keep the machinery turning over. This means not being nice to, but being involved with, the industry being regulated. We next examine an advanced case of institutional symbiosis.

10. THAT NICE OLD MISUNDERSTOOD INTERSTATE COMMERCE COMMISSION

Noble Qualities of the ICC. Regulation of Nothing Much. Mergers. Case of the Right Grandfathers (Chaos and Competition). Symbiosis. Law of Institutional Symbiosis. Word of Warning.

The Interstate Commerce Commission is the oldest of the federal regulatory agencies. Since 1887 it has dealt with railroads, and in more modern times with trucks, barges, and even strange, second-level carriers which ride on their other carriers.[1] The ICC's formal printed decisions now occupy over three hundred volumes in one series, plus over one hundred volumes of Motor Carrier Cases, and only a fraction of all decisions are printed. The ICC is informed: it collects statistics diligently, and the records of its proceedings as well as the decisions of the agency and its seventy-nine examiners bristle with facts and figures.

Yet, despite its age and these formidable evidences of its expert knowledge, the ICC finds itself attacked on all sides. It

---

[1] Known in the trade as "Part IV Forwarders."

has been Naderized, in a report with the cruelly memorable title of *The Interstate Commerce Omission.* [2] It is often charged with old age, stultification, and hardening of the regulatory arteries. The abolition of its collegial decision-making has been proposed, on dubious grounds, but by a Presidential Commission. [3] Its merger with the other transport regulating bodies is seriously proposed. Still more ominous, there are heard charges that the ICC's regulation has had what economists delight in calling "dis-benefits" for the public. (If an economist had written the Bible, the manna in the desert would have been called "incremental nutrition.") No lesser authorities than the Council of Economic Advisers [4] and the Office of the President are murmuring of the delights of deregulation, untasted for generations. And, added to all these unpleasantries, an ICC official cannot sit down to a plate of vulcanized chicken at an industry gathering without ever after hearing a charge of "industry captive."

Noble Qualities of the ICC

It is worth inquiring what has brought the doyen of regulatory bodies into such public disrepute. For despite the whispering campaign, the old agency leads a fairly upright life.

To prove one's honesty and diligence, like one's patriotism, is difficult. It is no easier for an agency to defend itself against personal accusations than for an individual to prove he is not a security risk. Unless you know personally the people who work in any institution, you cannot judge the charges

---

[2] Robert Fellmeth (Grossman, 1970).

[3] *A New Regulatory Framework* (the "Ash Report"), President's Advisory Council on Executive Organization (GPO, 1971).

[4] *Annual Report* of the Council of Economic Advisers (GPO, 1971).

against them. Accordingly, at this point you will have to accept
the following statements:

1. The employees of the ICC are hardworking and diligent; they come to work and they work.
2. The employees of the ICC are usually competent to
perform their assigned tasks.
3. The employees of the ICC believe in the value of what
they are doing.
4. The employees of the ICC have too much work to do
—they are, and regard themselves as, overburdened.
5. The employees of the ICC are honest—an offer of a
bribe would be a one-way ticket to jail.
6. The employees of the ICC are not "industry captives."
Nor, with a few arrogant exceptions, are their minds set
in industry-oriented concrete.[5]

While you must accept on faith and authority the statements as to the individual merits of the ICC staff, there is
objective proof that the charge of captivity is false. No captives
would devote so much time and effort to activities that are
burdensome, expensive and offensive to their captors. A great
deal of the daily work of the ICC costs the regulated industry
time (e.g., floods of reports, investigations) or money (e.g., fines
or fees) or even directly interferes with the way the industry is
doing business (changed rules and responsibilities).

Many of the charges of "captivity" are ridiculous on their
face. For example, the *Interstate Commerce Omission* says:
"Another trip that might better have been avoided was Mrs.
[Commissioner] Brown's recent excursion (June 17, 1969) to

---

[5]All six statements could be made at any time about most federal regulatory
agencies. Corruption in the federal regulatory agencies, while it exists, is universally believed to be extremely rare. There is, however, from time to time some
evidence of off-the-record pressure on the agencies, but very little ground for
thinking that money changes hands.

Minneapolis, Minnesota, for a luncheon address before the Accounting Division of the Association of American Railroads." Now, without in the least underestimating the social charm of rail accountants, a visit to Minneapolis to address them is hardly a frolic worthy of the term "excursion." And, since luncheons of rail accountants are not fairly classifiable as orgies, admissions to them cannot be called a bribe. It would be as fair to call the good railroad accountants a "captive" audience for Commissioner Brown's gripping speech as to charge the Commissioner with being a "captive" to the pleasure of their company.

So the staff is clean. Our next inquiry is: what is the result of so much hard work by so many excellent people? What public benefits flow? Here the answer is not so heartening. Whether the question is rates or routes, the agency is hard at work—but to what end?

Regulation of Nothing Much

In the previous chapter we discussed in very general terms the rate base doctrine of rate-making; this doctrine is adopted by the ICC for railroad rate regulation. But many railroads are in deep financial trouble, and all have enormous surplus plants. Thus, as railroads propose further general rate increases—an event which now occurs with metronomic regularity—the ICC duly holds a giant *Ex Parte* investigation and duly finds that the average rate of return on rail property is two or three percent, which is duly found to be low.[6]

A more interesting inquiry as to rail rates might be to find

---

[6]In its report in Ex Parte No. 265, *Increased Freight Rates, 1970*, and Ex Parte No. 267, *Increased Freight Rates, 1971*, the Commission found an average rail return of 1.76 percent on net investment in the twelve months ended September 30, 1970.

out why every commodity pays a different rate.[7] Such dark
thoughts of paying the same rate for the same service are firmly
excluded by the ICC, as well as other regulatory agencies.

Since railroads generally never earn enough money to war-
rant holding down their overall rate of return, and since the
ICC has no requirements as to individual rail rate/cost relationships, the only meaningful ICC business with rail rates lies in
the field of discriminations between shippers of like commodities. In this selected field, rail rates may be corrected, but on
standards never really laid down in precise words. An attack on
an individual rail rate remains an expensive luxury for well-
heeled litigants. And, as ever, the real question is what public
benefit can come from administrative proceedings where the
standards of decision cannot be enunciated.

Mergers

The ICC has done a fairly brisk trade in rail mergers,
exercising its plenary statutory powers to approve mergers
"consistent with the public interest" and to forbid mergers not
"consistent with the public interest." Again the standards of
approval are unexpressed, and the merger proceedings take
years to complete. Following the most famous of these mergers,
between the Pennsylvania and the New York Central, the com-
bined companies confounded all predictions of their future ro-
bust economic health, and the Penn Central is now in bankruptcy, calling urgently for federal aid.

Clearly, dealing with mergers in an ailing industry is a
damned-if-you-do and damned-if-you-don't task. Approve the

---

[7]Rates are different among commodities, of course, because the carrier maximizes
revenues by discriminating in pricing (charges what the traffic will bear, in
noneconomic language). The nice question is whether a regulated industry
should be allowed to so discriminate.

merger and the ICC is blamed for a bankruptcy; refuse the merger and the ICC would be blamed for preventing the predicted merger economies, leading to two big bankruptcies instead of one giant one. Again, however, there is a nagging doubt: what is the public benefit, if any, from all the administrative activity? Of course, only mergers in the "public interest" are to be approved. Apparently, though the "public interest" is so veiled as to be nondeterminable without a five-year inter-industry struggle and so complex as to be inexpressible. In terms now familiar, the function of administering mergers has become the only perceived or perceivable purpose of administration.

Of course, a rail merger well may result in public or private benefits. If the benefits sought were defined and precisely stated, the ICC would have the training and ability to produce the benefits so defined and stated. Perhaps the ICC should have the power to *require* mergers. But, when the standards of merger approval are inexpressibly vague, or when the standards of rate regulation are inexpressible, or in general when the purpose can only be defined by the whirring of the agency machinery, then our Third Axiom states that the only meaningful purpose *is* the whirring of the agency machinery.

Case of the Right Grandfathers
(Chaos and Competition)

A look at another branch of the ICC's business is similarly instructive. In terms of sheer numbers of matters, by all odds the chief business of the ICC is regulating trucking. Prior to 1935 the country was exposed to the manifold dangers of unregulated trucking. Since then interstate transportation for hire by motor carrier can be provided only with benefit of an ICC license called "a certificate of public convenience and necessity" for a common carrier.

Licensing truckers is for the ICC what automobile accident litigation is for our courts. The ICC drowns in its trucking regulation (both routes and rates). Thousands of motor carrier applications are filed in a year (7,508 in 1969).

Do not conceive of the ICC's licensing of motor carriers as the product of a wise long-range plan. Quite the contrary is true. There is no ICC plan for a national trucking network, designed to fill the public needs. Instead, when Congress first provided for licensing of trucks, it required the issuance of licenses to every then existing trucker—a process called granting "grandfather rights." These "grandfather rights" extend no farther than what the trucker was doing in 1935. If he was carrying soap from Chicago to Denver, that is the extent of his grandfather rights. If he was carrying iron and steel objects from Pittsburgh to Pocatello, he has those rights, and only those, and so on, in luxuriant proliferation of detail of commodity and route.

To extend a trucking business beyond the grandfather scope, an application must be filed with the ICC. Public notice is issued, all other truckers with any conceivable competitive interest object, and the administrative engine cranks up. The inordinate detail of the applications can only be appreciated by a sample list. By looking in the *Traffic World* of June 14, 1971, we find a list covering four pages of tightly packed small print, three columns per page. The list covers motor carrier applications of which notice was given on the day of June 10, 1971. The whole list is paralyzing. Here are some sample entries:

> MC–65626, Sub. 26, Fredonia Express, Inc., Fredonia, N.Y. Irregular routes, malt beverages, Baltimore, Maryland, to points in New York and empty containers, on return from points in New York to Baltimore, Md. Note: No tacking.

MC-113267, Sub. 264, Central & Southern Truck
Lines, Inc. Caseyville, Ill. Irregular routes, bags, and
bagging, (1) Birmingham, Ala. to points in Ga., La.,
Miss., and Tenn., and (2) New Orleans, La. to Birmingham, Ala. Note: No tacking, common control
may be involved.

MC-114312, Sub. 21, Abbott Trucking, Inc., Delta,
O. Irregular routes, fertilizer and fertilizer ingredi-
ents, Marseilles, Ill. to points in lower peninsula of
Michigan. Note: No tacking.

Again, with respect for the brave staff of the ICC, desperately trying to channel this torrent of applications, the question
arises: what public purpose is served by the whole administrative exercise?

The answer often provided is that regulation "prevents
chaos." On its face, this is not so. The system of regulation
began by freezing in to the trucking network whatever chaos
existed in 1935. There is no reason to believe that 1935's chaos
is preferable to 1975's chaos, particularly in 1975. Further, it
is by no means clear that the path out of chaos toward a rational
transportation structure consists of relying upon grant or denial
of piecemeal applications—and applications for pretty unimportant pieces at that. And finally, as the antitrust-minded
frequently remark, they have a suspicion that "chaos" should
be translated "competition."

We cannot purport here to decide whether certification of
motor carriers is or is not beneficial to the public. It may or may
not be: our point is that whether it is useful is unknown.

To the Commission, of course, the operation of the Third
Axiom has left no room for doubt as to the wisdom of certifying
motor carriers. The internal machinery certifies, and certification is the institution's real purpose. In fact, the Third has
operated with such overwhelming force that the ICC has even

claimed that regulation creates trucks. Thus, the ICC's 83rd *Annual Report* says:

> The great majority of the Commission's proceedings work involves the handling of applications for operating authority to transport property. Over 75 per cent of our formal cases is in this area. The carriers themselves respect this economic regulation and are aware that the tremendous transport capacity of our national system is a direct product thereof. Both intra- and intermodally, the proceedings are often hotly contested, but the shipping public and the public generally are the ultimate beneficiaries of the resulting strong and viable system.

Please do not think that the language just quoted was written with tongue in cheek. It was not. To see a "strong and viable" system and "tremendous transport capacity" as effects, and petty litigation as the cause, is a remarkable demonstration of the truth of the Third Axiom.

Symbiosis

The certification system has definite attraction for those who hold the grandfather certificates—as in so many other walks of life, it is important to have the right grandfather. A motor carrier certificate is now a valuable asset, bought, sold, mortgaged and worthy of appearance on a balance sheet. Thus truckers who now hold such valuable rights, far from groaning under the lash of regulation, are instead the stoutest defenders of the system of certification. Once again, we have an excellent example of symbiosis. The ICC is *not* "captive" to the truckers, but the running of the ICC's machinery appears to have self-defining purpose both to the ICC and to those whose affairs are the subject matter of the regulatory machinery. Applying the

Institutional Imperative to this symbiotic relationship we must conclude that the agency must support such a relationship as will keep the agency's machinery operating. Thus, there is derived the following:

LAW OF INSTITUTIONAL SYMBIOSIS

An Institution will maintain a relationship that provides it with the subject matter of its operations.

Here, then, is the source of claims that the ICC or other agencies are "captives." With rare exceptions, the claims of captivity are false. The ICC is no more a "captive" of the carriers than the carriers are "captives" of the agency. The relationship is symbiotic. Of a captive we would predict no action harming or annoying to the captor. Of a symbiote, we predict maintenance of the symbiotic relationship, which can and does include control, punishment and other unwelcome attentions.

Symbiotic relationships exist between all regulatory agencies and their regulated industries, and also between many other kinds of agencies and those they deal with. The Law of Institutional Symbiosis is as applicable to the relationship of purchaser and supplier as to regulator and regulated. It applies most particularly to the misnamed "military-industrial complex."

Word of Warning

There are a number of schemes circulating for shaking up the ICC and similar agencies. Most of the critics propose to create vigorous, hard-hitting agencies, fit and ready to do battle. Famous victories are promised, but the battle is not described in very precise terms and it is never quite clear who is the enemy.

There is little danger in what the regulatory agencies are doing. Most regulatory activities are of little public consequence, and their continuation gives gainful and innocent employment to many. Equally, there would be only little danger in abolishing the agencies. In most instances the argument is as strong for deregulation as for regulation. Chaotic competition to carry yak fat would break out, but the yak fat shippers just might prefer a little competition for their business.[8]

The real danger is that the agencies will be radically restructured without an understanding of what they do, or ought to do, or what any future agency would necessarily do in the same way.

An example of a proposed cure that would be notably worse than the regulatory disease is found in the Ash Report, *A New Regulatory Framework* (GPO, 1971), wherein it is proposed to put some zip in the regulatory agencies by placing a single administrator at the head of each instead of a board. No reason appearing to prefer a single powerful regulator's prejudices to a group decision, the Ash Report recommendations have been received without enthusiasm.

The Laws of Institutional Behavior argue against putting any zip in any agency until the agency (1) has a real purpose and (2) has internal machinery designed to achieve that purpose. Otherwise, do not fool with the machinery.

---

[8]Yak fat was the imaginary commodity in the most famous ICC hoax. A trucker named Robert Hilt got tired of constant railroad protests to all his trucking rates. In 1965 he published a rate on "Yak Fat," the railroads protested the rate as too low, and the ICC suspended the rate: "I.&S. M-19432, Yak Fat, Omaha to Chicago . . ." The story is regularly revived by the deregulators: see *Traffic World,* May 22, 1972.

11. RAPACITY REVISITED, *OR* ADAM SMITH WAS WRONG

Three Fairy Tales About Business: The Hard-Eyed Businessman, The Wonderful Strip Mine, The Adam Smith Story. Sheer Greed is Not Enough: The Institutional Explanation. The Arithmetic of Corporate Investment (Results of Money-Grubbing). The Wall Street Story: How to Turn a Dollar Into Eighty-Four Cents.

Three Fairy Tales About Business

American beliefs about big business are composed of a number of inconsistent myths. Consequently, the state of public understanding of the economic system is at about the same level physics would be were it based on the unexpurgated edition of the *Oz* books. The study of institutional behavior can improve the situation.

The Hard-Eyed Businessman

One of the most popular myths is that businesses are run by hard-faced types in expensive suits with dollar signs in their eyeballs. These tailored gentlemen are supposedly interested only in the last cent of profit. Their daily occupation, the story runs, is ordering the speedup of the production line, thus converting the oppressed workers (all of whom bear a suspicious resemblance to Charlie Chaplin) into overworked automatons. For relaxation, our captains of industry close the old textile mill, thereby sending Mary Pickford off to a life of shame in the city.

When their beliefs are challenged, those who believe this first myth will talk of automobiles with a curious tendency to shed rear wheels like confetti, or recite the latest figures for tonnage of heavy metal poisons discharged into the rivers. As further evidence for this view of industry as devoted only to constantly increasing profit, there is the flood of unnecessary products foisted upon the public by unbelievable, but mysteriously effective, false advertising.

To be fair to the believers, it is evident that many of the principal products of American industry are ill-designed to do useful work. The inflated and bechromed American automobile is an object of well-deserved ridicule. Some of the funnier productions of the 1971–1972 advertising season were the ads announcing proudly that the new bumpers could take a collision at the fantastic speed of 2½ miles per hour. Surely, the argument runs, the manufacture of automobiles with the durability of Christmas tree ornaments justifies the belief that the wizards of Detroit are motivated solely by the desire for gain.

The Wonderful Strip Mine

A counter-myth is now in circulation, or at least in paid circulation. Public relation advisors have been called into to retouch the damaged image of industry. If the glossy productions refurbishing the industrial image are to be believed, American corporations are consumed with a vision of the better life for all. A strip mine is stripped solely to be converted thereafter to a verdant park; the healthful effluent of a steel mill is in all medical respects the equal of the waters at Vichy. According to this second myth, the goal of industry is the improvement of products in order that the public may be served both cheaper and better. And again, to be fair, there is observable a regular improvement in many articles of manufacture. Your new refrigerator refrigerates better and makes ice besides, your air conditioner conditions so well that the electric utilities can no longer fill the summer demand, your TV set now delivers its wondrous messages in full color. Even your after-dinner cigar is mentholated, with the improved filter tips suitable for consumption by both liberated sexes. With such a flow of marvels, can industry be all bad?

The Adam Smith Story

A third myth about business explains both the good and the bad results of commerce on a higher intellectual level. According to this explanation, dating back to Adam Smith, businessmen are indeed evilly motivated. A businessman seeks only profit, a base motive which need not be disguised. Yet, by the workings of the marketplace, the base profit motive serves the higher ends of society, for the greed of thousands of individual suppliers is converted by the pressures of competition to the service of consumers. What the housewife wants, the housewife gets, so long as General Dishmop competes to the death for the housewife's dollar with Amalgamated Washrag.

Through the centuries, the original Adam Smith story of beneficial competition has acquired all the respectable academic trappings. Impressive graphs are set before freshman students of economics, demonstrating by the crossing of supply-and-demand curves how the market produces precisely the right amount of everything, at a price of X given the consumer's desire of an intensity of Y. The Antitrust Section of the United

States Department of Justice is stationed at the intersection of X and Y and ordered to defend the crossing to the last lawyer.

Unfortunately, the myth of competition does not fit with precision the observable facts of modern-day life. The fundamentalist economic theologians are in some disarray as prices, wages, and production deviate from the predictions of the accepted equations. These deviations are all explicable, no doubt, but the old gospel loses its appeal to faith when every happening in the real world has to be explained as an exception.

There is much in the behavior of the modern corporation that fits no accepted myth of business motivation. It is plainly true, for example, that many of the very largest businesses have had their profit drive surgically removed. For example, there is the peculiar phenomenon of mutual ownership. Billions upon billions of dollars of insurance are written by mutual companies —that is, by companies with no stockholders. It is hard to see how a mutual company can be driven by the desire for gain when there is no one to hold the corporate executives to the stern standard of maximizing profits. If, as *Forbes* magazine reports, 4,850 of the 5,550 savings and loan associations are mutuals, with no stockholders, then 4850/5550ths of this industry lacks the accepted motivation of greed for the benefit of its owners.[1]

The behavior of a mutual insurance company, or mutual savings and loan or a mutual bank is in all respects similar to the behavior of a privately owned company in the same business. New accounts are sought, money is collected with avidity and paid out with reluctance. The absence of a profit motive has

---

[1] *Forbes*, July 1, 1972, p. 18. The story reports that if a mutual savings and loan is allowed to "go public" (which means "go private," and distribute its stock to depositors), the depositors would reap "windfall gains." Yet, the prospect of these fat gains is opposed by many savings and loan executives because if allowed, the depositors "will bring pressure to convert." How strange that "pressure to convert"—to make money—is opposed by businessmen. For the institutional explanation, see below.

no apparent effect on the daily work of the business. Somehow, Adam Smith must be wrong, and we must seek further for the motives to explain business behavior.

Sheer Greed is Not Enough: The Institutional Explanation

Any business fits our definition of institution as "a continued recognizable group of individuals working together, where the group's existence is not measured by a human life." Corporations outlast their founders, and the group of corporate executives and employees is continuing and recognizable. It follows that if our laws of institutional behavior are valid, they must apply to businesses.

From our point of view, the institutional machinery of a business is like any other institutional machinery. Individuals have assigned tasks; they believe these tasks to be important, and they gain in personal importance by performing them. The head of a multi-billion dollar mutual insurance company is as important a fellow, as deserving of the esteem of his peers and himself, as the president of IBM, or the secretary of a government department. What is more, the individual workers in most businesses are plainly not concerned in their daily tasks by the lure of potential profits to the corporation. A salesman, for example, is supposed to sell, and a production man to produce. It is a matter of considerable concern in any properly run business to assure that the salesmen do not sell or the production men produce so eagerly that the company goes broke.[2]

Our body of Institutional Laws declares that in a business, as in any other institution, the prime motive is to keep the

---

[2]See the section "Institution, on Not Becoming An" in Townsend, *Up the Organization* (Knopf, 1970).

machinery of the institution running. The iron command of the Institutional Imperative applies as inexorably to a business as to a collective farm.

Each of the institutional laws applies to a business organization. The Law of the Institutional Irrelevance of Truth declares:

> **When the making of a statement is seen as necessary to the continued working of the institutional machinery, the statement will be made, and its truth is irrelevant.**

This law predicts—no, it requires—the existence of false advertising. The law does not say that all advertising claims are false. Not at all. What the law says is that false or true, the advertising claim will be made if it is institutionally necessary. The sales manager would doubtless be just as happy if the advertising claim were true. If the new improved deodorant would assure its users of a sensationally active sex life, that would be dandy. But what sells deodorants is the claim that underarm confidence assures marital (or extramarital) bliss, and that claim *will be made.*

The Laws of Institutional Behavior explain those less attractive business practices which come to public attention at least once a generation. An illustrious line of alarmists stretching back for generations have told us to watch out for the products of industry. Years ago, Upton Sinclair revealed that the meatpackers' salami was unsafe as any feed. Recently, Ralph Nader earned his first recognition as a hunter for proclaiming that a line of cars had emerged from Detroit with a bad habit—they shed their wheels out of season.

Now, it would be pretty stupid for an automobile manufacturer to make a car that kills its customers at a rate higher than normal. That is bad business. It is also pretty stupid to believe, against all the evidence to the contrary, that any institution will automatically dedicate itself to the public safety, the public health, or any other aspect of the public good. No really safe automobile is manufactured because no institutional reason exists to make one. Stuff sold as food may be wholesome or it may be 99 and 44/100 percent free of nutritive value—the difference is institutionally irrelevant.

The Law of Institutional Irrelevance of Morality and Humanity requires that: "If the operation of the institutional machinery (of a business) requires an action, morality and humanity are irrelevant." When the institutional action required is the sale of an unsafe motor car, the unsafe car will be sold. Note (because it is an important distinction) that we say institutional necessity can require the sale of an unsafe car, not just profit motive. Selling an unsafe car is a risk not to be taken by any sensible business motivated by greed alone. But if a new model car is designed in the designing sub-institution of a large manufacturing corporation, advertised by the advertising sub-institution, market-researched by the marketing sub-institution —such a new model is institutionally required to be sold, safe or not. The command of the institutional law is as absolute for shoddy merchandise as for shoddy foreign policy.[3]

The regular appearance of thousands of new products, of good, bad and indifferent merit, is likewise predicted by the Laws of Institutional Behavior. There are research departments, and sales departments and distribution departments, and they all function. Perhaps a mentholated cigar is an abomination, and perhaps not. Perhaps no one really needs chickweed-flavored chewing gum. No matter; the machinery exists and it operates, whether the new product is good or not,

---

[3]This year's bumper sticker reads, "Vietnam is an Edsel," recalling the works of a certain McNamara who was President of Ford and then Secretary of Defense. This recognizes that the institutional reasons for a dopey car and a dud of a war are the same.

and whether its production is a sensible profit risk or not.

This last is a most significant point. Ultimately and institutionally, profit is not the real purpose. Not that profit is unimportant—not at all. In a well-run business a lot of attention is paid to making money; but profit is not the mainspring of business behavior—if it were, a mutual insurance company could not exist. The profit motive in a business is at best a secondary, desirable, goal. Greed is not indispensable. If the business makes a good profit or a good product, both are secondarily desirable. First and foremost, however, comes the functioning of the machinery.

The bigger the company, the more important the jobs of the executives. The last decade has seen a trend to conglomeration of American industry. Corporations have made the sometimes fatal mistake of creating offices in charge of acquisitions. The Vice-President for Acquisitions has a job and a staff, and the acquisitions follow as the night the day. Naturally the conglomerate conglomerates in the name of "profit," as much as the Air Force bombs in the name of "defense." Quite often, though, the acquisitions result in a dreadful case of corporate indigestion. There is, after all, no reason to expect a management skilled in the manufacture of whiskbrooms to be automatically competent to drill for offshore oil, or to bake rolls. Just the same, United Whiskbroom is out with a liberal tender offer for control of Texas Platforms and Poppyseed. In later years the corporate annual report will note sadly that "some divisions of the corporation are not making their full contribution to profits." A Vice-President for Divestiture will then be named.

The Arithmetic of Corporate Investment
(Results of Money-Grubbing)

An arithmetical exercise permits a rough test of corporate motives, to determine whether the idea is to do business (to keep the machinery running) or to make a profit. The test is suggested by the following quotation (one of many examples to be found in the business press): "An investment [by Union Carbide] of more than $3 billion in plant and equipment over a decade has added $1.4 billion to sales but zilch to profits."[4]

This is an interesting statement since Union Carbide has about 60 million shares outstanding, and "over $3 billion" therefore amounts to over $50 per share of stock. Since the stock has been selling at *less* than $50 a share, it almost looks as if some factor other than greed has been dictating the corporate investment policy.

To follow this line of thought, it is interesting to assemble some figures for other big companies. Luckily, stock market speculators are like horseplayers and believe that if only enough statistics about past performance can be assembled, the future can be calculated with certainty. Since no one is sure just what statistics are relevant to this exercise, masses of all sorts of figures must be available. The *Value Line Investment Survey* is one respected source of corporate data, and the following table is distilled from the decade's results (1962–1971) for three big companies:

---

[4]*Forbes*, July 1, 1972, p. 42.

| | 1962–1971 | | |
Company	10-Year Total Sales per Share	10-Year Total Capital Spending per share	10-Year Total Dividends per share
U.S. Steel Corp ($4.9 billion sales in 1971)	$803.68	$80.75	$22.25
Aluminum Co. of America ($1.4 billion sales in 1971)	$592.03	$84.72	$15.65
Allied Chemical ($1.3 billion sales in 1971)	$419.05	$50.39	$16.01
Average	$604.92	$71.95	$17.97

In other words, for these companies a decade of money-grubbing has not grubbed much money for the stockholders. For each share, on the average, $600's worth of business was done, $72 was spent on new plant, and only $18 fell into the hands of the greedy owners for whom, according to myth, the whole game was played.

If the game is played for the stockholders, they lost. The score was 33 to one for sales (that is, running the institutional machinery) over dividends and 4 to one for buying more plant (that is, perpetuating the machinery) over dividends.[5]

There are, surely, a number of sound explanations for

---

[5]Letters rebutting the foregoing analysis will not be answered. True, profits were somewhat greater than dividends and some "growth" companies pay no dividends but command high stock market prices. Also true, the three big companies experienced a difficult decade (stock prices of all three declined). Also true, it could be argued that each company would have made less money if it had not sunk so much in newer plant. Finally, it is true that Polaroid and Xerox made fortunes for their lucky stockholders. But after all, the table could have included Libby, McNeill & Libby: sales $542.05 per share (1962–1971), capital spending $14.61 per share and dividends 16 cents. In this case, the $14.61 spent on plant is more than double the current stock price per share. So what was the point of the ten-year exercise?

everything that went on in Big Steel, Big Aluminum, and Medium Big Chemical over the decade. The Laws of Institutional Behavior state that there are always good reasons and good explanations. Just the same, there are sound grounds for suspecting that keeping up the old market share was somehow more important than bowing to the rapacious demands of the owners of these enterprises. The first rule of business as an institution is: business for business' sake.[6]

Other examples of doing business for its own sake abound. From time to time, corporate planners bring off their own versions of the Bay of Pigs—spectacular financial disasters. First General Dynamics and then Lockheed contracted to build new airplanes at prices so far below cost they almost sunk themselves. RCA just got out of the computer business for a neat half-billion dollar loss.[7] There are daily examples of corporations taking enormous risks simply to maintain their size. Similarly, there are always some examples of companies worth more dead than alive, where the corporate management stubbornly refuses to liquidate, and Adam Smith be damned.

Indeed, the corporate "raiders" are feared by just those corporations whose assets are worth more than their stock. The awful raider wants to swoop down, seize the hapless institution and strip off enough fat from the carcass to repay the price of buying the company. The profit motives of the raider are regularly slandered by the resisting management, which obviously prefers continuing institutional existence to making some dirty money.

---

[6]Mr. Wilson, first the president of General Motors and then a Secretary of Defense, was much criticized for saying "What's good for General Motors is good for the country." A better statement is: What's good for General Motors isn't necessarily good for the stockholders of General Motors.

[7]Only $490 million, to be exact. One wonders how the corporate underling announces a goof of this magnitude. What does the divisional vice-president of General Foods say: "Uh, Chief, about those new hamburger stands—you know, Burger Chef? Well we had a little loss, you know, relish, buns, that sort of thing . . . about $39 million. . . . Chief? Chief?"

The Wall Street Story: How to Turn a Dollar into Eighty-Four Cents

Mention of money brings us to a final demonstration of the subservience of business to the institutional laws. As everyone knows, the very flintiest-eyed capitalists roost on Wall Street. Here are the real raptors, for whom every emotion is secondary to the blood lust for gain. Does it not follow, then, that every investor desiring to profit should confide his capital to the care of the men of Wall Street? No, it does not.

The proof that the Wall Street institutions are subject to the same institutional laws as all others is direct and conclusive. The subject matter of the proof is a group of Wall Street institutions called "closed-end" funds. These funds are collections of money, held by a corporation that invests the money for profit. The asset value of the closed-end fund is easily calculated: it is the market value of the securities held by the fund.[8] Surely these funds are the epitome of capitalism, corporations with no functions but profitable investment. Karl Marx would shudder.

The closed-end funds are managed by Wall Street men, presumably all hard-eyed and clear-headed experts. Now for the test: surely, if the capitalist myth can be believed, a dollar in the care of a rapacious Wall Street money man must be worth more than a prosaic dollar in the bank. If, in contrast, these Wall Street institutions are like all others, a dollar inside a fund loses value, because the fund (being an institution) runs for reasons other than just making a profit.

Barron's financial weekly publishes a list covering closed-end funds, giving both (1) asset value per share and (2) the amount the market price of a fund share is above or below asset value. On June 26, 1972, thirty closed-end funds were listed, of

---

[8] A "closed-end" fund keeps its lump of money until it decides to pay dividends. An "open-end" fund, in contrast, promises to buy back its stock at the net asset value of its shares.

which no fewer than twenty-five sold *below* net asset value. The average discount was 15.9 percent. A dollar confided to this selected group of institutions, all presumably devoted single-mindedly to gain, was worth, on the average, 84.1 cents. The missing 15.9 cents represented the institutional discount—the market's assessment of the degree by which the institutional purposes of the fund defeat the expectations of the stockholder.

As they say on the Street, the market doesn't lie. The pity is, there is no similar *Barron's* weekly report of the discount to be applied to our foreign policy.

12. "IN THE INTEREST OF THE PEOPLE": THREE SELF-RIGHTEOUS INSTITUTIONS

Case of the Congress. Multiple Functions: The Whole Congress, The Fund-Raising Congress, The Congressional Complaint Bureau, State and Local Politics, The Committee Complex (The Honorable, The Committee on Rubber and Blubber). Hypocrisy. Case of the Nader. The Indignant Institutions of the Young and the Black.

Every institution congratulates itself on its successes. Such preening is normal and unimportant. Somewhat more significant is constant self-congratulation from the very highest motives: we blow our institutional nose solely "in the interest of the people of the United States." This sort of self-approval is either deeply hypocritical or, perhaps worse, really believed. We look now at both hypocrisy, Congressional division, and earnest reform, Indignant Institutions division.

Case of the Congress

The American voter is more than a little cynical about his Senators and Representatives. The voters' standards may be too high, perhaps raised by the conventional descriptions of the abilities of the founding fathers. Perhaps the present average is not up to Jefferson or Hamilton, or perhaps they were not either.

Shall we waste any time sympathizing with the Congressman, his burdens, his responsibilities, the pressures of his office? Grant to the Honorable Member or Senator that he runs around a lot, and inquire whether the running produces anything of value.

By the standards of performance expected from responsible bodies—say the ninth-grade student council—the Congress is doing a terrible job. The members of both Houses are uninformed or uninformable on major issues; many or most are observably at the service of one or another special-interest group. Urgent and painful issues are avoided with gladness; pompous flag-day orations are never to be missed. Its powers fading, the Congress has conceded to the Executive many of its Constitutional functions, most recently the right to decide where and when we will be at war. And perhaps worst of all, the Congress talks what can only be called the most awful guff. A millennium from now, scholars poring over the *Congressional Record* will wonder why the country did not collapse back into the Stone Age.[1]

The expert, called in to diagnose the Congressional sickness, will begin by observing that Congress is not one but many institutions. Only rarely does the Congress function as a single institutional unit. A dissection will clarify the organization's multiple functions.

---

[1] A competent future scholar reading the Extensions of Remarks (Appendix) to the *Record* might well conclude that it was a random computer printout.

Multiple Functions

1. The Whole Congress.

For an individual to be a member of an institution, by our definition, there must be institutional discipline. The Congress looks on internal discipline with the enthusiasm others reserve for acne. In recent time, only Joe McCarthy and Thomas Dodd on the Senate side and Adam Clayton Powell on the House side have been punished for behavior felt to discredit the institution of Congress as a whole. Ordinary fraud is readily accepted— a sort of Eagle Scout merit badge.[2]

There are, of course, a few occasions where the Congress as a whole follows the Institutional Imperative and assures its continued operations. The Congress as a whole will censure citizens who do not want to talk to Congressional committees. Sometimes also, but rarely, there will be talk of a Congressional "revolt," the banner of independence from the Executive will be raised, and a Supreme Court nomination rejected. But, since the Executive Departments do quite well in keeping individual Congressmen happy, and the President is a powerful fellow, this does not come to much. There is always someone else to nominate for the Court.

2. The Fund-Raising Congress.

While the individual member is little disciplined by the institution of the Congress, he needs to be reelected very

---

[2]Cynical reports persist that some Representatives and Senators regard their office as affording a good opportunity to get rich. Informed opinion is that the reports are true more than sometimes. The Congress refuses to police itself and is all but unpoliceable from the outside. Most Washington types believe that much more money changes hands on the Hill than in all the executive departments put together. The real purpose of some members is to get rich by selling favors, and this cannot be neglected in explaining some of the seamier aspects of Congressional behavior. Too bad if true, but probably true in an unfortunate number of cases.

urgently indeed. The golden saying is: "First get elected."

The Congress has imprudently arranged for licensing TV stations as monopolies with unregulated rates. The stations pay nothing for their licenses, but they charge for their time what the traffic will bear, which is plenty. Some day the legislators may wake up and require the stations to cede back a few hours for political debates. Meanwhile, a candidate needs a big pile of money, and he spends a lot of time shoveling.

The first, foremost, and faithful contributors are what are called politely "special interests." The remarkable thing about a successful "special interest" is that it has been found indistinguishable from the "public interest." To achieve this fortunate identity for his industry, the Washington representative of the garbanzo bean[3] growers is around and about spreading the word. His act of faith is the consumption of soggy hors d'oeuvres at fund-raisings. His reward is the canonization of the garbanzo bean as a protected national resource.

While you are free to be as cynical as you like about the real need for a garbanzo bean subsidy, please do not make the mistake of thinking that the sponsor of special-interest legislation does not believe in it. Not at all, for fund-raising and lobbying are quite institutionalized. It should not be necessary to repeat the Third Axiom: those within the institution perceive the operation of its machinery as its purpose. Sometimes, instead of usefully raising money, they hold big self-congratulating dinners. They honor the Congressman who pushed for the garbanzo bean subsidy; they applaud the Assistant Secretary who so valiantly fought to expand his agency's duties under the National Garbanzo Preservation Act; even the Garbanzo Pickers Union is present in force, enjoying the brotherhood and good will. By the time the orgy of good feeling is over, everybody present sincerely believes. When the distinguished Congressman finally retires, he will look back with satisfaction

---

[3]Chick-pea.

on a lifetime of fighting for the good, the right, the clean
bean.

3. The Congressional Complaint Bureau.

It is useful to consider the member and the voters of his
district as parts of a functioning institution. Votes can be obtained not only by appearances on TV, but also by "service" to
the voters. "Service" means the assignment of nine-tenths of the
staff of every member's office to handling voter complaints,
getting handouts, gathering information and generally serving
as all-purpose errand boys between the individual voter and the
great federal machine.

In the Scandinavian countries an "ombudsman" is named
to police the bureaucracy. In the American system the ombudsman, the tribune of the people against their Government, is the
individual Representative or Senator.

This role of the member is universally despised by those
within the Executive institutions. Congressional pressure, Congressional demands for out-of-routine treatment, Congressional
requests for "your early attention to the application of George
W. Voter," all are seen as offensive, unprincipled, flowing from
the lowest of motives.

As anyone in Washington will tell you, almost all the
pressure in town, fair or unfair, comes from the Hill (some
comes from the White House). The member of Congress wants
special treatment, special benefits, special expedition. In short,
the member wants meaningful particular results, while the Executive department wants to continue running its machinery
the way it is running, without interference. The Congressman
wants Jose X or Inga Y admitted by Immigration; Immigration
is off following its own rules. Since the institutional machinery
is quite capable of running without reference to any meaningful
results (as Immigration does), there is a conflict. The result the

member seeks is a particular, meaningful dispensation for Jose or Inga. That this result would be different if the machinery ran in its ordinary way does not necessarily mean the Congressman is wrong and the agency would be right.

The Congressman's function as ward boss dealing with city hall for his people is a vital one. If the government institutions fail to preserve the virtures of decency and humanity, and they do so fail, then the politician has to claim "special"—that is, human—treatment for his constituents. A Congressman's desire to be useful to a constituent who does not want a road through his house is no less public-spirited than the government agency's effort to pave over Rhode Island.

True, Congressional pressure (as well as White House pressure) often means the public suffers. Pressure produces some unattractive results, all the way down to bribes, intimidation[4] and obvious raids on the Treasury. Perhaps, the solution lies in more Congressional attention to defining the purposes of the legislation so busily administered by the Executive. If we knew where the roads were going, and why, we would not need so much Congressional influence to keep them out of our back yards.

4. State and Local Politics.

A member of Congress is, quite clearly, a part of the institution of his state political party. (Members are little subject to national party discipline and generally get little national help.) Much of the behavior of the member is explicable by regarding him as a functioning part of the local party, not a national statesman. The local Imperative is a weighty Imperative indeed.

---

[4]The penalty for any member of Congress threatening "I'll have your job if . . . " ought to be that he has to take the job.

5. The Committee Complex.

Congressional committees do 99 percent of all significant Congressional work. The committees are the most stable institutions of the Congress, lasting far beyond individual
elections, outliving the longest-lived members, and display-
ing all the institutional earmarks required by our body of
Institutional Laws. To avoid the laws of libel, we shall have
to consider an example of a real committee given an imaginary name.

The Honorable, the Committee
on Rubber and Blubber

Internally there is a good deal of discipline on Rubber and
Blubber. The seniority system operates, but in order to become
senior member and eventually chairman of a significant subcommittee, you have to first be named to it by the party elders.
Solid service is rewarded by appointments. Aberrational behavior is discouraged.

The relationship of the Committee on Rubber and Blubber
with its industry (latex and whales) is remarkably similar to the
relationship of a regulatory agency with a regulated industry.
In fact, it *is* the same symbiotic relationship. The staff of R&B,
and the R&B members, regard it as important work to keep
tinkering with the laws governing their industry. Hearings must
be held into the effects of importing natural rubber, and on the
stimulation of production of artificial blubber. The actions of
the executive departments must be criticized and investigated
at length. Perhaps a quota system is required, raising the
domestic blubber price above the world level; the National
Blubber-Boiler's Association so proposes. It is all technical, a

matter of expertise, a matter requiring (at great personal sacrifice) attendance at the quadrennial International Blubber Convention in Monaco.

Indeed, the institutional relationship of a Congressional committee and its industry is far cozier than that of regulator and regulatee. Those who regulate may not properly accept anything of value from the regulated industry. All proper Congressmen or Senators are (regularly) shocked to hear of such improprieties. But, at the fund-raising party for the good friends of Congressman Aaron Elastic, you should not be unduly astonished to find that the good friends and healthy contributors are most actively engaged in the rubber and blubber industry. The Committee has no subcommittee on hypocrisy.

As you look about in the Congress for some controls over the institutional machinery of the committees, you will find none of significance (there are super-important committees, of course: Rules, Appropriations, etc.). Absent a political upheaval, committee-recommended legislation passes. What does the outside member know about blubber? Nothing. What will the individual junior member get if he questions the judgment of the wise chairman and senior members, or makes the perfectly valid charge that they are part of the Congressional-industrial-blubber complex? An appointment to the Committee for the Preservation of the Papers of Millard Fillmore, that's what he will get.

In short, the Congressional committees are classic examples of institutions, and obey the precepts of our Institutional Laws in detail. The committees constantly continue their important work (the Institutional Imperative); they largely generate their own subject matter (General Law of Institutional Self-Occupation); they live in passionate and profitable institutional symbiosis with their subject matter; and they are quite capable of actions and decisions to which truth, or morality or good sense are strangers. Applying the Three Principles of Institutional Results, it appears that many of the failures of Congressional committees are congenital: the committee machinery is not designed to reach a meaningful goal, but to keep operating. When it comes to a real, hard, meaningful decision, a Congressional committee is the full equal of any bureaucracy in avoiding the issue. The business of Congress is done by committees, and a committee's business is . . . well, the committee.

Hypocrisy

A final word on the vice of hypocrisy. Here, if ever, is an unattractive vice, with none of the allure of lust and none of the rewards of avarice or sloth. Hypocrisy is a kind of athlete's foot of vices—contagious, unappealing, but not serious enough to be crippling.

A good Congressman has a mild case of hypocrisy; a bad one talks nothing but baloney (see any *Congressional Record*). The oversupply of hypocrisy springs from an institutionalized fear that if the voters knew just what their trusted spokesmen were doing, the representative would be retired to gainful employment. The Senator or Representative knows perfectly well why he votes as he does: the vote is dictated by the committee system. This truth is never revealed to his constituency, which has no consuming hunger for news of rubber or blubber.

Instead of the truth, the Congressman spouts off about the public interest. As we have tried to make plain, no one knows where the public interest lies in matters of rubber and blubber. Just possibly, the public will be well served by a vote pleasing to the National Association of Blubber Boilers. More likely, the Public will be raped. No matter, the legislator will declare he has voted only in the highest public interest. Apply the Law of

Institutional Irrelevance of Truth, and do not believe him.[5] He says that because he thinks he has to.

Case of the Nader

We have already mentioned some aspects of the institutional behavior of our corporations. They are in popular myth mere money machines, and in actual fact self-perpetuating institutions capable of considerable cruelty and waste, as well as efficient production.

The job of criticizing corporations for many good and valid reasons has been taken over by a number of institutions. The environment is being protected from some of the inroads of industry. The Sequoia forests may yet be saved from the lumberman; even the Artic tundra is stoutly defended: the musk ox can live a better life than the resident of New York City.

In an earlier generation, writers exposed the unspeakable contents of the hot dog, or the seventy two-hour work week thoughtfully provided to occupy the nine-year-old. In the 1960s the name of Ralph Nader led all the rest.

He has told us all, quite correctly as we have seen, that the automobile industry sells cars, not safety. Building upon his first success, Nader has created an entire institutional center

---

[5]An almost perfect example of Congressional hypocrisy is the death grip of the committees on the District of Columbia. The Congress is weekly concerned with such urgent affairs as the regulation of the practice of Podiatry in the District of Columbia (see 92 *Cong. Rec. H 7592*). A committee of each House, and two Appropriations subcommittees, labor over District affairs *ad nauseam*. Proposals to make the District self-governing have been made for generations; citizens groups in the District grow old and die parading for Home Rule. The interests of the citizens of the District are said to suffer; and the Congress as a whole plainly wastes time. And still there continues to be a District Committee in House and Senate, and staffs, and a lot of wasted effort. As soon as the committee, and not the Congress, is seen as the relevant institution, such a result is readily predictable.

devoted to investigation, denunciation, and publication, all in the sacred name of the public interest.[6]

Yet, while the well-deserved telegrams of congratulation are still coming in, the apparatus for a national conscience is beginning to show its own disturbing institutional characteristics. The apparatus is accusatory, almost exclusively. No headlines are earned, no attention is caught, by announcements like "Good Job by Bureau of Marmalade Inspection, Report Nader's Raiders."

An institution whose machinery is designed to accuse will find subjects to accuse. The General Law of Institutional Self-Occupation and the Special Law of the Security Office govern the Raiders of Nader as well as any Bureau of Employee Security. As the nets of the Raiders spread wider, the clues to corruption are beginning to be found where corruption is not, and industry-government conspiracies are being uncovered where they do not exist.

In short, the institutional Nader view of Government operations is beginning to be quite often institutionally wrong. Not that there should not be criticism—not at all. But every warmed-over chicken dinner is not a bribe. Every meeting of industry and government is not a conspiracy; on the contrary, as we have shown in the case of the ICC, they often get on each other's nerves.

There is a need for exposure of useless or foolish institutions. There is a descrepancy between ostensible Government purposes and what is actually being done. Many government and private institutions can be caught diligently working against the public interest. There is plenty of good stuff to be found, plenty of muck to rake.

---

[6]The investigations are of varying degrees of thoroughness. Some are fine; some of them occupy the entire summer vacation of a college student.

But, all that needs to be exposed is not going to be found out, or if found and proclaimed, the glad news of salvation will not be believed, if the saviors are always in the grip of an absolute institutional requirement to accuse. Who shall watch the watchers, and who shall expose the institutional failure of exposers of institutions?

The Indignant Institutions of
The Young and The Black

The human urge to institutionalize being what it is, there is now an ever-growing list of institutions designed to fight institutions. Caught by the inexorable Laws, these anti-institutions now begin to display all the signs of institutionality.

In a very broad sense, "the young" form an institution, with a certain amount of institutional discipline present (a fellow wearing a jacket and tie and with a haircut is out). There are professional youths, devoted to organizing protests and expressing indignation. The job does not pay much, but it is a job.

People are clear-sighted when young, and today's youth, under pressure, has seen and recognized some of the more vicious excesses of our institutions. Right, or even right on. But this essentially correct glimpse has been generalized to a condemnation of the entire "establishment" as purposefully evil. The picture is of a bunch of generals, politicians and pigs plotting human misery and war. It is a simplistic picture, and wrong, as anyone knows who has any experience with the "establishment" so pictured. Not that the establishment's results are not miserable; they surely are. The motivation is more subtle, and requires a deeper understanding of the forces at work.

The anti-establishment institutions show the same signs of decay as the institutions they attack. The underground newspapers,[7] and even the accepted youth-talk are crudely untruthful; the Law of Institutional Irrelevancy of Truth applies to the anti-establishment because it, too, is an institution. So too, hateful acts are committed in the name of "love"; neither the corner cop nor the corner Air Force general is treated as a human being. All is as predicted by the Institutional Laws; the anti-institution has become what it denounces, and the anti-institutions inexorably keep their machinery operating. There is a vision lacking, and that is the vision that virtue is an individual, not a group, attribute.

So also, the institutions with the noble purpose of seeking to better the lot of those who are black are falling into the same institutional excesses. That black people have been shamefully treated is surely true. This cannot mean that every trial of a black man for murder should call forth torrents of anti-white institutional indignation. A man is a man; a black can kill as murderously as a white, and as well deserve punishment if there is purpose in punishment.

Ethnics are in, and today, being a professional black is an expanding job classification. Professional blacks have the same institutional demands in all situations. Part of what they call for is simple justice and as such should be given, out of human respect. Part of what they demand is simple nonsense and should be treated as such, out of human respect.

The violent institutions of the anti-establishment merit special condemnation. A city in which the Weathermen are the dominant institution would not be a better place to live than Chicago is today. The justification of all black violence against whites because some other whites were once violent to some

---

[7]An underground newspaper, with its limited vocabulary of four-letter words, is as institutional a production as a Pentagon position paper. In each case the style signals the suppression of truth.

other blacks is ethically repellent and inhuman. It is an institutional justification, and one not above the level of the justifications of the worst bigots.

Also to be guarded against by the attacking institutions is the tendency to find whatever it is necessary to find to keep the attack going (General Law of Institutional Self-Occupation). The John Birch Society is an institution, and its paranoid ravings are constantly fueled by the discovery of the necessary plots and conspiracies. The Birchites believe what they say, and this ought to be strong warning for all those who are professionally indignant on any subject. The right rule is facts first, indignation second. The indignant institution's rule easily becomes indignation first, facts found to suit.

There is an institutional commandment punishing those who hate for a living. The commandment cannot be escaped, for it reads: you shall become what you hate.

13. THE PENTAGON BUSYNESS

Guidebooks. The Four Primal Elements: Replication, Independence, Attributes of Importance, Discipline. Jurisdictional Infighting. Over-Capability. Over-Coordination and Over-Planning. Over-Procurement: The Santa Claus Complex. The Dr. Strangelove Question.

Guidebooks

No study of Washington institutions can skip the Pentagon; it would be like writing about tropical plants and omitting to mention the jungle. There is, of course, much more to the Department of Defense than the Pentagon building, but the building, with its five rings of nested pentagons, and weblike corridors, is a brilliant symbol, now universally used to refer to the department. The Pentagon, then, is a huge hothouse in which the institutions within the department grow in luxuriant profusion, reaching unnatural proportions and assuming strange forms and colors as they reach for light, air and power. If our Laws of Institutional Behavior are valid, then here is their real test—a giant botanical experiment with all the institutional nutriments supplied without stint by a generous Congress.

There are three current guides to the jungle. The first is the

1970 Fitzhugh Report,[1] a not-too-critical institutional critique which still serves to describe the major topographical features.

A second, more specialized guide to the behavior of the jungle inhabitants is *Inside Bureaucracy* by Anthony Downs.[2] Downs is particularly good when describing the desperate efforts of the men at the top to "control" their institutions, the staffs they create to achieve control, the staffs created to control the staffs, and so on.

The third guide to the Pentagon is recommended to the serious student who wishes to do original field work in the jungle. Such a student, after getting the necessary series of immunizations, should purchase the Department of Defense Telephone Directory. Here is institutional life in the raw.

Buy the book ($2.50 from the Government Printing Office, Washington, D.C. 20402), and turn to the yellow pages—the "Organization Section."[3] Here you will find the flora in their natural habitat, neatly classified. Here is the specialization within specialization: the "Beach Jumper & Psychological Warfare Sec" of the "Naval Inshore Warfare Br" of the "Amphibious, Mine, and Special Warfare Divn" of the Office of the "Deputy Chief of Naval Operations (Surface)." Here is administration within administration: not only the Assistant Secretary of Defense (Administration) Hon. Robert F. Froehlke, Room 3E822, but his Executive Assistant, Lt. Col. Alfred H. Uhalt Jr., and his Principal Deputy Assistant Secretary of Defense (Administration), David O. Cooke. Here are plans within plans: the "LOG Doc & Sys Dev Ofc" in the office of the "Spec Asst for Plans and Programs" in the office of the "Asst Dep Ch of Staff for Logistics (Pers Doctrine & Sys)" in

---

[1] *Report to the President and the Secretary of Defense by The Blue Ribbon Defense Panel,* July 1, 1970, Washington, D.C., GPO (Gilbert W. Fitzhugh, Chairman of the Board of Metropolitan Life, was panel chairman).

[2] Little Brown & Co. (Boston, 1966).

[3] Just as a sample, some pages are reproduced in the Appendix.

the office of the "Deputy Chief of Staff for Logistics (PNT)" in the Department of the Army.

Buy the book, but bring your machete to cut your way out.[4]

The Four Primal Elements

Several factors cooperate to produce the luxuriant tangle of the Pentagon. When the forces are understood, the organization becomes comprehensible, just as the numbering of rooms in the building itself has a logic of its own (3E822: third floor, E ring, room 822).

The first factor at work is duplication, or better, *replication*. The Pentagon is not one institution but many, each of which is fully equipped with all institutional organs. At the top there is the Secretary of Defense, Monarch of the Realm, disposer of seventy billions of dollars annually, keeper of the instruments of total human destruction, and many similar titles as awesome as those of any oriental potentate. Shall such a man, such a giant among men, concern himself with the unimportant questions of bases and supplies? Most certainly not! Let there be, then, an Assistant Secretary of Defense for Installations and Logistics (or "I and L"). As esquires to this noble, let there be a Principal Deputy Assistant Secretary of Defense ("I and L"), a Special Assistant, four Deputy Assistant Secretaries and their staffs and bearers.

As there were to the ancients the four elements of earth, air, fire and water, so there are in the armed services of the United States, fighters of the earth, of the air and of the water.

---

[4]Do not omit to read the front of the book, including the "Joint Uniform Telephone Communications Precedence Chart" (i.e., a list giving the ranks of "Routine," "Priority," "Immediate," "Flash" and "Flash Override" to communications).

(The element of fire is presumably in the care of Research and Development—"R and D.")

That mighty chief of the forces of the earth, the Secretary of the Army—shall he be concerned with mundane matters of Army bases and Army supplies? Certainly not! Let there be an Assistant Secretary of the Army for Installations and Logistics, and a Principal Deputy for him, and four other Deputies, and assistants and trumpeters to suit. And let there be an Assistant Secretary of the Navy for "I and L" and an Assistant Secretary of the Air Force, also. Are we at an end? By no means.

These Secretaries, Assistants and Deputy Assistants are all but mere civilians. They do not fight on the earth, in the air or in the water: they control or direct or administer those who fight. Within the Army itself there must be those others who actually Install and Logist. Therefore, in the Pentagon let there be men in uniform, and of high rank, who will be sure that the Army does what the Assistant for "I and L" tells it to do. (Vocabulary: "military counterpart" of a civilian; "civilian counterpart" of a military officer. Also, "action agency"—the branch which will eventually do something: an action agency is "designated" as such.)[5]

Do not forget that there must be an overall military counterpart for the Secretary of Defense. Therefore, create a uniformed organization called the Joint Chiefs of Staff, and add to it all that is appropriate to its global importance.

You now begin to get the idea of the Pentagon: the same function is *replicated* (1) in the individual armed service, (2) in the Joint Chiefs, (3) in the appropriate service Secretary's office and (4) "at the Secretary of Defense level" within an Assistant Secretary's office.[6] Press on.

The second force at work in the halls of the Pentagon is

---

[5] "Inaction agencies" exist but are not so designated.

[6] "The result is a multiplicity of largely independent, parallel managements of the Department from the top . . ." Fitzhugh Report, p. 25.)

independence, an institutional drive for self-sufficiency. Every sub-institution attempts to be complete in all respects. Each must have its own "I and L" as well as "R and D" functions; each must have communications, intelligence; each must plan; each must indeed have a foreign policy, a domestic policy and a direct link with the Congress which shovels out the funds.[7] The result is not only a vertical replication of function, but also horizontal redundancy. Create an Assistant Secretary of Defense for Systems Analysis (as was done), and within each service the systems analysts will pop up overnight. (Vocabulary: "capability" is the goal; the shop should have "intelligence capability," or "research capability," or, if astrology is a recognized function, "horoscopic capability.")

The third force at work in the Pentagon tangle is the wild overgrowth of all the Attributes of Importance. In any Government institution modesty and humility are well underemphasized. In the military services the pomp and perquisites of rank are already prized. Plant all the military services together in the hothouse, and the forces of natural selection urgently require emphasis on every attribute of importance: Activity, Authority, Security, Urgency and Panoply.

In the Pentagon, Activity is a pearl beyond price; nervous, eager hands are ready for any work, clean or dirty. Just name any job, from wiretapping a convention to winning a war, and every service is ready. Similarly each service and each office within each service is desperate for every shred of Authority, preferably command Authority, but at least consultative Authority (committee-sitting).

Security and Urgency are not just casual incidents of Pentagon existence, they are the staff of daily life. Everything in sight is classified, and the higher the better. No office is so mean

---

[7]For an authentic dowager-in-the-burlesque-house expression of scorn and distaste, listen to an Army/Navy man saying: "We are dependent on the Navy/Army for [support, intelligence, or whatever]."

as not to have its secure file and its security-warning sign.

The brilliant flowers of Panoply riot in the Pentagon jungle, particularly (1) Technological Panoply and (2) Panoply of Staff. The technological panoply far exceeds any Hollywood special effects. The communications machinery, the computers, the displays, are all there, replicated as many times as possible. It is very well done and vastly impressive to those whom it is designed to impress (that is, those who use it).

In the Department of Defense, Panoply of Staff reaches extremes no less-well-funded agencies can afford. Like the rich man who could live on the income from his income, the Pentagon staffs can have staffs. The Fitzhugh Report notes, for example, that the Office of the Secretary of Defense has a staff of 3,500. The statutory limitation on the staff of the Joint Chiefs of Staff to 400 has "proved to be of no practical consequence," and JCS staff was 2,145 in 1969. No one can control an organization of two or three thousand without a staff: therefore the staffs have staffs (the "Chairman's Staff Group" and "Director of the Joint Staff" and Directors J-I through J-6, and the "Joint Secretariat" of the JCS).

The fourth, final and obvious force making the Pentagon what it is, is a high degree of institutional discipline. The Army man follows orders, and so does everybody else in the Pentagon, with rare exceptions. A Fitzgerald, in an auditor's fury, criticizing the C-5A, and an Ellsberg, in an agony of conscience, releasing the Pentagon Papers are rare birds, very rare.

While there are other factors operating within the Pentagon, the forces just described suffice to predict how the Department of Defense works. Most of the institution's attention, as predicted by our Laws, is turned inward.

Jurisdictional Infighting

Institutional survival within the Pentagon is bought at the price of constant battles to protect jurisdiction. If an enemy really wants to put the machinery of the Department of Defense out of action (a dubious objective), it should devote all its resources to reinventing Tom Swift's favorite vehicle: a land-water-aircraft. Show this around the Pentagon, and the Army, Navy, and Air Force would fight to the last memorandum to get control. Success of an enemy airdrop on Des Moines would then be assured—it would not have a high enough priority to be reported. The five-sided corridors would be empty because everyone was in meetings to decide control of the Swiftian super-weapon.

The jurisdictional fight in the Pentagon is fought on not five but fifty fronts. Civilians fight the military, often all the way to the halls of Congress. The services fight each other, bitterly.[8] The line fights the staff, all the way up. The staffs try to take over operations, all kinds of operations. The offices devoted to any form of expert activity get in each other's way and fight for control of functions residing in the field.

It would be absurd to think that the public interest has much to do with these jurisdictional fights. It does not, and could not. Why should not the Navy do as good a job as the Army, or the Air Force as either? Is there any reason to think that the Army's Assistant Secretary for Astrological Analysis is not as capable as the Navy's Chief Astrologer? Certainly not. But, a fight to be first in Astrology can work wonders for the research budgets of university professors commissioned to do research.

---

[8]The Fitzhugh Report (p. 21) speaks of " . . . continued adversary relations between the Military Services, which, although usually confined to the internal paper wars that constitute the Department's decision-making process, severely inhibit the achievement of economy and effectiveness . . ."

In short, the Institutional Imperative operates without check in the Pentagon jungle. All actions and decisions are taken to keep the institutional machinery running, and there are an awful lot of institutional machines. As the Law of Institutional Expertise requires, the expert judgment of each sub-institution is that it must continue its operations. Within the Pentagon, such expert opinions are mere small arms fire in the jurisdictional skirmishing.

Over-Capability

Contrary to the impressions of some, the Pentagon is not staffed with dumbbells—not by a long shot. The men, military and civilian, are smart. Those civilians who have reached the higher jobs and survived are very glossy performers indeed, with that aura of forcefulness that comes only from a hundred bureaucratic battles won and a thousand enemies vanquished memo-to-memo.

These capable men are distributed among services and sub-institutions each of which has had its machinery designed to perform, to be capable, to be self-supporting. It follows, therefore, that the Pentagon is overcapable; there is an enormous surplus of unused capability. Even professionally savvy observers forget this. For instance, many Washingtonians were surprised at the efficiency demonstrated in dealing with the Pentagon peace demonstrations, the Washington riots and the 1971 Mayday street blockages. Even the Fitzhugh Report marveled that the Pentagon machinery could function at all.

The truth is that the Department of Defense supervisory machinery is grossly overcapable. The Army could deal with all aspects of the riots from intelligence, to planning, to communications, to actual operations, and so could the Navy, the Marines and the Air Force, as well as probably half a dozen spe-

cial-operations groups. Ten offices in the Pentagon—no, fifty—
are capable of grasping, studying and disposing of any problem
set.

There is a great national asset going to waste in the Pentagon, and the waste is not the usually seen waste of lives in war,
or the waste of dollars in the billions, or the waste of time of
several million men spending years under arms. The waste is
the enormous capability of the giant, frustrated Pentagon machine. Turn some of the boys loose on something clearly
defined, something the country knows it wants, and watch the
results. Nominations are in order, starting with pollution, slums
and traffic jams.

Over-Coordination and Over-Planning

The Law of Conservation of Institutional Momentum
states that the quantity of institutional effort is independent of
the result; the Law of Reflexive Purpose states that if institutional machinery cannot function to achieve the designed purpose, the purpose will be altered.

The overcapable machineries of the Pentagon sub-institutions have too little hard work to do; daily operations are kid
stuff. They turn, instead, to those two favorite bureaucratic time
wasters (1) coordination and (2) planning.

Time-wasting coordination is easily foreseen. Creating ten
sub-institutions to do one job leads to incessant memo-writing,
coordination, liaison, paper shuffling, meetings, reviews. So
says the Fitzhugh Report (p. 38):

> Functional analysis of these [military headquarters]
> staffs reveals an astonishing lack of organizational
> focus and a highly excessive degree of "coordination,"
> a substantial portion of which entails the writing of

memoranda back and forth between lower echelons of parallel organizational elements and which serves no apparent useful or productive purpose.

The second great occupation of administrators with too little to administer is "planning." ("Planning" should be distinguished from "policy-making" because plans are the means to carry out a known policy. The distinction is important, but soon lost.) The sheer volume of "planning" in the Pentagon is staggering. A hint of its magnitude is the forty-seven volumes which the Pentagon Papers fill.

"Planning" as a reflexive purpose of an institution has great attraction: it sounds useful, it might even be useful, it does not appear to deny the institution's purpose. In the Pentagon, planning also produces good ammunition to be fired off in jurisdictional fights. The Institutional Imperative requires that "planning" be primarily designed to keep the institution's machinery running. Proof of the Imperative is provided by a careful, scholarly study of Air Force planning by Professor Perry McCoy Smith, of the Air Force Academy.[9]

Professor Smith shows that the Air Force planning for its postwar activities had little to do with either the larger public interest or the narrower "purpose" of the Air Force. Instead, the study concludes:

> The end sought was not national security through a properly balanced military defensive and deterrent force but rather an autonomous, powerful United States Air Force which would be the first line of defense, the largest of the three military services, and the recipient of the largest share of the defense budget. Assumptions . . . were drawn to lead to the end desired.

[9] *The Air Force Plans for Peace, 1943–1945* (Johns Hopkins, 1970).

Over-Procurement:
The Santa Claus Complex

One of the functions of the overcapable tangle of Pentagon institutions is the buying of weapons and supplies. Our body of Laws correctly predicts that this operation will be continued whenever possible, without regard to the need for or cost of the purchases. Our Laws do not predict, however, that the institution will attempt to enrich its suppliers. Yet, ever since President Eisenhower used it, the term "military-industrial-complex" is heard, with the meaning that the suppliers control the military. This is observably wrong.

When the toy buyers come to New York City, they are wined and dined by the toy sellers. Possibly they are even provided with song and with agreeable female companionship. The buyers then buy, the sellers profit. On occasion, a buyer knowing the toy business may become a salesman; or a salesman a buyer. Everybody knows almost everybody; the industry is close and gossipy. Does anyone talk about this "Santa Claus Complex" as a threat to the nation's children?

Corruption aside, an institution has no reason to assure to one seller either a dominant position, or inordinate profits. The buyer is in the best position if sellers are competing, hungry, with a real incentive to provide the most attractive inducements.

So, if the charge is that military procurement always unduly enriches the sellers to the military, the charge (although much pressed) is just wrong. It is to the institutional interest of the procurement planners, the reviewers of procurement policy, the reviewers of the reviewers of the reviewers and so on that they have something to do. Keeping the institutional machinery turning over means *administering* procurement, not abandoning administration to enrich the seller. The process of keeping military procurement well and truly overadministered is highly irritating and unprofitable to "defense" suppliers (there are no "aggression" suppliers).

Those who think supplying the military is a road to easy riches are invited to learn better by one of three methods: (1) try to sell something at a profit to the military; (2) read the annual reports of companies supplying military hardware and note the emphasis on diversifying to civilian lines (or, alternately, note the stock market's price-earnings ratio for military suppliers);[10] or (3) go read the decisions of the Armed Services Board of Contract Appeals (the Pentagon, of course, has its special Departmental court). Any of these routes leads to the conviction that the institutional interests of the Department of Defense may be to do business, may be to spend money, may be even to waste money, but they are not to enrich the suppliers. The Law of Institutional Symbiosis operates, but not always in the supplier's favor. So much for the Santa Claus complex.

There is another, dangerous, "military-industrial-complex." Control of Pentagon spending supposedly lies in the Congress. The control is little exercised, because the committee system produces a "Congressional committee-military-industrial-complex." The Committees on Rubber and Blubber, or Missiles and Fissiles, become one part of the interdependent super-institution in which everyone's back is scratched by spending more and more public money. In the three-way game, the Congressional committee benefits as directly from military contracts as the military or the suppliers. The institution produces contracts for ungainly weapons, but then contracts, not weapons of war, are what keep the machinery going.

---

[10]The Fitzhugh Report notes "the trend of the demonstrated reluctance by industry, whether justified or not, to commit resources to defense business." This is absolutely correct. The government is a lousy customer, difficult to please and disloyal when the next procurement comes around.

The Dr. Strangelove Question

A persistent bit of folk wisdom insists that, somehow, going to doctors causes sickness, hospitals cause death, and great war machines cause wars. The root of this folk belief is the General Law of Institutional Self-Occupation, stating that an institution will generate its own subject matter *if it can*.

A specific application of the General Law is the Particular Law of the Security Office ("Threats to security will be found"). Since the Department of Defense is a very large security office, and the Pentagon pressures to find work for the chronically underemployed planners are great indeed, the natural question arises: will the machinery promote a war for war's sake? Better put: is Dr. Strangelove in charge?

A careful answer is justified to a question of such magnitude. First, it must be noted that the Particular Law says: "*Threats* to security will be found." A *threat* to security need not be an attack, but only a threat of attack. The enemy threatens a ballistic missile attack, we must respond by building an anti-ballistic missile. They threaten to develop an anti-anti-ballistic missile missile, and we must respond. It is all very familiar, the swordmaker and the armormaker, and it keeps business brisk.

An experienced institutional threat-detector can turn even peace to good account. Secretary of Defense Laird proved his skills right after the first Strategic Arms Limitation Treaty with Russia. To Laird, arms limits were no reason at all to lower defense budgets. In fact, he said, the limits on some arms made it essential to go ahead with a new supersonic bomber, and a new submarine, all adequately complex and monstrously expensive.[11] There was no mention

---

[11]"Laird Would Kill Pacts if Congress Barred Arms Fund," *The New York Times*, June 21, 1972.

"Chief of Naval Operations Elmo Zumwalt insisted yesterday that new military spending was essential if the United States was to maintain a creditable

of an expanded research budget for supersonic bows and arrows.

While most of the Pentagon machinery keeps happy and busy with threats, the parts designed to function only in war cannot forever be satisfied with contingency planning and memo-writing. A shooting war is subject matter for some of the Defense institutions, and as subject matter, the need will be discovered. Note again that those who discover a need for war may believe in what they discover, believe it strongly, preach the need for action sincerely and with real conviction. They can also be dead wrong.

The Dr. Strangelove question is whether the Pentagon *can* generate its own most dangerous subject matter—war. The Constitution's answer is no, because only the Congress declares war. The Congress has abandoned this Constitutional function to the President. Thus the nub of the question is whether the Pentagon, or other institutions, can impel a President to find a threat so grave as to require a war. The answer depends on the design of the White House supervisory apparatus, and as to that, read on.

nuclear deterrent under the Strategic Arms Limitation Treaty with the Soviet Union." *The Washington Post,* July 22, 1972.

14. THE (UGH) FOREIGN POLICY OF THE UNITED STATES

There's No Policy Like Foreign Policy. Case of the Pushed Cookie. The Policy Wheel. The Insignificant Institutional Product. To Arms! The Chinese Are Coming (Quemoy and Matsu). The Secret Foreign Policy Role of the Interstate Commerce Commission.

There's No Policy Like Foreign Policy

Sir or Madam, as the case may be, do not train your child to be a doctor or a bank president. Send him into the foreign policy business, particularly if he has a talent for failure.

Most businesses do not like failure; they discourage it. In the foreign policy business, failure is routine and thumping disaster is unremarkable. At the time of the Suez crisis, for example, John Foster Dulles managed to be hanged in effigy both in Tel Aviv and in Cairo, and for good measure he was roundly cursed out in London, Paris, and of course Moscow. Such audience reaction is normal for a Secretary of State. In show business and foreign policy business there are a lot of flops, but the difference is, in foreign policy the same turkey goes on the next day, starring the same cast.

At times it is difficult to discover what our foreign policy is. Always it is difficult to discover why it is. When all possible

186

explanations for our policy are nonsense, the public is told the matter is too secret to be understood. The phrase is "you haven't read the cables," cable-reading presumably being the sole fount of enlightenment. Of course, you understand, the cables are *secret,* and so enlightenment is limited to a small group.

Still, cableful or cableless, the policy doesn't seem to work. Our foreign military aid poses a constant paradox. If we give country A a gun, then surely we do not expect country B, the historic enemy of A, to be pleased. But surely, country A should be happy. Somehow, though, neither A nor B loves us when we are through passing out the shooting irons. India is furious at us for arming Pakistan; Pakistan hates us for arming India;[1] and China expresses displeasure when we tell both India and Pakistan to shoot only toward China. Not only do the recipients pay no attention to the instructions packed with the guns, but they are also totally unappreciative of our pains in enclosing the instructions with the gift.

It is a matter of pride that wherever in the world a military dictatorship takes over, it must use equipment labeled "made in U.S.A." It is not too hard, then, to understand why the unhorsed government, either in jail or in exile, believes the military coup itself was made in U.S.A. This is at present the strong belief of many Greek democrats, observing the rapid resumption of American military aid to the Greek military junta. While it is well to be polite and overlook the errors of one's friends, there is some sentiment that the Greek junta's tendency to torture called for a longer wait before sending presents.

Military uniforms attract military aid in obedience to the

---

[1]More precisely, in 1972 Pakistan hates us for letting India slice off Bangladesh, and India hates us for our "Tilt Toward the Paks" (Dr. Kissinger's phrase—see the National Security Council minutes "released" by Jack Anderson to the leading papers on January 5, 1972).

Definition of the Critical Mass of Colonels: one colonel is "a patriot"; three colonels are "friendly elements"; and five are a critical mass entitled to recognition as a "free democratic government."

Once the flow of military aid has started, it is irresistible. The attitude of the foreign government toward American companies, Americans, or free enterprise ideology arrests the flow not at all. Often, the explanation for arms shipments is a variant of Wall Street's greater-fool theory:[2] "If we don't, the Russians [or Chinese] will." The Marxist explanation of our foreign policy (that we are assisting the giant capitalistic monopolies) may make good material for a *Pravda* editorial, but it has little basis in fact.[3]

In short, our foreign policy is neither highly ethical nor highly greedy. Instead, it is highly unsatisfactory. Our policy could be one of elevated ethical tone, supporting only countries with freely elected governments and with personal freedoms for the citizens guaranteed. Such a policy makes sense, and has purpose and bite.

Alternatively, our foreign policy could be coldly calculating, aiming at either military or financial advantage. The Arabs have the oil? Play ball with them. The Jews have a superb army? Break a matzoh with them. Is there money in trading with China? Trade. A good sharp self-interested foreign policy has much to recommend it.

Either way, ethical or self-interested, a foreign policy would make sense if it either rewarded our friends and not our

---

[2] If I buy this stock for a hundred dollars, some greater fool will pay me a hundred and fifty.

[3] This chapter was written before the publication of Richard Barnet's *The Roots of War* (Atheneum, 1972). Part I of the Barnet book contains much fine material corroborating the operation of the national security machinery. Part II, however, argues that foreign policy is profoundly affected by an urge to advance business interests. Usually, the evidence is largely against this, as is evident when one tries to advance an interest with U.S. Government help.

enemies or if it gained us some advantage. Any visible and attainable purpose would do. Since World War II, American foreign policy is plainly neither moral nor practical, but only irritating and expensive. Yet, an enormous Government institution is devoted to assembling this Edsel.

Now playing in its second decade, our foreign policy production in Vietnam has been the ultimate flop. Even those abroad who still gave us some faint credit for good intentions now regard Vietnam as a total failure of purpose and policy. None of our usual friends approve, while our enemies have rejoiced in the daily proofs of our cruelty and deception. Our policy has not looked good for years, and now it looks terrible. We diagnose a wasting institutional disease.

Case of the Pushed Cookie

The view of the State Department held in common by American businessmen, American citizens abroad in trouble, Hollywood screen writers and certain Congressmen has remained consistent for two generations. All these believe that the State Department will not stir itself to help an American. All believe that in some way the State Department is manned by supercilious cookie-pushers in striped pants representing foreign governments and afraid to do anything in the interest of the real Americans—an outfit offensive to every red-blooded boy.[4]

While the view of the State Department as an agent of foreign interests is greatly overstated, there is some truth in it. No one who has ever tried to get the State Department to help

---

[4]Here is a quote from a speech by Rep. Garmatz (75 *Congressional Information Bureau Bulletin* 139): "As a matter of fact, I have often remarked that—when it comes to standing up for our rights among the nations of the world—the State Department has about as much backbone as a tomato."

an American business abroad can retain the illusion that the Department thinks itself an agent of capitalist expansion. Sometimes, individual third secretaries have been helpful to citizens in trouble, but the Department thinks it a tiresome chore to dig Americans out of foreign jails.

In terms of our theory, the product of any institution is what the institutional machinery is designed to make: reports, discussions, impressions or whatever. Further, whatever the machinery does produce will be regarded from within as its purpose (Third Axiom). The truth is, the State Department has little institutional reason to assist either people or corporations. The Department's view of its own purpose is aristocratic. The diplomat's role is to create impressions, hold discussions, be dignified as befits one gentleman visiting another. No need to ask if dignified discussions should not have further ends, because the machinery is not designed to reach further ends (Corollary to the Institutional Imperative).

The diplomatic machinery, then, matches quite well the impression of the frustrated U.S. businessman. The State Department is not out to bludgeon some foreign government into accepting a chain of Monsterburger stands on the Gobi. The State Department is out to build rapport, a commodity so precious it cannot be exposed to our side's nagging demands (nagging demands from abroad are received with sympathy and understanding).

The Policy Wheel

At this low point, a fellow named John Franklin Campbell has written a book with the snappy title *The Foreign Policy Fudge Factory.*[5] In it, he makes two immensely valuable points:

---

[5](Basic Books, 1971). The "fudge factory" crack is attributed to Joseph Kraft, and it fits with all the assurance of the right insult at the right time.

first, that the fudge factory is not just the State Department, but the State Department *plus* the Department of Defense *plus* the Central Intelligence Agency, *plus,* and a very important plus—the White House staff machinery. This huge complex is the factory, and our policy is the fudge. Second, says Campbell, the whole thing is much too large; radical pruning is needed; most elements should be cut back, and some totally sawed off.[6]

At the higher level of most Government departments, foreign policy-making has the fascination of an addictive drug. Great staffs in the Department of Defense dabble in foreign affairs. There is an Assistant Secretary of Defense for International Security Affairs with a staff, the Joint Chiefs of Staff with a huge staff, the Defense Intelligence Agency—and Army, Navy and Air Force Intelligence—and a lot more besides, one suspects.[7]

Added to Defense is the Central Intelligence Agency, which not only reports on what goes on abroad (again, another part of the diplomat's job description) but conducts spy business. CIA appropriations are secret, but hefty, and all can see a big secret white building on a parkway right outside Washington. Security is preserved by not putting a sign on the parkway. Whether this CIA machinery produces useful or used intelligence is unknown. What is known is that on some occasions it produces events abroad[8] for which a foreign policy becomes necessary in a hurry.

And then, finally, since all the machineries of State, De-

---

[6]The third Campbell argument is that we should go back to an elite striped-pants foreign service corps. Aside from the obvious desirability of an all-star team in any sport, what is the purpose of the game?

[7]Campbell reports that the Pentagon has more men at embassies abroad than the State Department has. Isn't "International Security" the job of the State Department?

[8]The CIA stage-manages "operations" in the field abroad, but—with the exception of such items as the Bay of Pigs performance—what it does is supposed to be secret. The CIA therefore gets blamed for a little of what it does, and for much that it does not do.

fense and CIA are unmanageable, the President has a National Security Council, upon which sit the Secretaries of State and Defense and the Chairman of the Joint Chiefs of Staff and the CIA's director, and in addition that very important gentleman, the Assistant to the President for National Security Affairs (again, another title that seems to be a good job description for the Secretary of State). The National Security Council has its staff, of course.

The Law of Attributed Importance declares that every job is given the maximum quantity of the Attributes it can sustain, and jobs in the foreign policy complex can sustain a great deal. War, and particularly nuclear war, is the most frightful and important of all national concerns, and since foreign policy deals with war, the natural assumption is that the foreign policy complex is the all-important activity.

Thus, secret and urgent messages are normal within the policy factory. Crisis arrives as surely as Christmas. With a crisis, the activity redoubles, the cables bulge, the planes fly in and out with summoned ambassadors and dispatched special envoys, and the President is awakened at inconvenient small hours of the morning. At times the peak of communications importance is reached, and that super-instrument, the Great Telex, the hot line to Moscow, is opened. All these activities are conducted by those concerned with total twenty-four-hour devotion to their jobs, and with the absolute maximum belief in the Importance of the work, and in the Importance of those doing the work (Personnel Postulate).

The Insignificant Institutional Product

It is time, then, to consider the critical question: what is the product of all this enormously Important labor? It may be assumed that the presence of multiple and competing institutions within the complex takes up a great deal of time in coordinating, jurisdictional infighting, memo-writing and all the rest. But even allowing for memos, a complex numbering its workers in six figures must produce something. What is this product?

This last is an unfriendly question, and will receive from those involved the brusque answer that the machinery exists "to deal with crises." Such answers alert the antennae of the institutional investigator. A crisis is subject matter for an institution dealing with crises. A great national foreign policy crisis is Important subject matter, very Important and Secret and Urgent subject matter, to be dealt with by Very Important People.

The General Law of Institutional Self-Occupation declares that institutions will generate their own subject matter if they can. The Personnel Postulate states that every individual action affirms the Importance of the work. Applying these principles to the crisis-handling functions of the complex, it must be noted that the crisis-identifying and the crisis-handling machinery are within the same institution—in fact the two are largely identical. Thus, the conditions of the Law are met, and the unsettling conclusion follows that foreign policy crises can be and will be generated by the crisis-handling institution.

This is a serious conclusion, and it is important to be precise. The Law does not state that *all* subject matter is self-generated. Plainly, such a statement is not true. When a joint Cuban-Albanian strike force lands in Miami Beach and is working its way up Collins Avenue, the crisis is externally generated. But with the present scarcity of hostile amphibious action against the Fontainebleau, one must look elsewhere, if the foreign policy machinery is to be kept running.

To Arms! The Chinese Are Coming! (Quemoy and Matsu)

Off the Fukien coast of mainland China, near the harbors of two ports, lie the small islands of Quemoy (Chinmen Tao) and Matsu, 70 and 7 square miles, respectively. Quemoy is 17 miles from the mainland—Matsu perhaps 6. They are of no economic importance whatsoever.

It happened that these two islands, although right by the mainland ports, had remained under the control of the Nationalist (Formosa) regime at the time the Chinese Communists took over the mainland. It pleased the mainland Chinese as much to have these close-in islands under hostile control as it would please the United States to have Fidel Castro Veterans' Post 211 camped in New York harbor, hanging a beard on the Statue of Liberty.

The United States took the position that these two scraps of land were outposts of freedom, which under no circumstances could fall to the Red aggressor. Warships steamed to the straits, and we shook a big stick.

The Quemoy and Matsu "crisis"[9] is a fair example of self-generation. If the geographic realities had been recognized, the Red Chinese would have been allowed to take over. Such realities had been recognized when Russian troops took over Hungary in 1956 and Czechoslovakia in 1968 and no "crises" developed (except for Hungarians and Czechs). The United States could have declared a crisis, but did not—so there was none. In the case of Quemoy and Matsu, the crisis-handling machinery was activated by a declaration that there was a crisis to be "handled."

Here it may be objected that the Quemoy and Matsu crisis was real because "loss" of Quemoy and Matsu could have

---

[9]Also called the "Second Taiwan Straits Crisis" (1958).

meant much "loss of face." The reply is that this is a justification of the United States' behavior, and naturally there are Important reasons to be given for whatever was done (Law of Institutional Self-Justification). There were also Important reasons for doing nothing while face was lost as the Russians moved in Hungary and Czechoslovakia, or when the Chinese took over Tibet. There are always Important reasons, because whatever is decided is Important.

The Secret Foreign Policy Role of the Interstate Commerce Commission

There is a very pretty parallellism between the subdivisions of the Interstate Commerce Commission and the divisions of the foreign policy machine. The ICC has its inspectors, its experts, its enforcers. The ICC rules that a trucker is "compliance-minded" and worthy of a certificate; the foreign policy machinery awards a few hundred millions in military hardware to qualified "friendly" applicants. (The ICC's standards of qualification are somewhat stricter.) The parallellism of structure is reflected in parallel functions: both the ICC and the FPC (Foreign Policy Complex) are engaged in defining the indefinable.

If one asks what *is* the United States policy which has been produced by the foreign policy machinery, the inquiry is unsettling. Where the policy is clearly known—say the policy that no armed forces of foreign powers shall cross the borders of the United States—then no huge machine is needed to develop it. If the policy is not known, then the answer must be that *the policy is whatever is developed by the machinery.* This is recognizably circular and by now familiar. The mystique is the same as regulating rates. Regulation is necessary to assure reasonableness of rates, and reasonableness can only be defined as the result of the regulatory process. So, policy machinery is necessary to create "policy" which can only be defined as the product of the machinery.

"Secrecy" is not a way out of the logical circle. It is not an answer to say "our policy is correct because it is based on secret cables only known to policy-makers." That does not meet the point at all. Reading all the cables is no guide to what result is desired with all the Top Secret intelligence thus acquired. Secrecy is romantic, secrecy conceals mistakes, secrecy is a wonderful plaything, but secrecy is not a goal in itself.

The only meaningful way out of the logical circularity is to have some external definition of the purpose of the institutional machinery.[10] There must be a plain statement of just what regulation is supposed to accomplish if there are to be useful regulatory agencies. If we are to try to regulate the world's affairs, as we seem to be trying,[11] there must be a plain statement of the goal of our foreign policy.

Our Institutional Laws contain several stern warnings of the inevitable results of creating institutional machinery without very sharp definition of its purpose. Every condition of the Laws is violated by the foreign policy complex, and the results are as predicted.

Take the Third Principle of Institutional Design:

> *If the desired result of the institution*
> *cannot be stated in terms meaningful to*
> *design of the institutional machinery, it*
> *will not be accomplished.*

---

[10]"Advancing the national interest" is no guide at all, since it means whatever a policymaker wants it to mean.

"The terrible problem for policy planners in mid-century America was that they did not and could not know what their long-term interests really were." Richard Barnet, *The Roots of War* (Atheneum, 1972)

[11]"Perhaps the most striking characteristic of bureaucratic language is the recurrence of the imagery of manipulation." Barnet, *ibid.*

In all fairness, suppressing with difficulty all value judgments, it is plain that the desired result of our recent foreign policy has never been stated in terms such that a group of men could be sat down and told: work toward this goal.

Yet, if a group of men cannot be told what goal they should reach, or more precisely if their work cannot be set for them, the institution simply cannot reach the unspecified result. It does not work to set up an institution and say make "reasonableness" or make "policy." The First Rule of Institutional Results says, "If the institutional machinery is designed not to accomplish anything, it won't." That is evidently the case with our foreign policy complex, which is busily operating with no designed purpose.

The same conclusion can be reached by applying the Second Principle of Institutional Design ("If the desired result is not achieved, the institutional machinery is not designed to accomplish it."). Apply the Second Principle to some foreign policy decision—say, the long losing fight to prevent admission of Red China to the United Nations. Begin by listing some possible desirable results of foreign policy, such as friendly relations with large powers, or spread of free democratic government, or getting our national head out of the sand. Whatever desirable result is stated, the "policy" of not admitting China's existence appears not to have achieved it. This "policy" is now changing; whether the new policy will have any desirable results is dubious—why should it, when the developers of "policy" have not had their work specified for them?

In short, our body of theory reveals that what is called foreign policy is not a meaningful policy with meaningful goals but simply institutional activity for the sake of institutional activity. John Kenneth Galbraith puts it harshly: ". . . the bureaucracy, the military and intelligence bureaucracy in particular, operates not in response to national need but in re-

sponse to its own need." Or again: "Not wickedness but the
dynamics of big organization is involved."[12]

Such a hard conclusion does not depend on whether the
foreign policy machinery is manned by Democrats, Republicans, or Whigs. Foreign policy will be consistently nonmean-
ingful unless the results desired are meaningfully stated. Car-
toonists are fond of the image of the ship of state, beset by
perilous seas, steering amid rocks and shoals. It is not a bad
image, for a ship is as great a piece of complex machinery as
the foreign policy institution, and perils there are aplenty. Still,
a successful voyage implies more than safe arrival nowhere;
passengers are not happy unless the ship arrives at destination.
The foreign policy of the United States is long on crew and
machinery but short on destinations. And after all, if we do not
know where the ship of state is going, how will we know when
it gets there?

---

[12]Galbraith, "Plain Lessons of a Bad Decade," *Foreign Policy,* Winter 1971;
reprinted in *Economics Peace and Laughter* (1972). Galbraith is full of wonderful insights into the institutional machinery of foreign policy. In the domestic
field, he apparently retains faith in the ability of government agencies to solve
all assigned problems. Not so; the dynamics of big organization apply to do-
gooders as well as do-badders.

PART IV

DIRECTIONS FOR ASSEMBLY AND CONTROL OF INSTITUTIONS

15. THE MAN
AT THE CONTROLS

Case of the Chief, Office of Isotopic Diversion, and His
Activities: Money-Grubbing, Territorial Defense, People
Accumulating, Playing Big Daddy, Speech Making,
Learning. Partial Table of Government Executive Activi-
ties and Effects. Virtue. Law of Non-Delegable Duties.
Fallacy of the Staff. Law of Individual Judgment.

In every institution there is one person who appears to be in
charge. He is uneasily astride the elephant at the head of the
parade, trying hard to look as if he knows where he is going.
He is both part of his institution and uniquely separate from it.
His behavior requires a careful look.

Case of the Chief, Office of Isotopic Diversion,
and His Activities

To begin with the man at the top of an institution, particularly a large Washington institution—have you ever seen him
in action on a typical day? It is a long day, and from the black
coffee at dawn to the dregs at dusk the picture is one of pressure,
hurry and work piling up. Whether or not much of what is

going on is mere activity to demonstrate importance is not critical now. The telephone—rather the telephones—are ringing; subordinates are entering with urgent problems; documents are sifting "in" but not "out" in their baskets—the circuits are overloaded. In fact, this image of the overloaded man at the top is so valid that in Government departments where the nominal head is less busy, there is inevitably someone on his staff who displays the same behavior. Sheer violent work overload is an infallible guide to the government man doing the work of the man at the top.

What is going on? A fair question and one to be answered in two parts. First, what the man at the top is doing and second, what he ought to be doing. What the man (call him D. Chief, head of the Office of Isotopic Diversion) is doing includes:

1. Money-Grubbing.

As the first duty of the head of a family is breadwinning, the first duty of a department head is to get his budget requests filled. Much time is consumed thereby. D. Chief must fight on many levels: (a) above his head if his is part of a larger department, dealing both with higher-up budget officers and with his subcabinet or cabinet superiors; (b) with the White House arm, the Office of Management and Budget, and doubtless with the part of the proliferating White House staff dealing with Isotopic Affairs; (c) at some point, if he is high enough up the tree, D. Chief must deal with the staff and then the members of at least four Congressional committees: the subcommittees on Isotopic Diversion and the full committees on Horticulture of both House and Senate, as well as the Appropriations subcommittees and full committees, including the possibility of both subcommittee and committee hearings. With the pressure on to deliver the fiscal goods, it is not surprising to find members of the industry interested in supplying the proposed $80 million of subsonic diverters assisting on the Congressional level, isotopic-diversion-complex-wise.

2. Territorial Defense.

As a feudal baron, D. Chief can never leave his frontiers unguarded. Raids on his borders occur almost daily. Some raids are serious and substantive: employees, or money, or worse, jurisdiction over some part of the outside world may be in real danger of being lost. For example, the CIA claims that the Bureau of Isotopic Intelligence ought to be transferred out of D. Chief's control. Agriculture claims it should run the Isotopic Experiment station on Bimini. These serious territorial battles occur relatively rarely. When they do, the losing agency may even be eaten alive by the victor.

Far more common though, are threats of loss of consultative authority. No one is going to grab the Experiment station, but Agriculture is heading the delegation to the big international meeting in Palma, and Isotopic Diversion is not represented. Bad news, and better get on this at once. In fact, to be sure such threats of loss of consultative authority are nipped in the bud, better be sure to attend all those interagency meetings, and how about appointing a permanent liaison to liaise with Agriculture?

3. People-Accumulating.

As the man at the top, D. Chief thinks his institution's success depends on getting good men around him. So a lot of time is spent on locating and arranging the right assistants and subchiefs. Civil Service regulations get in the way, and it will be necessary (a) to fight for higher grades and more supergrades to pay more, and (b) to change the whole institution around, creating a whole new organization chart in order to bring in new men. Also, personnel affairs (firing, listening to gripes) will take a good deal of time every day.

4. Playing Big Daddy.

D. Chief is at the top, and thus cannot escape settling jurisdictional disputes within the OID. He also is the man who takes the rap so he has to make the final decision on substantially everything, from letters to Congressmen to location of offices to whether secretaries can wear hot pants, he has to decide. The standard of decision is "What's best for the OID?"

5. Speech-Making.

D. Chief gives a number of speeches puffing the OID's business each month, some to Isotopic Industry dinners, some to prestigious citizen groups, some to professional societies. This keeps the Isotopic-industrial symbiosis polished up. He also talks regularly to his assembled staff, firing up the team spirit.

6. Learning.

Information is constantly being transfused into or drained from D. Chief. He is constantly being briefed. ("Briefing" means to communicate the minimum necessary information in the car on the way to the meeting. The student of administrative behavior will note that the briefer has a good degree of control over the contents of the briefee's brain.) The test for acquiring information is whether it affects OID. In turn, D. Chief may become a briefer, up the line.

This list could be continued on and on, adding meetings, telephone calls, special sessions, lunches, cha-chas with the Senator's wife at the annual party, and so on for pages.

Evidently, D. Chief is frantically busy all day, every day.

And equally evidently, while he is burning himself up in the interests of his institution, he is not giving much (if any) thought to the purpose (if any) of the OID. The anticipated public benefits from isotopic diversion, the purpose of the activities of the subdivisions of the OID, are subjects unlikely to occur in D. Chief's daily thoughts.

The all-consuming daily pressure of the institution prevents the head of the OID from exercising the precious prerogative which he alone possesses—that is, the possibility of *not* acting as part of the institution.

In the bulk of D. Chief's daily activities, not only is he acting without regard to public purpose or public interest, but also in all likelihood he is actively working against the public good. To tabulate:

Partial Table of
Government Executive Activities and Effects

PRINCIPAL EXECUTIVE ACTIVITIES IN INTEREST OF INSTITUTION	EFFECT OF ACTIVITIES ON PUBLIC INTEREST
1. *Money-Grubbing*—getting budget requests filled.	Spending without reference to public objective—i.e., waste of money.
2. *Territorial Defense*—protecting jurisdiction of the agency.	Distributing work without regard to public objective of doing work best—i.e., waste of effort.
3. *People-Accumulating*—hiring; pushing for higher wages; reorganizing in order to fire.	Assignment of talent without regard to public needs—i.e., waste of people.
4. *Playing Big Daddy*—making all decisions by the standard of what is good for the institution.	Good decisions only when the public interest is coincidentally the institution's interest.

5. *Speech-Making*—puffing the institution.	Promoting industry-government symbiosis for the institution's good.
6. *Learning*—acquiring information filtered through subordinates; dispensing it refiltered.	Collecting and dispensing slanted facts for the institution's good.

Again, our standard warning is necessary: a tabulation of the ill results of the hypothetical Federal Executive's daily labors is not to say the executive is a purposely evil fellow. Not at all. The hypothetical D. Chief and his actual counterparts are devoted men—each is devoted to the welfare of his institution as he sees it, devoted to the institution's employees; even devoted, he would claim, to the public interest furthered by the important activities of his institution. As we have seen before, however, the welfare of the institution means its continued operation, not what is necessarily the public weal.

Virtue

Well, the disgruntled Federal Executive may say, looking at the table demonstrating the negative results of his arduous labors: "What do you expect me to do, let the shop go down the drain?"[1] The question is worth answering.

President Harry S. Truman used to say proudly: "The buck stops here."[2] Chiefs, to the extent they are buck-stoppers,

---

[1] "Shop" is a useful Government word meaning the organization one heads; its homeliness indicates (1) easy control of the institutional apparatus; (2) a sense of proprietorship in the speaker; and (3) that something useful is manufactured.

[2] "BUCK: The buck is a token usually used to liven up the game of Draw Poker. Initially it goes to the winner of the first pot. When it becomes the turn of the player with the buck to deal he may either pass the buck to the player at his left or put the buck in the center and name what variation of poker he will deal." *Oswald Jacoby on Poker* (New York: Doubleday, 1957)

can do things that nonchiefs cannot. The principal glory and opportunity of a man who stops the buck is that he can behave like a human being. Those within the institution, subject to institutional discipline, are human beings to be sure, but they are human beings whose actions are inevitably part of the institutional action.

The man at the top, the chief, has at least a possibility of adding a few rare ingredients to his institution's actions. These ingredients are the human virtues.

Human virtues are the product of the judgments of an individual human mind. Charity and compassion, decency, and all the virtues both high and low cannot be attributed to an institution's action, but only to an individual's action. Morality is a concept with meaning only for a single human being; if I do good I am moral, and if I do evil I am immoral. An army, a hospital, a regulatory agency, any institution whatsoever does not partake of human virtue.

Our Laws demonstrate that the morality and the decency of an act and the truth of a statement are considerations institutionally irrelevant. The same demonstration could be carried forward to show that thrift is irrelevant, that compassion is irrelevant, that justice is irrelevant, that any human virtue is irrelevant to any institution's functioning. Such virtues can be added to institutional acts and decisions, but only by an individual not considering himself a part of the organization. Since we define virtues as attributes flowing only from the judgments of an individual human mind, the next Law follows at once:

LAW OF NON-DELEGABLE
DUTIES

The various virtues (e.g., morality, decency, common sense) are ingredients that can be added to institutional acts and decisions only by one not a part of the institution.

This Law is not a startling one, and was foreshadowed by the demonstration that morality and truth were irrelevant to institutional actions, because the institutional actions *must* be taken without moral judgment. Since an individual insider is (by definition) subject to institutional discipline, the insider *in his institutional capacity* cannot be depended upon to act humanely, or truthfully. In his personal, or noninstitutional, or human-being capacity a man can be kind, compassionate and honest; as a part of an institution he cannot.[3]

When the preacher gets on the subject of Virtue, the congregation begins to shift uneasily in the pews. There is something boring about Virtue. We are always told that we should be virtuous and that we are not sufficiently so. At the same time, the virtues are dull things indeed compared to the vices. Each of the seven deadly sins has its own glitter. A little gluttony, a little lust, a little sloth, makes the day pass. In contrast, the cardinal virtues are joyless negatives: "Continence, anybody?" As a result, lectures on Virtue are to be avoided at all cost, and even the penetrating reader of this book may be indignant at suddenly coming upon an old and dull subject. It is much more amusing to prove that a Government institution is amoral than it is to consider how it could be made moral.

---

[3] "The individual bureaucrat cannot squirm out of the apparatus in which he is harnessed . . . in the great majority of cases, he is only a single cog in an ever-moving mechanism which prescribes to him an essentially fixed route of march." Gerth and Mills, *From Max Weber* (Oxford, 1958).

Nevertheless, with apologies, and at the risk of glazing the eyes of the audience, a few more words on the subject of Virtue are required. If it will ease the pain, substitute the phrase "Sound Human Judgment" for "Virtue."

As the word "Virtues" is used in the Law of Non-Delegable Duties, it is a most inclusive term. Common sense and good taste are "Virtues" which must be added to institutional actions. They will not spontaneously appear on the scene. So is thrift a virtue; so is truthfulness; so is sufficient human decency to attend to it that political prisoners are not mangled, beaten or jabbed with electric goads.

Only a few brief examples need be offered of the institutional absence of the less recognizable Virtues. Thrift, for example, is not a widely observable attribute of institutions. Every salesman of hard goods to the Government knows that the month of June is a good month for orders. The reason is, of course, that the fiscal year ends on June 30, and monies appropriated but not spent for the dying fiscal year will suffer the irredeemable fate of being "returned to the Treasury." The Institutional Imperative predicts that funds will be spent, and spent they are, before midnight June 30. "Thrift" does not reside in institutional action; thrift resides only in the individual judgment that money need not be spent.

Good taste is another matter of personal judgment not often evident in institutional actions. A leading architectural example in Washington is the Rayburn (or third) House Office Building on Capitol Hill. There was the glory that was Greece, and the grandeur that was Rome, and now we have the expensive marble mishmash produced by the Office of the Architect of the Capitol.

The concept of good taste goes a little farther than artistic taste. It includes the sense not to propose digging ditches with atomic bombs; not to turn natural wonders into ranges for target practice; and not to publish a "body count" even assuming one is made.

As for truth, well, the lack of truthfulness now has an official name: "credibility gap." This is not a mountain pass in Montana, but Governmentese for the growing public realization that Government departments are not designed as organs of the truth.[4] The public's belief is solidly based on fact and, as demonstrated, on Institutional Law. The gap can never be closed without an individual personal judgment that the truth should be told.

High on the list of Virtues needed but institutionally lacking is that almost indefinable quality of common sense. This implies both seeing things in proper perspective and recognizing facts as facts. The flow of information to the head of an institution is almost perfectly designed to insure distorted perspective. The daily demands on the time of the institutional executive, and the resultant need to acquire predigested facts, reinforce the insider's view of the institution in relation to the world.

Viewed from the inside, of course, the high purpose of the institution is seen as whatever it is doing (Third Axiom). The head of the institution, if he sees himself as a part of it, will share this view. All facts reaching him are first passed through the Institutional filter and selected with the perceived purpose of the institution always in mind. A moment's thought shows that the filtering of facts—briefing—*is* an institutional action and is subject to the Institutional Imperative. Thus, the fact-filtering always produces facts designed to continue institutional activities.[5]

---

[4] Note the institutional reaction to being caught lying: apply a name to the shame like "credibility gap," and then consider it an institutional task to erase the public impression of lying (without stopping the lies).

[5] Evidence: within many federal agencies a daily press digest is prepared and circulated. The digester does not select articles of general or theoretical importance, but only "relevant" reports dealing with the institution's specific subject

The institutional absence of the virtues of decency and humanity has been dwelt upon at length above; the thumbscrew is an institutional device, as is the napalm bomb. Hospitals may heal the sick, but compassion belongs only to the single human being.

Without extending the sermon unduly, a final Virtue may be named: humility. The opposite of humility is arrogance, a quality every institution displays in great abundance. The reason is not far to seek: arrogance flows from the certainty of being right, and every institution is perceived from within as being always and eternally right and never, never wrong. (Law of Institutional Admissions).

It might be thought that the absence of human virtues might be repaired in institutions by appointing special institutional officers to assure their presence. Let there be, say, an Assistant Secretary of Defense for Thrift, an Under Secretary of State for Morality, and by all means, a Special White House Assistant for Humility. The nonexistence of such functionaries reveals a truth: nobody is trying to be thrifty, moral, and certainly not humble.

Fallacy of the Staff

The harassed man at the top of the institution invariably seeks help in the making of his decisions and the discharge of his apparently overflowing duties. The device for seeking help is the personal staff, a group of employees whose ostensible purpose is to help the top man do his job.

---

matter. An Air Force press digest, for example, would not report a food riot in Harlem, a student sit-in in Ohio, or a taxpayer's strike in Kansas, although the Air Force might well need such information to make informed procurement judgments *if* procurement judgments would include judgments not to procure. Let some future Ph.D. candidate study the predisgested information flowing up to agency heads, and he will learn something about the perceived purpose of the agencies he studies.

To some extent, a staff is both inevitable and efficient. It is inevitable because the top man cannot answer his own phone, type his own letters, and rush about the department, the country and the world to see that his orders are carried out. A large staff may be required to be sure that a very large institution responds to the top man's commands. If there were no way of assuring compliance with the top decisions, the institution would splinter into several parts. Administrators know that such splintering can occur. For example, although the FBI is nominally a part of the Department of Justice, in effect the head of the FBI has been independent of the Attorney General.[6]

The staff is thus seen as a desirable instrument for exercising command, and so it is. The temptation is then to use the staff in other fields, particularly those fields where the top man knows he can devote all too little time. One of these fields is thinking, and the attempt to delegate the operation is a failure, always and totally. The reason for the failure is that the staff is a sub-institution, that is to say, an institution responsive to the Institutional Laws already exposed. As an institution, the staff views the staff's work as the ultimate purpose; unconsciously or not the staff becomes arrogant, the staff believes the staff knows best.

Most business in or out of Washington is done with the staff—it has to be, because the top man is either too busy to see you or too uninformed to talk rationally to you. The staff man's attitude, not just sometimes but invariably, is that the staff man knows best. D. Chief doesn't know the details, so how could he decide? So the staff man decides. If he agrees, then the word is "leave it to me and I'll brief the Chief, and he'll go along." Naturally the chief will go along, because he will know nothing

---

[6]Anecdote: J. Howard McGrath, as Attorney General, applies for late night admission to the Department of Justice building. The guard does not recognize him and refuses entrance. McGrath: "But I'm the Attorney General!" Guard: "I don't care if you're J. Edgar Hoover, you can't get in."

about the affair but what the staff man tells him. As every lawyer knows, if you let me state the facts, you can argue the law all you want.

These characteristics of the staff have been known for centuries. In *War and Peace* there is "the peculiar contempt with which a commander in chief's orderly speaks to officers . . ."[7] It is easy to imagine the same scene in the Egypt of the Pharaohs.

As we noted earlier, while there are no Assistant Secretaries for Humility in Government, there are assistant thinkers— Deputies for Ratiocination. These are actually titled policy planners; every respectably sized agency has its policy staff.

The concept of a policy staff is a very odd one, no matter what "policy" means. First, if "policy" means what the institution *should* be doing—that is, what the institution's purpose is —why does the institution exist at all if its purpose is not known? The Fire Department doesn't need a policy staff to say why the Fire Department exists. Second, if "policy" means the selection of methods to achieve an established goal, then it would be better called "planning"; one "plans" how to get to a desired objective. Third, if "policy" means the setting of rules of right action, then "policy" decisions ought to be moral, decent, humane—in short, virtuous. For example, "policy" statements should read:

(a) "It is our policy not to ship arms to dictatorships."

(b) "It is our policy not to kill innocent civilians."

(c) "It is our policy not to waste the public's money."

---

[7] *War and Peace,* Maude & Maude translation (New York: Simon & Schuster, 1954).

(d) "It is our policy to tell the truth,
     even when we have been wrong."

All the foregoing are evidently desirable policies, and all are equally evidently the exact opposite of institutional policies in force. It seems as if such good policy judgments cannot emerge from a "policy" staff. And our body of Laws confirms this at once. A staff, including a policy staff, is an institution, and as we have seen, the Virtues are (and are defined as) the product of an individual human mind. By the Institutional Imperative, institutional actions and decisions must continue the work of the institutional machinery—truth, morality and all other Virtues are irrelevant. Hence, there follows the:

LAW OF INDIVIDUAL JUDGMENT

**The judgments of an individual human
mind resulting in the virtues cannot be
created by a staff.**

In other words, a staff cannot make what we have called "virtuous" decisions because the staff adopts overriding institutional goals. A staff decision cannot be moral if the institution's purpose is more important than morality. Although this is evidently true in practice, two objections can be raised, which can be disposed of quickly.

First, it may be objected, why cannot a group of men, a staff, agree to be moral? If A can make a moral judgment, cannot A call in B, C and D and tell them to go confer and come back with moral judgments? Those making such an objection have missed the whole point. Agreed that Messrs. B, C, and D *individually* are just as capable of moral judgments as A, the man at the top. But when B, C, and D are functioning at A's direction, under the institutional discipline of A's institution, they must accept whatever the institution does. They thus cannot *act* virtuously because they must accept what the institution ultimately does even if they think it wrong. Or to put it another way, the man at the top cannot delegate his individual moral responsibility.

A second and currently popular way of trying to squirm off the moral hook is the "option" method. The option method goes halfway and admits that the man at the top must bear the responsibility. But then, since he is so busy, let there be assigned to the eager staff the task of looking into all possible alternative actions, listing all the pros and cons, putting them all in a fat black notebook and giving the notebook to the man at the top. In this way the man at the top will decide, and the decision will not be institutional, but virtuous. Right? No. Dead wrong.

The business of the option book is but a way of concealing the staff's position—that is, the institutional action of the staff. "All the options" do not appear in the option book, because the staff has selected only "feasible" options. That is, the options selected as "feasible" are feasible in the staff's opinion. Hence the staff has already made an institutional, nonmoral judgment. Further, and any lawyer knows this, the arguments pro and con, the selected options, *must* of necessity contain staff judgments: there is no need to mention this point, that point is foolish, here is a point to be stressed. Still further, the option book is limited in size. The man at the top has little time. The Pentagon Papers occupied forty-seven volumes, ran only through 1968 and, so it was said, were still not the "whole story." So, in the option book, you may be sure that there is a radical selection of "important" facts—again, an institutional decision.

Finally, as we have proved, the option book cannot ever contain a moral argument. Nowhere in the Pentagon Papers is there a thought for the civilians killed. Institutions, which means staffs, cannot talk morally.

The White House, where the buck stops, is the place to test these conclusions. If our Institutional Laws apply in the White House as elsewhere, we shall have run out of test cases, and we will then claim the Laws are true.

16. INSTITUTIONAL DISASTERS AT THE WHITE HOUSE

True Democratic and Republican Anecdote. "Honchos."
Duties of the Staff—Honchos in Action. Do-It-Yourself.
Predigested Thinking. Case of the Bay of Pigs. Vietnam.

In late twentieth-century America, the President of the United
States is the focus of all Government power and the fount of
all policies. The Congress is visibly reduced to a set of petty
baronies, incapable of either defining purpose or seeing to it that
the Executive Department carries out such duties as the Congress lays upon it.

It has long been evident that no one human being could
discharge the President's duties. It would be easier to grow an
extra head than to do all that the people of the United States
expect of a President. The President needs assistance, and this
assistance must be provided by a staff. The staff of the President
is an institution with a phenomenal growth rate. As usual, the
institutional expansion has nothing to do with its success. Neither Democratic nor Republican staffs have appreciated their
institutional limits. For instance:

217

True Democratic Anecdote

An important member of President Johnson's staff was asked off the record: How was the basic mistake about Vietnam made? How did the President make such an error, how did his advisers permit it? The answer was institutionally predictable. The Important man shook his head. "I just don't understand it. We did everything possible, we analyzed the problem every possible way. Why, we identified twenty-five separate options for the President to consider, with reasons for and against each one! I just don't understand it."

True Republican Anecdote

A member of President Nixon's staff, now translated to higher office, described his work as follows: "Every morning we meet to see what Congress is up to, and then we decide what our policy is."

"Honchos"

Before considering the import of these vignettes, a bit of vocabulary is in order. "Honcho," noun, means the man who has the staff job of seeing that something is done with the authority of the top man; he is the "can do" man, the expediter, the performer.[1] Of course, by immutable rules of Washington grammar, "honcho" is also a verb. Usage:

"Who is your honcho on the Persimmon Negotiations?"

"Jones, you honcho Project Pomegranate."

---

[1] Current usage as a noun: "One of Attorney General John Mitchell's top honchos is on the pan on Capitol Hill . . ." *The Washington Sunday Star*, August 15, 1971.

The White House honcho is a very important honcho, naturally. He is also a relative newcomer on the Washington scene (the word is probably a Lyndon Johnson-era usage). The question is: is he a desirable addition?

Duties of the Staff—Honchos in Action

Since the office existed, the President has had a staff. Their accepted functions have included:

1. *Service and ceremony*—no one expects the President to answer the telephone or write flowery citations.

2. *Enforcement*—a President needs someone to see that his orders are carried out.

3. *Personal representation*—a President often needs a trusty man to carry a special message or make a little political deal with a useful mayor.

4. *Advice*—the Senate's constitutional function of advising and consenting being a little hard for a President to take, Presidents have always had private advisers, kitchen cabinets, Bernard Baruchs. Bourbon is the preferred drink in the kitchen.

In recent years these functions have been overshadowed by the huge staffs devoted to (5) *field operations* and (6) *doing the President's thinking.* Item 5 is, of course, the specialty of the honcho. He goes out and gets things done—in fact, he does them himself. He becomes for the moment an executive department, with more power in the premises than any of the departments. Naturally, honchoing is a tough job, and naturally the honcho requires a staff. Since the honcho's business is by definition Very Important, the staff will grow very rapidly. In short, the honcho becomes an instant institution, complete in all respects. The Office of the Honcho is then subject to the immutable Institutional Laws, with results to be noted shortly.

Do-It-Yourself

Presidents who think it important to be active find it almost irresistible to appoint honchos. They come into office faced with a monster bureaucracy. Their plans, wise or not, disappear into the fog as soon as they are proclaimed. The job of reorganizing the departments is lengthy and unattractive, and the idea of asking Cabinet officers to spend their time in redesigning institutions does not occur. Besides, the Cabinet officers are as new as the President, and could not redesign the machinery if they wanted to. Thus, the way to get something done is to create a new institution right in the President's office, ready to do his bidding. This move is especially attractive if the President regards the existing Government machinery as staffed with enemies from the preceding Administration. It is also attractive to Presidents who lack experience with institutional operations and insight into the way institutions work. All in all, the temptations to do-it-yourself around the White House are irresistible. But, doing it yourself works no better around the White House than around most other houses.

One trouble with the do-it-yourself solution ought to be easily recognized. The President is not doing it himself, he is only adding one more layer of institution to the already existing layers of institutions. The inevitable consequences are the duplications, coordinations, liaison meetings, briefings and the rest.

The second danger of doing-it-yourself is equally familiar in terms of our Laws. The Office of the Honcho is an institution, and it is driven by the Institutional Imperative to keep functioning. When an ordinary institutional part of the Government presents its inevitable arguments for keeping the institution busy, at least in theory, the President can reject them. If the Bureau of Colossal Projects wants to build a twelve-lane super-highway down Pennsylvania Avenue for all the appropriately urgent reasons, the President can say no. But the moment the Office of the President has set up machinery to build twelve-lane roads, then twelve-lane roads we shall have. The dangers are obvious.

The General Law of Institutional Self-Occupation applies with immense force to the White House staff, right at the top, dealing with crisis, war and peace, life and death. If the staff becomes a Special Operations Group, men of steel (with supporting staffs) ready to move in on any detected crisis, the General Law dictates that crisis will be detected. Battleship admirals will find needs for battleships, welfare agencies will astutely discover welfare cases, and White House honchos will find crises worthy of their mettle.

Finally, there is a more indirect effect of White House overactivity. This is the slow corrosion of the great officers of Government heading the departments. Our Laws reveal that a very heavy set of nondelegable duties rests on the man at the top of any institution. He alone can add to his institution's actions the indispensable ingredients of morality, decency, and common sense. And thus, if he is left in charge, he can be properly accused of dereliction in his most important duties if his institution's actions have not been moral, or decent, or sensible. Once the White House takes over a portion of the operation, the Cabinet officer has lost personal, human responsibility. He has become part of the institution and he has, in a serious way, lost his ability to be virtuous. By relieving Cabinet officers of the hard personal decisions, the President robs himself of responsible assistance when he most badly needs it.

Former Secretary of State Dean Acheson describes the right and the wrong way in *Present at the Creation:*[2]

> President Truman's strength lay not only in knowing that he was the President and that the buck stopped with him, but that neither he nor the White House staff was the Secretary of State, or Defense, or Treasury, or any other. To him the heads of departments were secretaries of state and members of his staff, as Lord Burghley was to the first Elizabeth. He made the ultimate decisions upon full and detailed knowledge, leaving to lieutenants the execution. This conception of the supreme role runs the risk that a lieutenant may fail as Longstreet did at Gettysburg or MacArthur in North Korea. The other conception runs the greater and more hazardous risk that the chief will fail in his infinitely more important role. It was such a failure, I fear, that blighted the high promise of President Johnson's administration.

Predigested Thinking

The last branch of modern White House staff activity consists of trying to do the President's thinking. The staff digests, the staff analyzes, the staff runs up reasons pro and con and presents options in option books. The reasons why the act of thinking cannot be delegated have been covered at length in the previous chapter; the result is summarized in the Law of Individual Judgment: individual human judgment cannot be created by a staff. It cannot be done, it will not work.

Staff thinking is institutional action; it results in expert judgments which cannot be believed (Law of Institutional Expertise) and to which truth and morality, if not strangers, are at least irrelevant (Laws of Institutional Irrelevancy of Truth,

---
[2]Signet ed., 1969.

Morality, and Humanity). The institutionalized staff admits no mistakes (Law of Institutional Admissions), and it finds important reasons justifying its action (Law of Institutional Self-Justification).

A few examples give tangible meaning to these predicted results of institutionalizing the staff. The Democratic anecdote at the beginning of this chapter is a fair example. The staff gets up a list of twenty-five different possibilities in Vietnam, and somehow the result is not just punk but putrid. Of course it is. The inevitable process of selection, of institutional processing, assured that the list would be not only useless but also positively harmful, because it only *appeared* to include "all possibilities." While the list of twenty-five options is not public, it is a safe bet that the real hard questions and tough arguments were not on it.

Or consider the Republican anecdote at the start of the chapter. Machinery is set up to review Congress' work. To what purpose? That is not specified. The machinery is there, and it had better operate—see what Congress is doing and tell them to stop it.

A very bright professor said, warning of the dangers of staffs: "The staff on which modern executives come to depend develop a momentum of their own. What starts out as an aid to decision-makers often turns into a practically autonomous organization whose internal problems structure and sometimes compound the issues which it was originally designed to solve . . . The internal requirements of the bureaucracy may come to predominate over the purposes which it was intended to serve." He added, "serving the machine becomes a more absorbing occupation than defining its purpose."[3] The author was Dr. Henry Kissinger, in the days before he followed his teachings and became President Nixon's Assistant for National Security

---

[3] *American Foreign Policy, Three Essays* (New York: Norton, 1969).

Affairs. He saw that "The ultimate decision often depends less on knowledge than on the ability to brief the top administrator . . ."

Further following the teachings of Professor Kissinger, Presidential Assistant Kissinger's White House staff is growing like crabgrass, and the Doctor is daily taking more and more operating responsibility himself. Whether any policy of Dr. Kissinger is brilliant or flawed is not in issue. The real danger is the one he himself both saw and succumbed to.

Case of the Bay of Pigs

A famous example of a really bad White House decision is John F. Kennedy's decision to approve the invasion of Castro's Cuba at the Bay of Pigs. A relevant inquiry is, what was missing?

Surely one could not say expert opinion was missing. President Kennedy had the advice of the CIA, whose operation it was, as well as all the other experts in the field: State, Defense and the whole crowd. He did not lack for a White House staff of accredited intellectuals. Yet on the morning after, the whole adventure was a shambles, the American image was battered, men died—it was a total failure.

Our Laws reveal two causes for the disaster. First and obviously, President Kennedy forgot the institutional theory he knew as a successful Washington operative. He was impressed by the Attributes of Importance, the Aura of Expertness with which phony judgments were handed him. He knew—he had to know—that an institution's advice and opinions will keep the institution's machinery functioning—he knew the Imperative, but he forgot until the next morning reminded him.

The second cause in the disaster was the lack of that indispensable ingredient—common sense. Common sense is a virtue that, our Law states, does not reside in institutional actions or advices. The common sense of the Cuban situation at the time was this: (1) Castro had just thrown out the highly corrupt and unpopular Batista regime; (2) Castro had just divided up the land holdings among the peasantry and opened the private beach clubs to the city dwellers; (3) the revolution had been received with every show of popular enthusiasm—it was too early for staged mass meetings. Items 1, 2 and 3 are not after-the-fact insights but matters painfully obvious at the time. Every American businessman confirmed the previous corruption; the newspapers reported Castro's decrees; and all travelers reported the strong initial enthusiasm for Castro. Beards were definitely in.

The question of common sense was: would the peasants rush to beaches to welcome back the landlords?[4] To state the question is to answer it—so it must be assumed that the question was not so put to the President. So much for the option book.

A President, however, has a nondelegable duty of exercising his common sense. Common sense must be exercised in the face of the most urgent, expert and important reasons to make a decision a particular way, because *all* decisions recommended to a President are urgent and important and recommended by the most weighty experts. Only urgent matters get to a President. Only expert opinions are laid before him as evidence. A President needs to recite the Law of Institutional Expertise once an hour.

---

4 "And the operation as a whole was a humiliating and costly flop. The wisdom of hindsight suggests that it never should have been launched in the first place —or at least, not without considerably more convincing evidence that the invaders would be welcome." Crozier, *The Masters of Power* (Boston: Little, Brown, 1969).

Vietnam

We return, for the last time, to the war in Vietnam. One President was broken by the adventure, a second has had immense difficulties in disengaging.

The first cause of the Vietnam mistake is plainly the direct involvement of the White House staff with the whole mess. As Vietnam became a White House Operation, as the decisions were White House decisions, as the White House staff and the President himself became part of the institution running the war, the Laws of Institutional Behavior applied with a vengeance. It is impossible for an institution to admit a mistake (by Law[5]). It is impossible, within the institution, to see any purpose but running the machinery.[6]

The rapid, fungoid growth of the Vietnam involvement is the direct result of the General Law of Institutional Self-Occupation. Set up a working group, give it Vietnam as its subject, and the rest follows inexorably.

The failure of institutional design was complete. We read in the Pentagon Papers a memorandum from McGeorge Bundy, special assistant for national security affairs, *written during a trip by Bundy* and department officials to Vietnam: *"We believe* that the best available way of increasing our chance of success in Vietnam is the development and execution of a policy of *sustained reprisal* against North Vietnam . . ."[7] Instead of reviewing and advising, Bundy is out in the field, operating.

---

[5]Mistakes are not called mistakes, but "hard decisions." So today, many of the White House advisers to President Johnson still insist that the Vietnam policy —their policy—was correct. No doubt they honestly believe what they say. Yet these same men would see their work product as a failure if it had been someone else's policy, someone else's operation.

[6]"The American war effort had, then, become almost entirely solipsistic: the United States government was trying to save 'American prestige' for Americans alone, to convince itself of American superiority." Frances Fitzgerald, "Vietnam," *The New Yorker*, July 22, 1972.

[7]*The Pentagon Papers* (Bantam ed., 1971), Document #92, McGeorge Bundy to President Johnson, February 7, 1965.

No one was left outside the Vietnam institution to advise the President. Bundy was one of the "we" believing, and his memoranda are institutional products—perfectly predictable in that they recommend carrying on the work of the institution. The memoranda are also classic institutional products in that they are cold, ice cold, inhuman and inhumane.[8]

Finally, we see in the White House action groups the causes contributing to the very worst aspects of the Vietnam War, the lying, the "body counts," the defoliation, the destruction of the people and the country. Of institutions, our Laws show that such immoral behavior can be expected. The man at the top of the institution has the nondelegable duty to be moral. This duty is shirked when the most important control, the man at the top, is absorbed into the institution itself.[9]

---

[8]The Pentagon Papers also illuminate the expected military advice. Here is a memorandum from the Joint Chiefs of Staff of October 14, 1966, responding to a disillusioned McNamara's conclusions that bombing North Vietnam was a failure. "I see no reasonable way to bring the war to an end soon," said McNamara. Instantly ("obviously forewarned"), the Joint Chiefs whip out a counter-memo:

> "Certainly no one—American or foreigner—except those who are determined not to be convinced, can doubt the sincerity, the generosity, the altruism of U. S. actions and objectives." *The Pentagon Papers* (Bantam ed., 1971), Document #119, Joint Chiefs to Secretary McNamara, October 14, 1966.

Plainly, when the Joint Chiefs are giving advice on the subjects of generosity and altruism, there is a serious flaw in the design of the institution. The proper functions of the Joint Chiefs and the College of Cardinals are separate.

[9]Not for a minute should the men close to the top, the Bundys, et al., be excused from their moral duties. These fellows are always upset when booed at a lecture, as if being a Presidential adviser was a license to kill. Boo!

17. HOW TO GET THERE FROM HERE (INSTITUTIONAL SUCCESS)

The Technological Labors of Hercules. Aspects of Success: First, Identity of Ostensible and Internal Purpose; Second, Setting the Pattern of Work; Third, Money (Case of Project Seltzer); Fourth, Czardoms. Final Aspect of Success: Operation of the Law of Reflexive Purpose.

The evidence of the preceding pages to the contrary, not every institution is a disaster. Sometimes the institution's budget would be better deposited directly in the can marked "waste"; but sometimes, somehow, the machinery works.

You need not look far for examples of institutions in glowing health. How about, say, the National Football League? There is institutional success for you, profit, glory, broken legs, satisfied customers. Horse racing is well and happy as a sport and a business; so is crap-shooting in Nevada.

On occasion, even the big jobs come off. To build the pyramids required men and organization. Somewhere under the sands there are the Pharaoh's organization charts for Project Pyramid or Operation Sphinx, complete with Bureaus of Hieroglyphic Design and Deputy Assistant High Priests for

Incantations. Yet the pyramids were built, to the greater glory
of a vanished institution, and we too have our successes.

The Technological
Labors of Hercules

The power of properly designed institutional machinery is
awesome to contemplate. In the good old days when the monarch commanded the sea to lie still, or to roll back, it was
considered a distinct mark of divine intervention when the sea
obeyed. Today, to get the children of Israel across the sea
dry-shod would be a minor exercise in hydraulic engineering—
the only question would be whether the State Department ap-
proves the children of Israel crossing any more national bound-
aries.

Of the labors set modern institutions, three commands
capture the imagination:

1. Walk on the Moon.

2. Create a Nuclear Explosion.

3. Cure Infantile Paralysis.

The first labor was accomplished by the National
Aeronautics and Space Administration; the second by the Manhattan District and the other predecessors of the Atomic Energy Commission; the third by a private institution, the National Foundation for Infantile Paralysis (the "March of
Dimes"). If the human race returns to nomadic savagery a few
years from now, these miracles will be reported with Biblical
awe: "And the President said unto them, walk thou on the
Moon, and Lo! they walked."

The methods of scientific investigation employed by

NASA, the Atomic Bomb project, and the March of Dimes appear to be broadly similar. In each case, a great deal of money was spent. In each case, all possible promising lines of investigation were followed. The methods of the Manhattan District are well documented.[1] Every possible method of accumulating sufficient radioactive material to reach a critical mass was energetically explored, from gas diffusion to mass spectroscopy, often at great cost. The work was pressed forward on several fronts at once, although in the end some methods were dropped as impractical. The Smyth Report explains:

> In a memorandum written to Bush on May 14, 1942
> . . . Conant estimated that there were five separation
> or production methods which were about equally
> likely to succeed. . . . All were considered about ready
> for pilot plant construction and perhaps even for
> preliminary design of production plants. If the methods were to be pushed to the production stage, a
> commitment of five hundred million dollars would be
> entailed. Although it was too early to estimate the
> relative merits of the different methods accurately, it
> was presumed that some methods would prove to be
> more rapid and efficient than others. It was feared,
> however, that elimination of any one method might
> result in a serious delay.

Approximately the same procedure was followed by the infantile paralysis researchers, who labored in many vineyards for thirty years before one vine bore fruit. Many of NASA's problems appear to have been attacked in similar fashion, with various alternatives explored before the lunar hardware took its final and successful shape.

Several common aspects of these great successes strike the eye at once:

---

[1]See the famous Smyth Report, published under the terse title *A General Account of the Methods of Using Atomic Energy for Military Purposes under the Auspices of the United States Government* (GPO, 1945).

First Aspect of Success:
Identity of Ostensible and Internal Purpose.

First to be noted as of prime significance is that *the ostensible purposes and the purposes of the institutional machinery were identical.* The *ostensible purpose* of any institution is, of course, always something very high-sounding: defense, health, security. The *purpose of the institutional machinery,* however, is what counts, for that is what the machinery does—which is all the institution does (First Axiom). "Purpose of the institutional machinery" is the same as "perceived purpose within the institution" (Third Axiom).

In any event, the ostensible purposes in our three examples were evidenced in the institutional machinery. To create explosive nuclear fission was the purpose of the Project, as well as the purpose of each major part of the machinery. You could not point at any large segment of the work of NASA, of the Manhattan District, or the polio research effort and say that the work going on in the sub-institutional segment was not directed to the institutional goal. To achieve such unity of ostensible and perceived purpose required that another, second, condition be satisfied.

Second Aspect of Success:
Setting the Pattern of Work

Second, in order to achieve equation of institutional purpose with ostensible purpose, *the goal was stated simply in terms which had solid operational meaning.* Each of the three goals under review could be and was stated in at most four simple English words: "Walk on the Moon." Each goal was solidly, concretely, expressed in terms of the operations of the institutional machinery. Such clarity and solid meaning are absolutely necessary if the ostensible purpose is to be reflected in what the institution really does.

If success in institutional design means creating an institution that will achieve its intended purpose, then the secret of success must boil down to this recipe:

1. The ostensible purpose—the goal—must be stated precisely.

2. The ostensible purpose must be expressed in words which have clear meaning in terms of setting the pattern of work within the institution (this *is* the institutional machinery—by definition).

3. If the pattern of work within the institution is set to correspond with the ostensible purpose, the institution will operate to accomplish its goal.

In even simpler terms: if you don't *know* what the goal of your institution is, the institution won't reach it. You don't *know* the goal (in any meaningful way), unless you can tell the workers within the institution what they ought to be doing.

For example, take the case of the rate-regulating agencies, discussed above. Personnel, knowledge, and energy are available. Why don't the agencies reach their goals? The answer is: they have not been given any meaningful goal. To command an agency to see that "rates are reasonable" is—in operational terms—meaningless. If you do not know what you mean by "reasonable," then how can the pattern of work within the agency be set? Exactly what is the Agency for Reasonableness Investigation supposed to investigate? And further, if you cannot define "reasonableness," how will you know whether the agency has ever achieved its goal? A goal which cannot be defined cannot be reached. To say "keep rates cheap" is meaningful, as it is to say "keep rates 10 percent above cost." To say "keep rates reasonable" is without meaning, and the agencies ought not be blamed for their futile labors.

Third Aspect of Success:
Money (Case of Project Seltzer)

Returning to the Moon walk, the bomb, and the Salk vaccine, a third common ingredient of success is visible. The secret ingredient is that popular favorite, money in large quantities. Money has both an obvious and a concealed function. Sufficient funds to buy equipment are of course necessary in any technical work, although it is hard to judge how much is really needed. Would success have been achieved with half the money? Probably so, if it were not for the concealed function of liberal funding.

This concealed function of liberality is to avoid internal fights over funds. The danger is not just time wasted by the infighting. The danger is that internal fights over funding have the inevitable effect of fragmenting the purposes of the parts of the institution. The effect of scarce money is automatic and devastating. It can be illustrated with an imaginary case.

Consider the Interstellar Travel Administration. Funds are not sufficient for all avenues of rocket-drive development. The part of the Administration devoted, say, to developing a krypton-fueled rocket drive comes into conflict for funds with the part developing a drive fueled with soda water. At once, the Office of Krypton Fuels redefines its purpose not as traveling to the stars, but as developing a krypton-fueled drive. The Office of Soda Water, no less squeezed by the implacable Institutional Imperative, at once takes action to continue the vital soda-water development ("Project Seltzer"). All expert energies are thereupon devoted to giving expert opinions pro-Seltzer or pro-Krypton (Law of Institutional Expertise). The goals of the sub-institutions have shifted from the stars to sheer institutional survival.

Demonstrations of operating Krypton-fueled rockets will be arranged convenient to Lake Tahoe by the Office of Krypton Fuels. The Soda-Water forces will counter with a trip to the

Virgin Islands test grounds of Project Seltzer for a subcommittee of six Congressmen to witness the giant siphon in action.
Whether anything gets done toward interstellar travel is dubious, but a lot gets done toward continuing krypton-fuel research and Project Seltzer.

Fourth Aspect of Success:
Czardoms

A fourth common ingredient of successes such as polio
vaccines, Moon shots and atomic bomb projects is well known.
In each case, a new institution was set up to do the assigned
task. The atomic bomb was developed in a special autonomous
project; NASA is not a part of the Bureau of Roads; all polio
funds were not handed over to some existing medical laboratory. New and separate institutions are created in the belief that
their goals will be better reached free of the entangling and
conflicting purposes of existing institutions. A separate institution is created to be single-minded and to ignore other goals.
The call is for a "czar" to see that a particular job is done. The
Army might have spent the atomic bomb money on tanks, the
Navy on ships. The Department of Transportation—had it
been in existence—might have spent the Moon-shot money on
subways or SSTs.

Creation of new institutions (always for high and overriding single purposes) calls into effect an equal and opposite
reaction. Conflicts with other institutions appear. "There has
not been a ranking of national priorities" it is said. Fragmenta-
tion is duly bemoaned, lack of coordination is noted, and steps
are taken. Typical steps are coordinating committees; liaison
representatives; interdepartmental planning groups; and, inevitably, super-agencies designed to swallow the existing pygmies.
A nongovernment example is the United Givers Fund; a Gov-

ernment example is supplied by any of the large departments
—for example, the absorption of the Agency for International
Development into the State Department.

Final Aspect of Success:
Operation of the Law
of Reflexive Purpose.

It is instructive to note what has happened to these three
institutions selected as examples of success. For in each case,
success implied that the institution had accomplished its reason
for being. The Law of Reflexive Purpose predicts what will
happen in such cases.

The Atomic Energy institution fared best. There were at
hand two excellent reasons for continued existence, related to
its original purpose. Further development of atomic weapons
was a natural substitute pastime, and so was peacetime use of
atomic reactors for making electricity. "Civilian control" of
atomic energy was the rallying cry in the fight for preservation
of a separate institution, and it worked: the AEC is not within
the Department of Defense. The shift in institutional purpose
was not accompanied without incident. Objections were heard
to endless development of weapons to overkill the enemy more
than ten times. Also, we have already noted the lack of wild
public enthusiasm for the Plowshare projects.[2] Water lily ponds
and canals are still dug without the benefits of atomic explo-
sives.

At the moment, NASA is in considerable trouble. The

---

[2]Some people remain unenthusiastic about nuclear electric power: "This touted
technology, defying human fallibility, sporting huge control panels, computers
and 'defense in depth,' all engineered by masters on the very edge of the impossible, accomplishes only one useful thing: it boils water." Senator Mike Gravel,
letter to *The Washington Post,* July 25, 1972.

Moon shots accomplished, it has not developed successful alternate reasons for existence, and seems headed for budgetary starvation. There was some talk of "keeping the team together" for some other urgent national project, but none turned up. The NASA technology, while stunning, seems difficult to apply to earthbound activities such as trash removal. NASA needs to discover some hostile Martians or a way to put no-return bottles in orbit around Mercury. Get into some growth business, fellows.

The fate of the third of the trio of successful agencies brings a rare smile to the face of the institutional theorist. The result is as perfect, and as predictable, as the forming of a precipitate in a test tube. The March of Dimes, brilliantly successful in that its disease has been wiped out, simply shifted diseases. The Dimes are now marching against birth defects.

18. MANUAL FOR INSTITUTIONAL REPAIR

Question (Again) of the President and Dr. Strangelove.
Three Recommendations. The Sweet Uses of Stupidity.
Sixteen Rules of Institutional Design. Afterword.

The existence of successful institutions proves that institutional machinery can produce results. Our Laws of Institutional Behavior tell us how the machinery always operates. We should be ready, then, not only to diagnose disease, but to prescribe some remedies. We are not going to hold a clinic for the entire sick list of institutions; instead, we provide the intern with a sample operation to view. The subject might as well be important.

Question of the President and Dr. Strangelove

In the chapter on the Pentagon, the question was asked: will the war machinery inevitably lead to war, that is, is Dr. Strangelove in charge? The answer was deferred.

As usual, precision is important, "War machinery" is vague, and can have two meanings. An army is a machine of war, but its internal machinery (the pattern of work assigned) need not cause an army to advocate (that is, see an urgent reason for) war. The Swiss have an army, but not a war. So can we.

The real question is whether we can have a great quantity of institutional machinery whose subject matter is crisis leading to war, without getting into a war. The answer to this depends first on how we design the crisis-dealing institutional machinery, and second, on the actions of those who can stand outside this machinery.

Three Recommendations

There are only a few design remedies, as follows:

I. Those determining that there is a crisis must never be those who deal with crisis (there must be no White House participation in war operations—none).

II. The machinery, that is, the pattern of work assigned to each man, must be extremely carefully designed so that each man knows why he is doing what he is doing; that is, what the institutional purpose of his job is. Thus, if the purpose is to sound alarms, alarms will be sounded. If the purpose is not to alarm but to predict, or advise, decent predictions or advice can be obtained.

III. The triplicated and quadruplicated foreign policy machinery must be disassembled. There is too much of it, it is all dangerous, and it produces nothing of value. There should be one State Department, much smaller, and outside the White House. The Secretary of Defense, the Joint Chiefs, the CIA and all the rest must stop playing State Department. The Secretary of State must be found, if possible, and given a hot meal, a suit of clothes, and a good job.

Even with these precautions, there will be great dangers unless the war and crisis machinery is controlled from the top. The top means the President. The essential qualities of a President are not energy and dash, or political acumen, or even a talent for cool organization. They are the simple human attributes of decency and sense, accompanied by the experience or wisdom to reject institutional pressures offending sense or decency. If he fails in this duty the machinery will run immorally, indecently and without making sense. Failing in his most basic duties, the President will fail as President.

The President's duty to think cannot be delegated. The thinking staffs are at best gadgets and at worst traps. Of course, a President needs advisers, but that is a different matter. An adviser is consulted on a particular matter, an adviser is a wise man talking to a man who needs counsel. A President needs wise men; he does not need his thinking predigested or channeled. There are ample institutions in Government capable of devising programs or canning facts. They must be left to their jobs, with their work product coming under properly suspicious scrutiny in the White House. Competence and success can be obtained institutionally, but virtue cannot.

A good share of the essential Presidential attributes ought to be present in the Cabinet officers. They are, unfortunately, all too quickly captured by the institutions they head; they turn into spokesmen for their business, stewards for their shops. It would be good sound Presidential policy to inform Cabinet officers that they too have non-delegable duties to think like human beings. If operations are returned to the Departments where they belong, Department heads should be responsible— morally responsible—for the actions of their institutions. The same doctrine applies farther down the line. The man who orders the machine-gunning should be as likely to be put on trial as the gunner. A Cabinet officer is as likely a war criminal as a Calley.

Thus, *if* the machinery is redesigned, and *if* the moral responsibilities of office are recognized, the question of Dr. Strangelove may be answered in the negative, and the institutions may be controlled. In the way that a work of art has of revealing the hidden truth, this answer appears in Kubrick's motion picture version of *Dr. Strangelove*. In the movie, you recall, Dr. Strangelove and the President of the United States were played by the same man.

The Sweet Uses of Stupidity

People at the top of the Washington heap, or at the top of any institution, are not dumb. Yet, as we have seen, paralytic institutions are constantly created, incapable of useful movement. Many of those institutions that can function are managed so that we all wish they could not. An extended list of institutions would confer a great boon on humanity by burning themselves to the ground (names on request).

If the creators and managers of institutions were stupid, their disasters could be excused. As they are not, we conclude that the failure is purposeful, and we ask why.

As a final example of a Federal agency chasing its tail, we can offer the Federal Communications Commission in its licensing of television stations. The number of TV channels is limited and so a license to run a TV station is valuable. The FCC has been described as standing on a corner handing out million-dollar bills.

The Congress could have provided the FCC with a fixed machinery for passing out licenses: they could be drawn from a hat, like lottery winners, or they might be auctioned off, with the money for the grant returning to the Treasury.

Instead of such sensible procedures, licenses are granted after hearings of all applicants, with some vague "public interest" standards applied. As nearly as can be ascertained, "public interest" means promising the maximum number of dull programs no one wants to watch (that is how programs are known as good, important, public interest stuff. If viewers *want* to watch a program, it isn't in the public interest). So, the TV applicant prevails who promises to run his station so it has the least viewers during the most hours.

The significant point here is not that the FCC licenses to no purpose. That is a familiar story. The question pressed is why such a charade was begun and continued. The answer is not stupidity, but the familiar vice of hypocrisy. There are worse things for a Congressman or an FCC Commissioner than running the Fun House as it is.

For the Congressman faced with a tough decision, the remedy is evasion. Of course a Congressman could think about a rational system of TV licensing, but why should he? Better to play dumb, take no risks and appoint a Commission with a "public interest" standard.

So also, the Commissioner even more than the Congressman knows the Commission is playing jacks all day. But the Commissioner has a job, and an agency staff he is responsible for, and a sense of self-importance. The temptation to be hypocritical is irresistible for Commissioner or Congressman, and the public interest is therefore exalted in name only.

Stupidity has its sweet uses; far better to be shocked by the inability of an agency to reach the incomprehensible goal than to come right out and say what has to be done. When the river is polluted, your Congressman knows the cause. The cure—which is obvious—is too hard, so your Congressman appoints a Commission, and the Commission disappears into the mucky depths.

All of us play dumb. The Laws of Institutional Behavior here set down are not truly strange. We know which institutions work, and which do not. Prisons do not work. But it is convenient to lock up criminals first and put aside for later the question of what the prison should be doing.

We all know more, a hell of a lot more, than we find it convenient to admit. If we wished, we could insist on moral, honest, purposeful performance from our public and private institutions. We do not, and we go along with the game, because thinking about right and wrong is painful, and fudging along is convenient.

The indictment suits our crimes, and there remains only one last futile attempt to evade personal responsibility for the mess. All this stuff, we may say in a surly tone, all this stuff is theory; a business or a war isn't run by professors of ethics but by practical men.

To a debater, his opponent's appeal to practicality rather than truth is the sign of an argument won. The flat-earthers are losing faith when all they can say is that a round world is not practical. Nevertheless, the challenge to be practical is accepted, and there follow some eminently practical rules. Observe them.

Sixteen Rules of Institutional Design

1. If the purpose of the institution cannot be specifically and solidly stated, do not create the institution. "Specifically and solidly" means with enough precision and content to tell every individual in the institution what his pattern of work is to be, with what objective.

2. The definition of the pattern of work of the individual determines all that will come from an institution. Define it carefully, and check it against the purpose—the result—

desired. Terminate any institutional function where the defined work pattern does not directly achieve the result desired. Most institutions will require an annual checkup, followed by surgery. Cut ruthlessly.

3. Reshuffling an institution's table of organization is largely futile, impressive citizens' commission recommendations to the contrary. If the desired result is not known, who cares how you do not reach it? The sound method is to terminate purposeless activity, not reorganize it.

4. If an organization is plainly not achieving a desired result, investigate to determine whether it has been forbidden to do so. If this is indeed the case, either terminate the institution or gather the courage to let it operate.

5. No institution that deals with emergencies can be allowed to determine the existence of its own emergencies unless they are self-evident (say, fires). Never let an institution create its own subject matter.

6. Do not assign the same work to more than one institution. This rule is so obvious that its regular breach is explicable only by hypocrisy. Two institutions cannot be assigned the same work unless a hard decision is thereby hypocritically avoided.

7. Liaison is the institutional equivalent of illicit sex. If two or more institutions are constantly coordinating, consulting, and attempting liaison, get rid of one or the other. (Do not create an additional coordinating institution.)

8. No personal staff should be allowed to conduct any operations whatsoever, at any time, under any circumstances. If the staff men are so able, make them generals in the field.

9. Never allow anyone on the staff even to purport to think in the name of the boss. If necessary, reassign responsibility for decisions to a subordinate within the institution.

10. Secrecy should be sharply limited, and totally discouraged when possible. The modern Theory of Games teaches

THE INSTITUTIONAL IMPERATIVE

that strategy cannot be successful if based on a secret.[1] Secrecy is used ninety times for effect or to cover ignorance or mistake to once where it is justified.

11. Any individual counseling action which enhances the importance of the individual should be viewed with deep suspicion.

12. Any institution counseling action which leads to enhancing the operation of the institution's machinery should be viewed with deep suspicion.

13. Those who find institutional error should be rewarded and protected; those who conceal it, punished. Cherish your honest Inspector Generals, there aren't many of them.

14. No lie should be countenanced unless it is to be publicly declared within thirty days.

15. The principal task of the individual heading any institution is insuring the operation of the institution in accordance with virtue: morality, decency, common sense. The head is directly and personally responsible, including criminal penalties as necessary, for any failures in this regard.[2] This applies without exception, whether the institution's employees insult the public or merely murder the public.

16. The head of any institution should be selected for two reasons: (a) his ability to judge whether operations are being conducted in accordance with the virtues of morality, decency and common sense, and (b) his ability to depend on his own judgment uninfluenced by experts, by panoply or by false institutional loyalty.

---

[1]Example: in the game of scissors/paper/rock, if you have a secret strategy of playing twice scissors, then twice paper, then twice rock, your opponent is very likely to win because he will discover your pattern.

[2]Distinguish the criminal operation *of the institution* for which the head man should be punished, from the fortuitous criminal act of a single employee of the institution. If the police department is institutionally brutal, the chief is responsible—but not if a single patrolman gets drunk.

Afterword

That concludes the instruction period, and a brief recapitulation is in order.

The Government of the United States of America is not working well. The malfunction is evidently systemic, not a matter of which party is in power or President in office. Failure is consistent. These institutional failures are the result of simple laws, intuitively known to those who need to know them, but stated with clarity only occasionally, and never applied consistently. The rate of institutional failure is accelerating: another Vietnam would collapse the societal foundations.

Our great institutions are out of control. They function as they must in accordance with institutional laws. They are powerful, wasteful and dangerous. Institutions can be better designed, and that is one lesson. Another is that only individual human judgment stands between any institution and a moral disaster.

Each of us has an inescapable human duty never to give our individual conscience to any institution. To those inside an institution, the institution's purpose will always seem to justify any act or depravity. It does not; a moral judgment, a judgment of justification, can be made only by an individual human mind. That, in the end, is what makes us human.

APPENDICES
A Preliminary Note on Method

One of the perpetual discouragements in the social sciences is the elusiveness of absolutes. A physicist sets down laws which the physical world for all practical purposes obeys with alacrity. A chemist predicts the outcome of a reaction, and subsequent analysis proves him chemically correct. The luckless social scientist is in a much worse spot.

The demand for reliable predictions is rising, but the supply of laws of behavior of social man remains inadequate. No formulas exist for arranging a society to produce a Renaissance on request. The reasons why a stable democracy exists here and a dictatorship there are not known with sufficient precision to permit a reliable forecast.

Knowing that thousands of forces are acting on man in civilization, the social scientist has generally avoided the enunciation of predictive laws. With the exception of economists, who predict freely (and often in contradiction one of another), the professional student of society makes no absolutes.

The Laws of Institutional Behavior set forth in this book are a crude beginning in a corner of social science where laws can be discerned to be operating. The nature of the Laws deserves a little special attention.

Many of the deduced Laws of Institutional Behavior come from negative deductions. There is one great guiding principle: that operation of the internal machinery is absolutely imperative. From this, it is simple indeed to deduce that truth, or morality, or common sense, or any other otherwise desirable goal must be irrelevant, because secondary.

Aside from the negative Laws, which are only the other side of the positive Institutional Imperative, there are also Laws which apply the Axioms to additional defined entities. Thus, for example, we define "virtue" and a "staff." Application of the Axioms to the definitions predicts whether a staff can be virtuous (it cannot, of course). This is a familiar process in all deductive systems; define "area" and "triangle" and the system of plane geometry will yield a formula for area of a triangle.

The kind of prediction possible by applying a Law of Institutional Behavior is not as complete as a prediction from a physical or mathematical law. We can say with certainty that an institution will not commit suicide by declaring itself superfluous. The certainty of this prediction is not much inferior to the certainty of predicting the conservation of momentum in a collision of two steel balls. Yet, the student of physics can predict with high accuracy the position and speed of physical objects thirty seconds after collision, while the student of institutions cannot predict with similar accuracy what the institutions will be doing thirty days from the moment of observation. We know with certainty what the institution will *not* be doing, its actions will obey the Institutional Laws. This is valuable, to be sure, but it would be still more valuable to be able to predict with mathematical precision exactly what the institution will be up to one month from today.

It seems highly likely that all valid laws about individual or group human behavior must share the characteristics of the Institutional Laws. One may predict with certainty that a person of a given race, religion, residence and affluence will not marry a ten-year old of the opposite sex. One may predict that of ten thousand such candidates for marriage over 90 percent will choose partners not more than ten years older, or that 62 percent will marry within their religion. What cannot be predicted is that a particular Sam Alpha will marry a specific Susan Beta.

So with institutions, our Laws simply exclude some fields of behavior. It is sure that the Annual Report of the Atomic Energy Commission will fail to advise discontinuation of its nuclear activities. This we know, but we do not know whether the AEC will propose a Project Plowshare to dig canals or a Project Long Johns to irradiate winter underwear. Such insights are mercifully withheld, and probably always will be.

To say that a science cannot be complete is by no means to say that it is useless. In any part of the social sciences, whatever can be set down with certainty by that much illuminates the darkness. The need is to penetrate back to a few basics —the Axioms on which a science must build. Take economics, a science that often enrages lawmakers and citizens as it fails to meet the demand for certainty. Economics has its laws. Gresham's Law (that bad money drives out good) is surely true. Gresham's Law is a shrewd observation with the flavor of a deduction from other, more basic principles describing the relationship of men and money. Yet such principles remain unstated. The fault is not in the labor invested in developing the science. Much of modern economics appears to the outsider to be more than adequately unintelligible, but economic predictions are still not satisfactory. Such a situation suggests that little time should be spent on further rococo decoration of the science until the foundations are reexamined.

So in this book, the Laws of Institutional Behavior are based on a few simple statements about the relationship of men and institutions. If the Laws are useful in their present form— good. If further Axioms should be added, and scholarship suggests further useful deductions—so much the better. If corrections are required, too bad, but let them be made. Additions, amplifications and corrections are all consistent with the method employed. If the method is fruitful in this corner of the social sciences, then application of the same method to other fields is a modest proposal.

Note on the Two Appendices

The first Appendix below is a completion of a Table of Equivalents begun in Chapter 3. The table is significant because it ties together the individual's view of his work within the institution with the product that emerges from the institution. If there were not a one-to-one correlation between the views of the embedded individual and the institution's actions, then our basic assumptions—the Axioms and Postulates—would be somewhere inconsistent. While an institution is a creature much different from a group of human beings, the ease with which institutional and personal equivalents can be found is strong evidence that the behavior of institutions draws motive power from the personal drive for importance.

Incidentally, much more detailed tables can be set up to match each particular institutional action—say, a decision of a regulatory agency—with the personal feelings of importance of the individuals within the machinery.

The second Appendix is supplied for those who do not ordinarily read telephone directories for fun. It consists of only a few sample pages from the 181-page "Organizational Section" of the Summer 1971 Telephone Directory of "Defense, Department of." The Directory is completely public, so there is no breach of security. Enough pages are reprinted to give some idea of the replication of functions. The pages are yellow in the original—let your fingers do the walking.

Appendix I

TABLE OF EQUIVALENTS

STATEMENT ABOUT INSTITUTIONAL BEHAVIOR	EQUIVALENT STATEMENT OF THE INDIVIDUAL
First Axiom: Any institutional action is merely the working of the institution's internal machinery.	My important work *is* the institution in action.
Second Axiom: Institutional existence depends upon the continual working of the internal machinery.	The institution's existence depends upon my important work.
Third Axiom: Whatever the internal machinery does is perceived within the institution as the real purpose of the institution (i.e., function is seen as purpose).	I perceive my important work to be the real purpose of the institution.
The Institutional Imperative: Every action or decision of an institution must be intended to keep the institutional machinery working.	Above all, my important work must continue.
Corollary to the I.I.; To speak of any goal or purpose of an institution other than keeping the machinery running is no more meaningful than to speak of the goal of an automobile exhaust or the purpose of the hum of a sewing machine.	If you understood my institution, you too would see that my work is the real purpose of the institution.
Every institutional job will be given the maximum possible quantity of the Attributes of Importance (i.e., the Law of Attributed Importance).	My work shows that what I do is important (i.e., the Personnel Postulate).

251

252]

TABLE OF EQUIVALENTS

Special Law of the Security Office: Threats to security will be found.

My security work is important, as I demonstrate by performing it.

General Law of Institutional Self-Occupation: If an institution can generate the subject matter of its operations, it will.

My work is so important that it must be done.

Law of Institutional Self-Justification: Reasons said to be Important will be given to justify every institutional action.

I will tell you the important reasons for my work.

Law of Institutional Expertise: The expert judgment of an institution, when the matters involve continuation of the institution's operations, is totally predictable (and hence totally worthless).

In my expert judgment, the importance of continuing my vital work is unquestionable.

Law of the Institutional Irrelevance of Truth: When the making of a statement is seen as necessary to the continued working of the institutional machinery, the statement is totally predictable and its truth is irrelevant.

I will tell you why I believe my important work must continue. (Direct lie: my work is so important I have to lie about it for your own good in this emergency.)

Law of Institutional Admissions: No institution can admit an error.

My work is so important I can't make mistakes.

Law of the Institutional Irrelevance of Morality and Humanity: If the operation of the institutional machinery requires an action, morality and humanity are irrelevant.

I must be tough: my work is too important for bleeding hearts.

Law of Invariable Accomplishment: An institution will always accomplish its internally perceived purpose.

My important work is well done.

Law of Reflexive Purpose: If the institutional machinery cannot function, the perceived purpose will be altered.

The institution has come around to my way of thinking about my important work.

Theorem of Institutional Inertia: The same institutional procedure will be repeated without reference to the results (if any) achieved.

I would not have done yesterday's important work incorrectly.

Law of Institutional Symbiosis: An institution will maintain a relationship that provides it with the subject matter of its operations.

I must continue my important work with my symbiote.

Law of Individual Judgment: The judgments of an individual human mind resulting in the virtues cannot be created by a staff.

The purpose of my important staff work is to see that the right things get done.

Appendix II

Organizational Section

DEFENSE, DEPARTMENT OF

(Pnt)
Personnel Locator------53241

SECRETARY OF DEFENSE Hon Melvin R Laird 3E880 --------55261
Mil Asst Brig Gen Robt E Pursley 3E880 --------55261
Mil Asst RADM Danl J Murphy USN 3E880 --------55261
Secy to the Secy of Defense Laura Hawley 3E880 --------55261
Secy to the Secy of Defense Thelma E Stubbs 3E880 --------55261
Secy to the Mil Assts Alice Blake 3E880 --------55261

DEPUTY SECRETARY OF DEFENSE Hon David Packard 3E921 --------56352
Mil Asst Col Ray B Furlong 3E928 --------50661
Mil Asst Col Jas G Boatner 3E928 --------50661
Secy Margaret Paull 3E928 --------56352
Secy Gwen Kinkead 3E928 --------56352

DIRECTOR OF DEFENSE RESEARCH & ENGINEERING
Hon John S Foster Jr 3E1006 --------79111
Exec Asst Saml E Clements 3E1006--------56556
Spec Asst Capt Benjamin F Sherman Jr USN 3E1030 --------71282
Prin Dep Dir Defense Research & Engineering
Eberhardt Rechtin 3E1014 --------57178

Dep Dir (Electronics & Information Sys) Herbert D Benington 3E110 --57345
Mil Asst Col Thos A Anderson 3E110 --------57345
Asst Dir (Information & Comm) Howard L Yudkin 3D1047 --------57245
Asst Dir (Intelligence) Manfred Eimer 3D1082 --------55240

Dep Dir (Engineering & Mgmt) LTGEN Robt E Coffin 3E1030 --------74176
Exec Asst Cdr David W Caswell 3E1031 --------70016
Asst Dir (R & D Policy) Edw L Ball Jr 3D1028 --------79125
Asst Dir (Programming) L A Knutson 3E1030 --------74994
Admin Officer J Russell Johanson 3E1031 --------72525

Dep Dir (Research & Advanced Technology) Gus D Dorough Jr 3E144 -55036
Mil Asst Lt Col John J McCambridge USAF 3E144 --------53042
Asst Dir (Engineering Technology) G R Makepeace 3D1085 --------77922
Asst Dir (Environmental & Life Sciences) Albert E Hayward 3D129--59604
Asst Dir (Laboratory Mgmt) Edw M Glass 3D115 --------59602
Asst Dir (Research) Edw M Reilly 3C128 --------74197
Dir of Tech Information W C Christensen 3E144 --------74789

Dep Dir (Southeast Asia Matters) Leonard Sullivan Jr 3E1082 --------74172
Exec Officer Maj Ronald A Johnson 3E1082 --------74431

Dep Dir (Strategic & Space Sys) Ben T Plymale 3E130 --------79386
Mil Asst RADM Roderick O Middleton 3E130 --------57417
Asst Dir (Defensive Sys) C Robt Wieser 3D136 --------75385
Asst Dir (Space Technology) (Actg) Howard P Barfield 3E139 --------77825
Asst Dir (Strat Sys Rev & Anal) Jas R Drake 3E130 --------74931
Asst Dir (Strategic Weapons) 3E129 --------74910
SALT Support Group 3E120 --------73712
Dep Dir (Tactical Warfare Programs) David R Heebner 3E1040 --------59713
Mil Asst Brig Gen C L Stansberry 3E1040 --------59715
Asst Dir (Air Warfare) Allan D Simon 3E1047 --------53015
Asst Dir (Combat Support) John W Klotz 3E1060 --------52754
Asst Dir (International Programs) R A Basil 3E1021 --------79203
Asst Dir (Land Warfare) Donald N Fredericksen 3D1075 --------73459
Asst Dir (Ocean Control) Stanley A Peterson 3D1048 --------72205
Asst Dir (Tactical Sys Plans & Analysis)
G Ronald Wenninger 3E1040 --------71130

Dep Dir (Test & Evaluation)
LTGEN Alfred D Starbird USA (RET) 3E153 --------79961
Asst Dir (Operational Test & Evaluation)
BrigGen Geo H Sylvester 3E1019 --------59284
Spec Asst (Threat Assessment) N F Wikner 3E1087 --------78970

Advanced Research Proj Agency (AB)
Dir Stephen J Lukasik 802 --------43007
Dep Dir (Actg) Donald R Cotter 802 --------43035
Dir Program Mgmt Russell W Beard 813 --------41440
Dir Advanced Engineering C J Wang 741 --------43998
Dir Advanced Sensors (Actg) A M Rubenstein 1029 --------41771
Dir Behavioral Sciences (Actg) Lt Col Austin W Kibler 713 --------45917
Dir Info Processing Techniques Lawrence G Roberts 731 --------45921
Dir Materials Sciences Maurice J Sinnott 709 -------- 43010
Dir Nuclear Monitoring Research Eric H Willis 913 --------43037
Dir Overseas Defense Research Donald R Cotter 1005 --------42440
Dir Strategic Technology David E Mann 3D155 Pnt --------57026
Admin Officer Myron E Huffman 827 --------43236

Weapons Sys Evaluation Group (400 Army Nv Dr)
Dir Lt Gen Arthur W Oberbeck --------76335
Sr Army Mbr Maj Gen B E Huffman --------79134
Sr Navy Mbr RAdm Emmett P Bonner --------75004
Sr Air Force Mbr Maj Gen Fred J Ascani --------74756
Exec Secy Col Clifford J Moore Jr --------76335
Dep Exec Secy Lt Col David W Odiorne Jr --------76335
Admin Ofc Capt Trevor E Bissey --------56933
Report & Document Control Bertha Eister --------75814
Security Ofc Capt Trevor E Bissey --------77312
Defense Science Board
Chairman Gerald F Tape 3D1040 --------54157
Exec Secy Leon Green Jr 3D1040 --------54157
ASSISTANT SECRETARY (ADMINISTRATION)
Hon Robt F Froehlke 3E822 --------78225
Exec Asst Lt Col Alfred H Uhalt Jr 3E827 --------57042
Prin Dep Asst Sec David O Cooke 3E822 --------54436

ASSISTANT SECRETARY (ADMINISTRATION)—Continued

Dep Asst Sec (Intelligence) VADM Harold G Bowen Jr 3C200 --------59732
Exec Dir Robt E Morrison 3C200 --------71882
Admin Officer Lt Robt C Taylor 3C200 --------52305
Mgmt Policy 3C200 --------71024
Programs & Resources 3C200 --------76987
Dep Asst Sec (Security Policy) Jos J Liebling 3C275 --------78233
Exec Asst LtCol John V Mackie 3C275 --------78233
Dir Security Plans & Programs Div Chas M Trammell Jr 3C272 ----50122
International Br Herbert Lewis 3C272 --------57141
Investigative & Personnel Br Wm T Cavaney 3C288 --------57116
Plans & Industrial Br Col Chas C Blossom Jr 3C269 --------55179
Dir Security Classification Mgmt Div Geo MacClain 3C285 --------73969
Asst Dir C Donald Garrett 3C285 --------75568
Dir Industrial Security Clearance Review Div
Wm J Scanlon 3D282 --------73256
Dept Counsel Rowland A Morrow 3D276 --------52354
Dir Admin Svcs Chas V Brewer 3B322 --------73111
Budget & Finance Div Carl W Fisher 3B287 --------76760
Budget Br Mark C Snyder 3B287 --------56342
Finance & Accounts Br Wm R Miller 3B269 --------76500
Travel Br Virginia Chambers 3B279 --------72304
Correspondence & Directives Div Maurice W Roche 3D949 --------78261
Cable Br Lt Col Richard J Uzee 3E925 --------78151
Correspondence Control Br Jas S Twitchell 3A948 --------59717
Classified Control 3A948 --------76131
Records & Reference 3A948--------79285
Reports & Mail Distribution 3A948 --------76395
Sub-Registry 3A948 --------79287
Unclassified Control 3A948 --------53133
White House Correspondence 3B923 --------56151
Directives Br Helen R Rimmer 3A938 --------74111
Records Mgmt Br Jas S Nash 3B925 --------50970
Personnel Div 3B321 --------73723
OSD Locator (Civilian & Military) --------53241
Dep Dir Geo D Boale 3B321 --------74211
Ch Benefits Br I Gene Hodges 3B340 --------71703
Ch Mil Pers Br Lt Col Wm R Palmer 3A336 --------75271
Dep Ch A P LaMantia 3A336 --------75272
SMS John E Gayda 3A336 --------75272
Army Rep SFC Jas E Kofoid 3A336 --------52621
Navy/MC Rep YNC Wm M Conger 3A336 --------75271
Air Force Rep TSgt Geo W Coram 3A336 --------55430
Ch Personnel Data Br Lucille Jacob 3A348 --------71759
Ch Personnel Mgmt Assistance Br 3B334 --------59794
Trng & Career Develop Spec Bobbie S Ellerbee 3B334 --------78373
Pers Mgmt Assistance Reps
Jas O Lewis 3B334 --------50511
Willard C Moore 3B334 --------78373
F Patrick Slattery 3B334 --------78373
Ch Staffing Br Earl L Payne 3B346 --------74212
Staffing Specialists
Lois Brissey 3B347 --------75171
Grace Cook 3B347 --------75171
Robt White 3B347 --------75171
Ch Position & Pay Mgmt Br Karl F Becker 3B329 --------78305
Position & Pay Mgmt Representatives
Howard Becker 3B329 --------78304
Bob G Jones 3B329 --------78304
Edith Kramer 3B329 --------78305
Michael Sekol 3B329 --------78304
Paul Wesson 3B329 --------73305
Clayton White 3B329 --------78304
Security Div Wm C Hunt 3B272 --------77171
Appraisal & Review Br Wm H Quinlan Jr 3B278 --------77173
Physical Security Br Maj Elbert M Marshall 3B272 --------77396
Security Oper Br Chas W White 3B278 --------77395
Security Information & Control Sec Marion R Beasley 3B278---77394
Visitor Certification Wm H Stewart 3B278 --------77394
Space Mgmt & Svcs Div Thos C Embrey 3B252 --------77241
Graphics & Presentations Br Robt B Logan 2A310 --------54266
Office Svcs Br Ronald E Deane 3B252 --------53144
Contract Liaison 3B252 --------53144
Facilities Sec Clarence C Smith 3B252 --------53207
Printing 3A1037 --------54313
Publications 3B200 --------52167
Reproduction 3A1037 --------54313
Supply & Svcs Sec John A Burrell 3B264 --------55184
Space Mgmt Br Leonard Aaronson 3C261 --------77281
Historical Staff Rudolph A Winnacker 3C321 --------74216
Spec Proj Staff John R Whittington 3B322 --------79241

Directorate of Organizational & Mgmt Planning
(Actg) Capt Donald S Ross USN 3C920 --------54278
Dir Defense Investigative Program Ofc 3D913 --------79586
Secy Def Investigative Rev Council 3D913 --------79647

ASSISTANT SECRETARY (COMPTROLLER) Hon Robt C Moot 3E854 ----53237
Exec Asst CDR S D Frost 3E854 --------71102
Asst for Admin Douglas Hall 3A862 --------75925
Analysis Group Opns Anal 3B866 --------57391
Prin Dep Asst Secy Don R Brazier 3E843 --------59252

DEFENSE, DEPARTMENT OF [255

O-6 DEFENSE, DEPARTMENT OF

ASSISTANT TO THE SECRETARY (LEGISLATIVE AFFAIRS)—Continued

Dep (M&RA) Col Allan W Farlow 3D920 --- 54131
Dep (R&E AE DCA DASA) Col Ricardo R Alvarado 3D920 --- 55497
Dir Ofc Research & Admin Col Chas W Anderson 3D930 --- 57470
Asst for Congressional Liaison (Budget Authorization)
Lt Col Richard L Fischer 3D930 --- 57456
Staff Asst Jos A Pitkiel 3D930 --- 57495
Staff Asst Lt Col Peggy Lou Schissell 3D930 --- 79166
Staff Asst Maj Francis G Hall Jr 3D930 --- 57495

ASSISTANT TO THE SECRETARY (TELECOMMUNICATIONS)

(Actg) David L Solomon 3D158 --- 53136
Exec Asst Lt Col Harry Jaffers 3E165 --- 50906
Dep Asst (Opers & Engineering) David L Solomon 3D158 --- 53136
Dir Willie L Moore 3D158 --- 76673
Dep Asst (Advanced Sys & Technology) 3D174 --- 52748
Dir (Actg) Dr Robt M Langelier 3D174 --- 52761
Dep Asst (Resource Mgmt) 3D161 --- 55970
Dir Alden P Sullivan 3D161 --- 55004

DEFENSE ADVISOR US MISSION TO NATO Ralph Earle II 4E840 --- 78101

JOINT CHIEFS OF STAFF

(Pnt)

Msg Center Duty Officer 2C940 --- 53337
JCS NMCC Oper Ch (Duty Ofcr) 2D877 --- 78322
Pers Locator --- 53241

The Chairman Joint Chiefs of Staff
Adm Thos H Moorer 2E873 --- 79121
The Asst to the Chairman Joint Chiefs of Staff
LtGen Richard T Knowles 2E873 --- 79124
Exec Asst & Senior Aide Capt Harry D Train II 2E872 --- 79121
Admin Aide LCdr Wm C Francis 2E872 --- 79121
Aide Lt Col W B Ratliff 2E873 --- 79829
Aide Maj M D Salmon 2E873 --- 79847
Social Secy Lt Janice N Buckles USN 2E873 --- 59512
Admin Asst Paul M Kearney 2E865 --- 55066
Chairman's Staff Group
RADM R C Robinson USN 2E860 --- 75367
Capt R P Hilton USN 2E860 --- 77359
Col B L Davis 2E860 --- 71480
Col J A Wickham 2E860 --- 56297
Col J A MacDonald 2E860 --- 75257
Asst LL Capt A J Valentine USN 2E859 --- 71309
Asst Pub Aff Cdr J C MacKercher 2E857 --- 71308

ASST TO THE CHAIRMAN JCS FOR STRATEGIC ARMS NEGOTIATIONS
LTG Royal B Allison 2E844 --- 59181
Exec Maj J D Dethlefsen 2E840 --- 59183
Dep Col P R Von Ins 1E843A --- 59178
Asst Dep Capt W O McLean 1E843A --- 59176
Qualitative Analysis Col J E Dalton 1E839 --- 50322
Quantitative Analysis Col L Fitzgerald 1E839 --- 70520
Admin Sec 1E841 --- 59166

DIRECTOR JOINT STAFF Lt Gen John W Vogt 2E936 --- 74084
Exec Col E O Post 2E936 --- 59088
Spec Asst for Joint Matters Col B Scowcroft 2E936 --- 72826
Dep Asst for Joint Matters Cdr W D Shaughnessy 2E921 --- 72563
Spec Asst for Public Affairs Col E O Post 2E937 --- 57665
Asst Exec Cdr J W Tomion 2E937 --- 57665
Legal Advisor Capt N Sabalos 2A886 --- 52107
Admin Asst to Dir W A Kemper 2E921 --- 56275
Secy to the Dir Nancy J Collins 2E936 --- 52713
Vice Dir VADM Mason B Freeman 2E932 --- 71297

OFC OF ASST FOR AUTOMATION
Asst for Automation Capt R M Thompson 2A886 --- 73453
Mil Asst Lt Col D E Slessman 2A886 --- 73453
Mil Asst Maj W E Campbell 2A886 --- 76476

DIRECTOR J-1 (PERSONNEL) BG P C Watson 1B738 --- 73062
Dep Dir Col R C Storey 1B738 --- 76364
Mil Secy LTC M K Chase Jr 1B743 --- 53842
Manpower Div Col W M Bledsoe 1B730 --- 75790
Unified & Specified Hq Br Col J L Jones 1B726 --- 74139
International Hqs & Def Agencies Br
Col J H Von Der Bruegge 1B728 --- 76257
Plans & Survey Br COL T U Harrold 1B735 --- 56446
Personnel Div Capt W H McCaughey 1B737 --- 76378
Pers & Plans Br Col J W Warren 1B737 --- 70870
Educations, Trng & Key Asgnments Br Capt W H Knueven 1B737C --- 72054
Mil Terminology Br O T Albertini 1B739 --- 55909

DIRECTOR J-3 (OPERATIONS) LTGEN M Zais 2D880 --- 73702
Vice Dir J-3 MGEN W G Johnson 2D878 --- 56243
Special Asst to the Dir J-3 J E Glick 2D874 --- 70436
Dep Dir for Opers (Strategic and General Opers)
BG J G Shanahan 2D874 --- 79031
Dep Dir for Opers (Command and Control) RADM J M James 2D874 --- 52403
Dep Dir for Opers (Reconnaissance)
RADM J C Donaldson Jr 2D921 --- 57356
Dep Dir for Opers (Environmental Services)
BG R F Long 1B679A --- 76668
Dep Dir for Opers (Regional Opers) BG J W Pauly 2D874 --- 50483
Dep Dir for Opers (SACSA) BG L J Manor 1E962 --- 59852
Dep Dir for Opers (NMCC) BG T J Camp Jr 2D901A1 --- 73229
Dep Dir for Opers (NMCC) BG E O Martin 2D901A1 --- 73229
Dep Dir for Opers (NMCC) BG W P Anderson 2D901A1 --- 73229
Dep Dir for Opers (NMCC) BG R O Miller 2D901A1 --- 73229
Dep Dir for Opers (NMCC) RADM J S Christiansen 2D901A1 --- 73229
Exec CAPT O I Svenson Jr 2D874 --- 78863
Exec Asst LTC J E Rogers 2D874 --- 78863
Admin Officer CDR S Hinden 2D860 --- 50000
Mil Secy LTC H E Miller 2C857 --- 54532
Mil Secy LTC W E Lozier 2C857 --- 54532
Atlantic/South and Central America/Alaska Div
COL J R Thompson 2A872A --- 53772
LANT Br CAPT W A Hardy 2A874A --- 53517
STRICOM/AL Br COL J C Reed 2A872A --- 50997

DEFENSE, DEPARTMENT OF O-6

JOINT CHIEFS OF STAFF—Continued

SOUTH Br COL B R Wright 2A878A --- 78757
European/Middle East AF SA Div COL M C Kettelhut 2B927 --- 54846
European Br COL R V Lee Jr 2B927 --- 71355
NATO-Spec Opns Br COL K E Buell 2B927 --- 75070
Middle East AF SA Br COL R W Rhea 2B927 --- 57903
General Operations Div COL J H Patterson 2B857B --- 73752
General Opers Br CAPT B C Spell 2B861 --- 53734
Exercise Br COL V H Williams 2B857C --- 53089
Pacific Div A J Coleman 2B885 --- 77921
Dep Chief CAPT E A Davidson 2B885 --- 77921
East Asia-Pacific Br COL R D Barrett 2B885 --- 77403
Force Reqmt-Deploy Prog Br CAPT P V Purkrabek 2B885 --- 54773
Southeast Asia Br COL A P Hobrecht 2B913 --- 74040
Strategic Opers Div COL E S Harris 2B865A --- 57920
Current Opers Br COL C H Holt 2B865F --- 78508
Strat Def Opers Br COL D B Ballou 2B865D --- 59297
Nuclear Weapons Br COL H A Thornhill 2B865E --- 53431
SIOP Br CAPT C Priest Jr 2B865C --- 78725
Plans & Analysis Div CAPT W E Munroe 2B864 --- 72203
Planning Sys Br CAPT C F Moul 2B877B --- 73679
Combat Analysis Br CAPT C C Carter 2B877C --- 54711
Info Systems Br LTC G T Sherron 2B868 --- 76324
Joint Recon Center COL J B Anderson 2D921G --- 57356
Recon and EW Programs Div COL L J Stevens 2D921G --- 50581
Recon Opers Div CAPT W J Wacker 2D921G --- 50583
Opers Div COL A DiSilvio 2B936 --- 59103
Opers Br COL C M Adams 2D881B --- 54212
Emergency Actions Br LTC W H Richardson 2B872 --- 59514
Weather Br CDR G L Rice 2D921H --- 76851
MOLINK Br LTC J Crutchfield 2D9013A --- 79240
Data Processing Div CAPT J W Crane 2B914 --- 50046
Opers Statistics Br COL L S Baumann 2B920 --- 75389
ADP Plans Br COL F L Maloy 2B926 --- 71509
Status of Forces Br LTC M W Hulse 2B884 --- 78368
Plans & Reqmts Div COL W K Farmer 1D831 --- 71934
NMCS Plans & Reqmts Br LTC A F Cochran 1D830 --- 73706
Sys Br COL K A Plant 1D825B --- 57155
WWMCCS Plans & Reqmts Br COL T E Ringwood 1D833C --- 71689
WWMCCS ADP Mgmt Div H B Goertzel 1D840A --- 74814
Dep Chief COL J A Ely 1D840A --- 74814
Design Br M R Billings 1D835 --- 50251
Standards Br D L Coates 1D836A --- 73413
Implementation Br COL B Clemmons 1D828A --- 53553
Support Br CAPT K F Walery 1D832A --- 53553
Environmental Services Div COL J R Anderson 1B682 --- 77383
Dep SACSA COL D F Schungel 1E962B --- 76815
Exec LTC W J Ryan 1E862 --- 54590
CI Opers Div CAPT L E Willson 1E957 --- 56507
PsyOps Div COL J B Hendricks Jr 1E939 --- 56319
Spec Opers Div COL E E Mayer 1E940 --- 55814
ANMCC COL R W Marshall --- 196x81454
NEACP COL R L Harris --- 185x4015

DIRECTOR J-4 (LOGISTICS) LTG Timothy F O'Keefe 2E828 --- 52732
Dep Dir J-4 (Strategic Mobility) MGEN W N Redling 2E828 --- 74121
Dep Dir J-4 RADM Wm R McKinney 2E828 --- 52934
Tech Advisor for Strategic Mobility W S Boone 2E829 --- 73687
Exec LTC R E Clouser 2E828 --- 71408
Mil Secy LCDR B F Doe 2D826 --- 55147
Mil Secy Maj J H Akin 2D826 --- 71844
Admin Officer Mona S McCracken 2D826 --- 71844
Documents Processing Br Betty H Reedy 2D826 --- 55147
Records Br Peggy W Rowe 2D823 --- 71018
Sys Data & Analysis LTC C J Hall 2D848 --- 75464
Logistic Readiness Center 2C836 --- 52213
EUR/MEAFSA Div Col G S Oliver 2D841 --- 52327
Plans & Oper Br Col E Hernandez 2D841 --- 53834
Regional Policy Capt J C Burkart USN 2D841 --- 72300
Mobility Opers Div Col G S Royal 2D840 --- 76256
Current Opers Br Col F K Fulton 2D840 --- 75635
Opers Plans Review & Analysis Br R P Clark 2D840 --- 73615
PAC/W HEM Div Capt Vincent L Murtha USN 2C822 --- 70634
Plans & Oper Br Capt J P Sundberg USN 2C822 --- 53665
Regional Policy Br Col E W Gramkow 2C822 --- 76928
Mobility Plans & Analysis Div Capt J X Miller USN 2D822 --- 71435
Requirements Br G O King 2D822 --- 74161
Capabilities & Allocations Br Col T E Benson 1B683 --- 77200
Policy Div Col J W Hanley 2C841 --- 71629
Guidance & Procedures Br Col Woodus A Carter 2C844 --- 50982
Logistic Objectives & Programs Br Col H L Gronewald 2C837 --- 59033
Resources Mgmt Br Col A E Halls 2C839 --- 56126
Services Div Col W H Lillie 2C828 --- 71713
Ammunition Br Capt E N Bouffard USN 2C828 --- 57742
Civil Engineering Br Col W H Lillie 2C828 --- 71535
Petroleum Br Capt H G Packard USN 2C828 --- 53819
JTB Secretariat Col G S Royal 2D840 --- 76256
Transportation Agency Liaison Officers 2D836 --- 54950

DIRECTOR J-5 (PLANS & POLICY) VADM J P Weinel 2E1000 --- 55618
Dep Dir J-5 MG R F Shaefer 2E1008 --- 71887
Dep Dir J-5 MG J H Elder Jr 2E996 --- 72101
Dep Dir J-5 MG F B Clay 2E984 --- 76628
Spec Asst COL W H Fletcher Jr 2E987 --- 76946
Spec Asst COL R N Joens 2E987 --- 76946
Spec Asst Capt K W Sharer 2E987 --- 76946
Spec Asst State C A Freshman 2E980 --- 71906
Exec Col S A Vale 2E996 --- 79716
Exec Asst Col G F Hoge 2E996 --- 77047
Spec Asst Col B S Hanson 2E987 --- 56147
Spec Asst Col J Roberts 2E987 --- 56147
Mil Secretaries
LTC C R Roper 2E987A --- 56702
LCdr J T Parker 2E987A --- 56702
LTC G P Reynolds 2E987A --- 56702
MAJ R R McKay 2E987A --- 56702
Staff Asst Jack Siegert 2E987 --- 56702

ARMY, DEPARTMENT OF THE

SECRETARY OF THE ARMY, OFFICE OF THE
(Pnt)

SECRETARY OF THE ARMY Hon Stanley R Resor 3E718 --------------53211
  Exec COL Jas L Kelly 3E718 ------------------------------53211
  Mil Asst COL Richard L Livermore 3E718 ----------------53211
  Mil Asst MAJ Donald S Pihl 3E718 -----------------------53211
  Mil Asst LTC Chas-W Bagnal 3E725 ---------------------79506
UNDER SECRETARY OF THE ARMY Hon Thaddeus R Beal 2E722 -----54311
  Exec COL Philip T Boerger 2E722 -----------------------76806
  Mil Asst COL John P Vollmer 2E722 --------------------52947
  Mil Asst LTC Clifford Wortliy Jr 2E725 ------------------77834
Dep Under Secy (Operations Research) Dr Wilbur B Payne 2E729 ---50083
  Asst Dep Under Secy Hunter M Woodall Jr 2E729 -------76742
Dep Under Secy (International Affairs) David H Ward 3E736 ------72241
  Exec COL Albert L Romaneski 3E736 -------------------72432
Spec Asst Francis X Plant 1E520 --------------------------------79641
Army Council of Review Boards
  Dir MG Herbert G Sparrow 1E474 ----------------------73071
  Dep Dir COL H C Hicks Jr 1E474 ----------------------73166
  Admin Officer LTC Edw P Brophy 1E474 ---------------73166
  Discharge Review Board 1E479 -----------------------54682
  Elimination & Security Review Boards 1E474 -----------73518
  Physical Disability Appeal Board 1E474 ---------------55074
Army Board for Correction of Military Records
  Exec Secy Raymond J Williams 1E512 ------------------74254
  Admin Asst Mary L Posey 1E517 ----------------------54298
Army & Air Force Clemency & Parole Board 1E486 --------------77775
National Board for the Promotion of Rifle Practice Dir of Civilian
  Marksmanship LTC Frank T Luhmann 1E053 FOR BG ------36460
ASST SECRETARY OF THE ARMY (FM) Hon Eugene M Becker 2E678---54291
Dep Asst Secy of the Army (FM) Richard L Saintsing 2E678 ------72121
  Exec COL Leslie R Sears 2E678 -----------------------75215
  Asst Exec MAJ Frederick S Benson III 2E678 ---------79581
  Ch Ofc of Program/Budget Leonard F Keenan 2E665 ----76146
  Ch Ofc Mgmt Data & Acctg Sys (Actg) Wm E Davis 2E665 ---74341
  Ch Ofc Working Capitol Funds John F Wallace 2E665 ----55951
  Ch Ofc Mgmt Information Robt E McKelvey 2E665 --------52909
  Ch Ofc Cost Analysis Harry S Hull 2E665 --------------55121
  Admin Ofc CW4 Russell W Clark 2E665 ----------------78805
ASST SECRETARY OF THE ARMY (I&L)
  (Actg) Vincent P Huggard 3E606 ---------------------52254
  Principal Dep Asst Secy (I&L) Vincent P Huggard 3E616 ---59000
  Dep Asst Secy (I&L)-MR&LMS Gerald B Russell 3E620 ----74443
  Exec COL Nevin L McCartney 3E606 -------------------52216
  Mil Asst CW3 O W Whytsell 3E606 --------------------52256
  Asst to Prin Dep Asst Secy (I&L) COL Paul K Shultz 3E616 ---77753
Asst for Vietnamization & Mat Readiness
  COL Mitchell J Hazam 3E619 -------------------------56869
Deputy for Family Housing Paul W Johnson 3D620 ------------78161
Deputy for Procurement BG V H Ellis 3E588 ----------------52647
Deputy for Supply Maintenance & Trans Jos C Zengerle Jr 3E613 ---79030
Deputy for Installations W R Shuler 3E591 ------------------50867
Army Small Business & Econ Utilization Pol Advisor
  Jack W Askins 1E464 ------------------------------78113
Army Contract Adjustment Board Chmn COL John S Benner 3E588 ---54101
Recorder Army Contract Adjustment Board COL Harvey S Boyd 2E569 -55705
Labor Relations Advisor LTC Carol E Minis 2C440 ------------54369
Advisor on Fraud Matters COL Chas W Bethany Jr 2C459 --------50240
ASST SECRETARY OF THE ARMY (M&RA) Hon Hadlai A Hull 2E594 ---79253
Dep Asst Secy (M&RA)-M&F Donald W Srull 2E594 -----------59721
Dep Asst Secy (M&RA)-PP&P John G Kester 2E665 -----------79185
Dep for Reserve Affairs Arthur W Allen Jr 2E594 ------------55291
  Asst for Civilian Aides Program Virginia Harris 2E725 ----78948
Dep for Civ Pers Pol & Equal Oppor 2E609 ----------------53372
  Spec Asst Prog Rev LTC Glenn K Otis 2E589 ----------52101
  Exec Asst MAJ Steve Chabon 2E594 -------------------71967
  Ch Mil Pers Pol COL Wm K Merrill 2E609 -------------54078
  Ch Proc Educ Research & Trng Chas F Parker 2E589 ------78201
  Ch Manpower LTC Glenn K Otis 2E589 ----------------53840
  Ch Forces LTC Chas L McNelli 2E589 -----------------71482
Employment Policy & Grievance Review Staff
  Dir Albert Kransdorf 1E482 --------------------------56062
ASST SECRETARY OF THE ARMY (R&D) Hon Robt L Johnson 3E390 ---56153
Dep Asst Secy of the Army (R&D) Chas L Poor 3E390 ----------53762
Dep Asst Secy of Army (R&D)-BMD Dr J B Gilstein 3E365 ------73558
Asst for Research Dr K C Emerson 3E379 ------------------57674
Exec & Asst for Air Mobility Col Leo D Turner 3E390 --------55749
Asst Exec CW3 Frank Stamey 3E390 ----------------------56742
Asst for Electronics Victor L Friedrich 3E379 --------------53515
Asst for SEA Clyde D Hardin 3E379 -----------------------79982
Asst for Programs Chas R Woodside 3E390 ----------------57616
Asst Exec & Asst for Combat Materiel COL Donald F Packard 3E390 -74995
Asst for Anti-ballistic Missiles COL Robt J Lunn 3E379 ------72653
Asst for Missiles COL Grayson D Tate Jr 3E379 ------------72653
DIR OF CIVIL DEFENSE John E Davis 3E346 ------------------74484
  Duty Officer (0830-1700 Saturday) ------------------74484
  Duty Officer (Non-Duty Hours Sunday &
  Holidays) --------------------163x5378 or 638-3983
  OCD Pers Locator -------------------------------71621
  CD Information --------------------------------59441
Exec Asst Robt E Young 3E346 ----------------------------53374
Dep Dir Georgiana H Sheldon 3E336 ----------------------55538
Spec Asst Herbert E Kunde 3E340 -------------------------56855
Dep Dir Richard C Kendall 3E334 --------------------------59372
Spec Asst Frank H Vogel 3E330 ---------------------------59384
Mil Advisor COL Wm H Pietsch Jr 3E330 --------------------59271
General Counsel Chas Manning 3C336 -----------------------53763
Asst Dir for Policy & Programs Bernard Rubinstein 3E318 ------71364
Asst Dir for Plans & Oper John W McConnell 3D347 ----------78314

SECRETARY OF THE ARMY, OFFICE OF THE—Continued
Asst Dir for Tech Svc Ren F Read 3C316 ------------------59611
Asst Dir for Mgmt Walter A Girstantas 3C322 --------------53402
Comptroller Troy V McKinney 3E326 -----------------------57120
Asst Dir for Research Walmer E Strope 3E314 --------------76258
Liaison Svcs Virgil L Couch 5D346 ------------------------55282
Information Svcs Vincent Otto 3E341 ----------------------59441
GENERAL COUNSEL (Actg) R Kenly Webster 2E614 -----------79235
Principal Dep R Kenly Webster 2E614 ---------------------74807
Dep Gen Counsel (Logistics) 2E621 ------------------------78029
Dep Gen Counsel (Mil & Civil Affairs) Bland West 2E614 ------76493
OFFICE OF CIVIL FUNCTIONS
  (Actg) Ch Civil Functions Chas R Ford 2E653 ----------76985
  Exec for Civil Functions COL Lewis A Pick Jr 2E653 -----79809
  Scientific Advisor Dr John R Sheaffer 4G026 FOR BG -----36276
  Dir Program Planning Group Dr Jim J Tozzi 4G026 FOR BG ---36588
CH OF PUBLIC INFORMATION (Office Secretary of the Army)
  Ch MG Winant Sidle 2E636 --------------------------55135
  Dep Ch BG DeWitt C Smith Jr 2E636 -----------------74482
  Ofc for the Freedom of Info Wm J Donohoo 2D655 -------76732
OFC CH OF LEGISLATIVE LIAISON
  Duty Officer -------------------------------------53524
  (If no answer call TAG Duty Officer) ------------------50163
  Ch MG Bernard W Rogers 2C631 ---------------------76767
  Dep Ch COL Jas R Brownell Jr 2C631 ----------------56368
  Spec Asst Roger M Currier 2C631 ------------------53918
  Exec LTC Henri E Mallet 2C631 --------------------53524
  Admin Ofc CW4 Standord J Gervasio 2C600 ----------56849
  Congressional Inquiry Div COL David A Thomason 2C628A ---78381
  Investigations Div Roy H Steele 2C634 --------------72106
  Legislative Div COL Hugh J Clausen 2C626 ----------70275
  Plans & Oper Div COL Philo A Hutcheson 2C638C ------54828
  Senate Liaison Div COL Jas E O'Leary 152 Old Sen Ofc Bg ---37446
  House Liaison Div COL Lloyd L Burke B325 Rayburn Bg ----37580
  Congressional Travel Marna Steger 2C630 ----------78843
ADMIN ASST John G Connell Jr 3E732 ---------------------52442
  Information --------------------------------------55378
  Dep Admin Asst R M Yingling 3E741 -----------------55879
  Admin Support Group A F Spada 3D718 ---------------55456
  Mgmt Analysis Staff Dir J J Harvatt 3E749 -----------76900
  Emergency Planning Officer Robt D McMaster 3E741 -----77176
  Mgmt Ofc Ch Peter Stein 3D736 ---------------------78600
    Program & Financial Mgmt Br Francis J Raeder 3D740 ----78600
    Mgmt Sys Br Hazel Elkins 3D749 -----------------50495
    Military Personnel Br CWO G E Campbell 3D746 -------77441
    Conference Reporting Br John J Lucas Jr 1D518 --------79424
    Admin Svc Br Ethel T Fuller 3D747 ---------------52244
    Graphics Arthur L Howard 3D745 -----------------56169
  Equal Empl Opportunity Officer Chas J Wartman 3D336 ----53823
Dept of the Army Welfare Fund
  Custodian Lois S VanSickler 1E230 ------------------52005
  Exec Secy Robt L Castile 3D736 -------------------72691
  Recreation Dir Karl F Edler Jr 3A146 ----------------73337
  Ticket Info (Pent Ticket Svc) 5E360 -----------------79747
  Travel Info (DOD Vacation Svc) 3A146 ---------------73337
  Mil Charter Info (United Svc Clubs) 3A146 -----------55104
  Forrestal Bg Office GP130 ------------------------35977
Ofc of the Personnel Manager
  Personnel Manager Robt L Castile 3D736 --------------72691
    Admin Br Eloise G Thomas 3D723 ----------------53858
    Labor Mgmt & Empl Relations Br Clair F Beck 3D731 ----53383
    Position & Pay Mgmt Br Edw L Zavilla 3D731 --------74213
    Recruitment & Placement Br 3D731 ---------------59504
    Trng & Development Br Orman D Suter 3D731 --------53383
    Personnel Support Br Ann Baucom 3D731 ----------59504
  Civilian Atty Career Program
    Technical Advisor Jas W Bagg 3D731 --------------73230
  OSA Service
    Security Officer Lester J Boykin 3D748 ------------79355
  Civilian Employees Security Program
    Dir Lester J Boykin 3D748 --------------------79355
Headquarters Svcs-Washington
  Coordinator R M Yingling 3E741 -------------------55879
  Comptroller W O Soderstrum 1E238 ----------------77964
  Employment Coordination Svcs-Washington
    Dir R L Merlilat 1A111 ------------------------70335
    Dep Dir C J Humphrey 1A111 -------------------70335
    Employment Information ----------------------70335
  Space Mgmt Svc-Washington
    Dir Dominic Ciango 1A127 ---------------------52242
Defense Supply Svc-Washington (See Dept of Defense-Miscellaneous)
  Dir Thos J Schelilk 1E230 -----------------------52005
Defense Telephone Svc-Washington
     (See Dept of Defense-Miscellaneous)
  Dir Jas T Bedsole 1A775 ----------------------52121
DA Planning Committee for Building Mgmt
  Chairman R M Yingling 3E741 --------------------55879
DOD Bg Administrator Edw Jirgl 3C748 ---------------78998
    (See Dept of Defense-Misc: Building Mgmt)

CHIEF OF STAFF, UNITED STATES ARMY
(Pnt)

OFFICE CHIEF OF STAFF
Ch of Staff GEN W C Westmoreland 3E668 -----------------52077
  Duty Officer 5A918 ------------------------------72727
  Exec & Sr Aide COL V F Warner 3E668 --------------54329
  Aide to Ch of Staff LTC V T Bullock 3E668 -----------54329
  Aide to Ch of Staff MAJ J O B Sewall 3E668 ---------54329

CHIEF OF STAFF, UNITED STATES ARMY—Continued

Admin Asst CW2 Richard A Sauer 3E668 --------------------75673
Social Secy Ann Webb 3E668 -------------------------------76931
Sergeant Major of the Army SMA Silas L Copeland 3E677 ---52150
Admin Asst MSG Bobby W Alexander 3E677 -----------------52152
Admin Asst SFC Floyd D Gluff 3E677 ----------------------52152
Spec Actions Unit COL Robt C Kerner 3D642 ---------------73207
Vice Ch of Staff GEN Bruce Palmer Jr 3E664 --------------54371
Asst Vice Ch of Staff LTG W E DePuy 3D656 ---------------50294
Secy of the General Staff MG Warren K Bennett 3E668 -----53542
Spec Advisor Dr F G A Kraemer 3C640 --------------------52365
Dir of Military Support LTG H M Exton BF751B -----------73147
Safeguard Sys Mgr LTG W P Leber CWB --------------------43061

OFC OF THE VICE CHIEF OF STAFF
Vice Ch of Staff GEN Bruce Palmer Jr 3E664 --------------54371
Exec COL Pat W Crizer 3E664 ----------------------------54372
Asst Exec & Aide Maj Lincoln Jones III 3E664 ------------73903
Admin Asst CW2 Will Wells 3E664 ------------------------54372

OFC OF THE ASST VICE CHIEF OF STAFF
Asst Vice Ch of Staff LTG W E DePuy 3D656 ---------------50294
Exec LTC H H Perritt Jr 3D656 ---------------------------50296
Asst Exec Ofcr E Lee Januski 3D668 ----------------------70871
Admin Asst CW2 G D Rothmeier 3D656 ---------------------50294
Coordinator of Army Studies
Coord LTC J W Seigle 3C626 -----------------------------70937
Planning & Programming Analysis Directorate
Dir BG H J McChrystal Jr 3C718 -------------------------54417
Dep Dir COL F G Gosling 3C718 ---------------------------71475
Exec LTC R M Wiser 3C720 -------------------------------75628
Force Planning & Anal Gp COL W E Manning 3C726 ---------70631
Prog & Fin Anal Gp D H Havermann 3B652 ----------------72832
Studies, Models, & Sys Gp COL P J Mueller 2B664 ---------78929
Mgmt Information Sys Directorate
Dir BG R L Fair 1D629 ----------------------------------50678
Dep Dir COL R J Petersen 1D625 --------------------------50040
Tech Adv M B Zimmerman 1D625 --------------------------55729
Exec LTC L J Riley 1D629 -------------------------------75503
Plans & Proj Office R P McLaughlin 1D626 ---------------50041
Mgt & Policy Gp LTC E D Bjorn 2A720 --------------------50313
HQ Sys Gp LTC D D Miller 1D626 -------------------------55353
Army Functional Sys Gp COL J C Griffith 1D636 ----------75076
Sys Integration Gp LTC W F Faught 1D616 ----------------52094
Opn & Fid Sys Gp LTC J H Ashhurst 1D667 ----------------50301
Weapon Sys Analysis Directorate
Dir R J Trainor 1E600 ----------------------------------57404
Dep Dir COL Ennis C Whitehead Jr 1E604 ----------------57264
Exec LTC W L Hatcher 1E600 -----------------------------57264
WSMCO Ofc Dr J G Honig 1E620 --------------------------71107
CS Sys Gp 1E613 ---------------------------------------50781
Fld Arty Sys Gp COL J T Wortham 1E633 -----------------50039
Armor/Inf Sys Gp COL D H Williamson 1E625 --------------76291
AD Sys Gp (Actg) COL J T Wortham 1E633 -----------------50039

OFFICE OF THE DEPUTY SECRETARY OF THE GENERAL STAFF (STAFF SERVICES)
Dep SGS (and White House Ln Officer) COL H S Long Jr 3E669 ----52776
WHLO Asst A E Schroff 3D689 ----------------------------77425
Exec LTC G R Giles 3E669 -------------------------------73658
Equal Empl Opportunity Officer Dr Bruce E Fleming 3C672 ----50534
Assoc EEOO Daisy B Patterson 3C672 ---------------------50534
Admin Div
Ch MAJ K D Meadows 3D685 ------------------------------76534
Sergeant Major SGM R L Higbee 3D685 -------------------72567
Mail & Records Svc Br Dorothy Whittet 3D671 -------------73210
Official Mail Room 3D671 -------------------------------53503
Pers Svc Br CW4 G L Beineman 3D681 ---------------------59685
Correspondence Div
Ch LTC H B Bynell 3C715 --------------------------------54185
Editor Sarah T Rigg 3C715 ------------------------------54185
Protocol Office
Ch LTC D K Doyle 3D676 --------------------------------53901
Asst SGS MAJ R J Torretto 3D676 ------------------------77051
Staff Civilian Pers Div
Info (Army Staff Civ Locator) 1D432 (0930-1600 Hrs) ----52926
Info (Employment) 1E444 Pnt (0800-1630 Hrs) -----------50133
Info (Employment) 7A175 FOR BG (0800-1600 Hrs) --------56540
Civ Pers Officer S G McDonald 1E416 --------------------56540
Dep Civ Pers Officer J F McDonald 1E416 ----------------78337
Personnel Mgmt Representatives
Wm Homan 1E416 ---------------------------------------50010
Robt L Smith 1E416 ------------------------------------50010
John W Stewart 7A189 FOR BG --------------------------35326
Tech Support Ofc
ADP Spt & Control Sec Marjorie R Hull 1D436 ------------54690
Analysis/Eval Sec Constance M Ewy 1E417 --------------75235
Admin Svc Sec Ina W Hartwell 1D432 --------------------79662
Mgmt-Empl Relations Br Harry O Maneman 1E428 ---------74127
Mgmt - Empl Counseling Sec #1 Warren L Jensen 1E421 ---52599
Mgmt - Empl Counseling Sec #2 Anthony C Hall 7A199 FOR BG---35309
Unions & Emol Prog Sec Anna Veremko 1E430 -------------53061
Posn & Pay Mgmt Br Gaylord E Sheller 1E422 ------------53881
Posn & Pay Mgmt Sec #1 Donna J Ashurst 1E422 ---------79889
Posn & Pay Mgmt Sec #2 Wm S Armstrong 1E422 ---------78338
Posn & Pay Mgmt Sec #3 A B Spikol 7A211 FOR BG -------35324
Recr & Placement Br Roberts Chickering 1E438 ----------74920
Fld Recr Sec W J Sellers 1E439 ------------------------56212
Merit Prom Sec R L Diehl 1E434 ------------------------59748
Career Placement Sec J T Clarke 1E443 ----------------57667
Spec Actions Sec Annie E Duke 1E440 ------------------59687
Trng & Dev Br Eugene T Wells 1E398 -------------------72172
Trng Programs Sec Dorothy Julian 1E398 ---------------55839
Supv Trng Sec (Actg) Wm W Wall 1E413 -----------------76057
Career Dev Sec G H Darmstadt 1D405 ------------------77589
Staff Comm Div
Ch LTC W S Burrus 5A926 -----------------------------55404
Oper Ofc LTC R H Horner 5A926 ----------------------55404

CHIEF OF STAFF, UNITED STATES ARMY—Continued

Production Br (24hr dy Officer) 5A858 -------------------57135
Admin Office SGM F B Johnson 5A928 ---------------------74153
OCSA Cables Officer LTC T A Austin 3E679 ---------------56894
Staff Mgmt Div
Ch COL J E Munnelly 3C678 ------------------------------77344
Plans & Studies Ofc LTC J J Mossellem 3C686 ------------78841
Financial Mgt & Manpower Con Br MAJ L S Boyd 3C680 -----71512
Org & Manpower Con Br LTC O G Price 3C681 --------------53485
Mgt Engr Br P R Kunberger 3C671 ------------------------77341

OFFICE OF THE DEPUTY SECRETARY OF THE GENERAL STAFF (STAFF ACTION CONTROL)
Dep SGS COL J B Wadsworth Jr 3E665 ---------------------57552
Exec MAJ C W Stiner 3E665 ------------------------------54574
Opns & Sp Tm COL W W Plummer Jr 3E661 ----------------77803
DCSLOG LTC H L Jones 3E661 ----------------------------52183
DCSOPS LTC R E Zastrow 3E661 --------------------------74268
COA LTC T R Hukkala 3E661 -----------------------------56410
CRD LTC C R Sykes --------------------------------------57922
Personnel Tm COL J N Brandenburg 3D652 ----------------78859
DCSPER LTC A DeBarardino 3D652 ------------------------73623
TAG LTC C W Gillis 3D652 -------------------------------74606

OFFICE OF THE DEPUTY SECRETARY OF THE GENERAL STAFF (COORDINATION & REPORTS)
Dep SGS COL R C Kingston 3D643 -------------------------73206
Coord Div COL W A Wood 3D641 --------------------------57208
Cong Act Div (Actg) LTC G C Mahan 3D636 ---------------55997
Reports Div COL B T Bashore 3D619 ----------------------53160

OFFICE OF THE SPEC ASST FOR THE MODERN VOLUNTEER ARMY (OSAMVA)
SAMVA LTG Geo I Forsythe 3D639 ------------------------76010
Dep SAMVA COL R M Montague Jr 3C645 ------------------54111
Exec MAJ E G Sills 3C639 -------------------------------76010
Ch Opers LTC J R Butler 3C565 --------------------------78059
Ch Plans LTC J L Anderson 2C574 ------------------------74441
Admin Officer CW3 D E Hess 3C637 -----------------------70202

ARMY RESERVE FORCES POLICY COMMITTEE
Ch MG Leonard Holland 3B747 ---------------------------74655
Subcommitee on Army National Guard Policy
Ch MG Leonard Holland 3B747 -------------------------74655
Mil Exec COL S L Underdown 3B747 -------------------73391
Subcommitee on Army Reserve Policy
Ch MG Felix A Davis 3B747 ----------------------------55746
Mil Exec COL R S Friedman 3B747 ---------------------74369

COMPTROLLER OF THE ARMY, OFFICE OF THE
Duty Officer 3A712 ------------------------------------53040
If no answer call TAG Duty Officer ---------------------50163
Official Mail Room 2B665 ------------------------------56069
The Comptroller of the Army LTG John M Wright Jr 3A712 ---52510
Staff Asst (Spec Projects) MAJ R J Suhosky 3A712 -------54160
Dep Comptroller of the Army Eckhard Bennewitz 3A712 ----76659
Spec Asst to the Comptroller of the Army MG Autrey J Maroun 3A712 ----72215
Staff Asst LTC P P Burns 3A712 ------------------------72215
Exec LTC D L Lawrence 3A712 ---------------------------72027
Asst Exec (Staff Actions) LTC D A Waller 3A712 --------53040
Asst Exec (Pers & Admin) LTC G R Green 2B680 ---------50431
Admin Officer H M Langwasser 2B680 ------------------52320
Graphic Arts Ofc E R Wood Jr 2B677 -------------------71463
Asst Comp-Fiscal Policy E L Tracy 3A686 --------------54296
Asst Compt-Foreign Financial Affairs E K Shultz 3A724 ---73289
Asst Compt-Fin & Compt Info Sys BG R J Richards Jr 2A712 ---50303
Dep Asst Compt Fin & Compt Sys
COL M E Richmond 2A712 ----------------------------50315
Exec COL G A Maloney 2A712 --------------------------50660
Dir Army Budget BG J A Kjellstrom 3A666 --------------73937
Dep Dir John P O'Hehir 3A662 ------------------------54575
Exec LTC A J Cade 3A662 ----------------------------54579
Bud Formulation Ofc W T McCormac 3A674 -------------76241
Fiscal Mgmt Ofc L G Morris 3A652 --------------------50817
Asst Dir (Programs) H D McGlade 3B670 ---------------55706
Mil Programs Div V S Young 3B662 -------------------73892
Mil Funds Div COL S M Bracey 3B717 ------------------54612
Mil Asst Ofc W H Ouderkirk 3B674 --------------------75887
Asst Dir (Resources) W J Cleary 2A680 --------------56819
Asst Dir (OMA) COL Leslie R Sears 3B671 --------------52063
Dep Asst Dir (OMA) C A Olson 3B671 -----------------74633
Proj Dev & Exec Div W M Means 3B684 ---------------54485
Operating Forces Div COL J W Kiely 3B715 ------------72639
Support Forces Div W E Mayo 3B714 -----------------54031
Dir of Mgmt, Review & Analysis BG J W Gunn 3B738 -----74693
Dep Dir G E McKinney 3B738 ------------------------77406
Exec LTC R E Price 3B738 --------------------------72232
Audit Compliance Ofc W P Revis 2A664 ---------------74327
Compt Career & Education Ofc T E Williams Jr 3B743 ---75320
Mgt Improvement Div (Actg) COL R J Sapenter 2A672 ---73550
Program Review Div J G Warner 3B733 --------------77201
Reports & Statistics Div R S Cochran 2A670 ----------55111
Dir of Cost Analysis T A Smith 2A684 ----------------76331
Dep Dir COL J G Mears 2A684 -----------------------70303
Spec Asst J Ratway 2A685 --------------------------70303
Exec LTC L F Skibbie 2A684 ------------------------76332
Plans & Econ Anal Office P Gund 302 CBB -----------50271
Data Analysis Div (Actg) E R McCauley 302 CBB ------77182
Materiel Analysis Div (Actg) COL J A Mears 2A684 ---76333
Force Analysis Div (Actg) J E Koletar 2B682 --------78136
CO U S Army Field Operating Cost Agency COL J R Maher CBB ----22230

DEPUTY CHIEF OF STAFF FOR LOGISTICS (PNT)
Duty Officer 3E560 (After Dy Hrs & Sat, Sun & Hols) -----72118
Dep Ch of Staff for Logistics LTG Jos M Heiser Jr 3E560 ----54102
Exec Asst to Dep Ch of Staff for Logistics LTC J H Kovach 3E560---54102

ABOUT THE AUTHOR

Robert N. Kharasch was born on December 13, 1926, and was educated at the University of Chicago for twenty years during the Robert
Maynard Hutchins era, from nursery school through Law School. He
received his Ph. B. in 1946, a B.S. in Mathematics in 1948, his J.D.
in 1951 and was a member of Phi Beta Kappa and Coif.

Since 1951 Mr. Kharasch has lived and worked as a lawyer in
Washington, D. C., where he is a partner in the law firm of Galland,
Kharasch, Calkins & Brown, specializing in administrative law for
U.S. and foreign clients. He is married to Shari Barton Kharasch, a
political scientist, and has two children, Mark and Frank, and two
step-children, Edward and Stacia Teele.

The inventor of a teaching machine, Mr. Kharasch is a terrible
but persistent tennis player, and a fair bridge player. Modesty forbids
a cribbage rating.